Editors:

Haivan V. Hoang

Peggy Woods

Anne Bello

Joshua Barsczewski

Chris Edwards

Melissa Hudasko

Patricia Matthews

Michael Schoch

Sarah Mazun Stetson

Benjamin Zender

Opening Conversations: A Writer's Reader

University of Massachusetts Amherst

Writing Program

HAYDEN

HM

McNEIL

Hayden-McNeil Sustainability

Hayden-McNeil's standard paper stock uses a minimum of 30% post-consumer waste. We offer higher % options by request, including a 100% recycled stock. Additionally, Hayden-McNeil Custom Digital provides authors with the opportunity to convert print products to a digital format. Hayden-McNeil is part of a larger sustainability initiative through Macmillan Higher Ed. Visit http://sustainability.macmillan.com to learn more.

Hayden-McNeil Publishing
14903 Pilot Drive
Plymouth, MI 48170
www.hmpublishing.com

Hoang 8021-5 F15

Table of Contents

✔ Introduction v

Why Happiness, Why Now?
Sara Ahmed 1

Death Metal and the Indian Identity
Akshay Ahuja 10

You Knock My Brains Out This Sunday and I Knock Your Brains
Out the Next Time We Meet
Steve Almond 19

How to Tame a Wild Tongue
Gloria Anzaldúa 34

From *On Immunity: An Inoculation*
Eula Biss 46

Outcomes, Testing, Learning: What's at Stake?
Peter Brooks 59

All Can Be Lost: The Risk of Putting Our Knowledge in the
Hands of Machines
Nicholas Carr 68

Vanishing Languages
David Crystal 78

Mail
Anne Fadiman 88

I Can't Afford to Get Sick
Leslie Feinberg 97

From "Vignettes: Locations of Writing"

Splintered Literacies
Amanda Hayes 104

Writing in Sacred Spaces: Tangible Practices for
Understanding Intangible Spirituality
Brian J. McNely 106

What's the Language of the Future?
Henry Hitchings 110

✓A Place Where the Soul Can Rest
bell hooks 118

The IRL Fetish
Nathan Jurgenson 126

No Man's Land
Tomás M. Kalmar 132

All Souls' Night
Michael Patrick MacDonald 159

Untitled Op-Art
Marjane Satrapi 166

Hejira
David Sedaris 168

Toward a Civil Society: Memory, History, and the *Enola Gay*
Andrea Useem 170

My Life as an Undocumented Immigrant
Jose Antonio Vargas 181

How to Make a Slave
Jerald Walker 192

Can You Picture This? Activism, Art, and Public Scholarship
Rachel Marie-Crane Williams 197

"Is Your Underwear Flame Retardant?": Sexuality and Sports
Dave Zirin 210

Glossary of Rhetorical Terms 235

Citation Credits 239

Introduction

Writing as Conversation

It's hard to imagine living in the world and *not* being a reader and writer of texts. Our culture is saturated with words and images. We may write emails and text messages to family and friends, compose essays for college course-work, complete job applications, post consumer reviews, voice our concerns about issues in public forums, and so on. We are called upon to write for personal, academic, professional, and civic purposes. Quite simply, writing is fundamental to our everyday lives.

In fact, in *The Rise of Writing: Redefining Mass Literacy*, literacy researcher Deborah Brandt argues that we are encountering a distinct moment in history when writing is becoming more common, more pervasive, and more integral to the mass public. College students have contributed to this groundswell in writing. Researcher Andrea Lunsford provides ample evidence of writing activity in her five-year study of 1,616 undergraduates and the approximately 15,000 pieces of writing they produced during that period. Interviewed for *Wired Magazine*, Lunsford contends, "I think we're in the midst of a literacy revolution the likes of which we haven't seen since Greek civilization" (qtd. in Thompson). Those who lament the decline of writing in society misunderstand this moment. "For Lunsford," *Wired* writer Clive Thompson explains, "technology isn't killing our ability to write. It's reviving it—and pushing our literacy in bold new directions."

Digital media have created opportunities for a greater volume of published texts, more rapid speed in their circulation, and potentially, more extensive reach to readers in our own communities and across the globe. In the 1990s, as the internet became publicly available and we became more attuned to globalization, there was a widespread belief that technology and globaliza-tion had a democratizing effect: *everyone* can write and circulate their writ-ing, *everyone* can be read, *everyone* will have a voice in our world. But is this true? Even in digital and global contexts, the past two decades have demon-strated that inequalities persist through uneven access to digital technologies and writing education, the prevalence of the English language and a related anxiety (even intolerance) about language diversity in the United States, and serious problems of power and privilege that enable some to be heard more than others. Many of us do have more opportunities to write and circulate our writing; however, the "literacy revolution" has turned out to be more complicated than we hoped.

One way to explore these issues is by reflecting on how we each fit into this literacy context. *How might you narrate your own reading and writing histories? What have reading and writing meant to you? What kinds of writing have you valued? Who or what has supported or hampered you in your writing life?* In this book, several essays invite us to think about our own writing biographies in relation to social histories of language and literacy. In the essay "How to Tame a Wild Tongue," Gloria Anzaldúa contends that language identity and ethnic identity are intimately connected. Contributing to "Vignettes: Locations of Writing," Amanda Hayes reflects on literate traditions that allowed her Appalachian family to pass on stories from generation to generation, but she also notes a later school-based prejudice against her Appalachian dialect and home literacies. In the same publication, Brian McNely asks about the role that writing plays in Catholic spiritual devotions; religious institutions have historically been important sponsors of literacy. And writing from her academic and activist identities, Rachel Marie-Crane Williams's graphic essay "Can You Picture This? Activism, Art, and Public Scholarship" narrates how she's come to see the purpose of her writing. These essays shed light on the various ways in which language, reading, and writing can be personally meaningful—to our cultural identity, familial relationships, spirituality, political beliefs, sense of self—and can exist in tension within larger societal norms.

The fact that texts can travel faster and farther than ever raises complex questions about communicating across borders and with diverse peoples. Writers learn about and draw from multiple cultures, language and writing traditions, and technologies. Writers and readers may not share the same cultural heritage, political beliefs, or economic privilege and constraints. And as a result, we may have different expectations about what constitutes good writing. Writing itself has become an increasingly complicated cognitive and social activity.

So what does it mean to write well in this brave new world? Learning to write well means learning how to effectively engage in a conversation in the context of cultural, social, economic, and political differences. Consider this well-worn metaphor for writing:

Imagine that you enter a parlor. You come late. When you arrive, others have long preceded you, and they are engaged in a heated discussion, a discussion too heated for them to pause and tell you exactly what it is about. In fact, the discussion had already begun long before any of them got there, so that no one present is qualified to retrace for you all the steps that had gone before. You listen for a while, until you decide that you have caught the tenor of the argument; then you put in your oar. Someone answers; you answer him; another comes to your defense; another aligns himself against you, to either the embarrassment or gratification of your opponent, depending upon the quality of your ally's assistance. However, the discussion is interminable. The hour grows late, you must depart. And you do depart, with the discussion still vigorously in progress. (Burke 110-111)

If the idea of a "parlor" seems quaint today, we can replace the parlor with a living room, a coffee shop, a blogging community, a political organization. The idea of *conversation*, however, is timeless and fundamental to writing. What conversations do we want to join, and why? As we compose our texts, how do we each draw on our writing traditions, language backgrounds, sociocultural contexts, and technological resources? And how do we engage with others who may not share our beliefs and worldviews? *I may no agree with what you say..*

Opening Conversations: A Writer's Reader is a collection of 24 nonfiction texts that all embody the spirit of writing as conversation; a committee of college writing instructors at the University of Massachusetts Amherst Writing Program designed this collection for writers, specifically those in college writing courses. There is certainly diversity here. These essays explore contemporary social issues—including language, immigration, technology, health care, sport, and more—and are wide-ranging in writerly perspective, essay form and style, and publication context. The editors made a decision to include essays that speak across difference—including but not limited to race, gender, sexuality, class, and language background—because these essays showcase writers who deftly compose texts for readers who may not share the same worldview. A writer's ability to engage readers from a variety of backgrounds is essential. With this collection, we recognize that, as a genre, the essay itself is versatile and flexible, far from uniform.

At the same time, we'd like to emphasize what these essays share: all of these essays illustrate the ways in which writers step into the parlor and join a conversation. While the parlor metaphor quoted above may imply oppositional conversations (note terms above: "defense," "ally," and "opponent"), this collection suggests purposes for writing that include but also go beyond argument:

+ writers who critically reflect on how their contexts have influenced their worldviews;

+ writers who respond to other writers—not simply to fall into facile agree-disagree arguments, but rather to engage in true dialogue;

+ writers who are open to discovery, who rethink an existing worldview;

+ writers who research and synthesize multiple sources to understand a conversation;

+ writers who *add* to the conversation, whose texts *do* something in the world.

For now, we cast writing as conversation in order to highlight that writing is about social engagement. It's important to remind ourselves that texts are integral to our social lives, and writing can act in meaningful ways to help us build relationships with others and create change in our communities.

In the end, writing has the potential to *impact* our worlds. And for this reason, writing can be powerful. As you read this collection, we urge you to read *as writers*: contemplate the choices that these writers have made to join and even re-imagine conversations. If writing is about acting on our worlds, then learning to write well requires learning to cultivate a rhetorical mindset.

The Rhetorical Situation

Rhetoric is the art of identifying and using symbolic resources (e.g., words, languages, genres, images) in order to communicate purposefully and effectively within a particular social context. Cultivating a rhetorical mindset means carefully examining the ways in which writers and speakers make decisions about symbolic resources according to one's purpose, audience, and contexts. When we communicate in writing and speech, many of us already adapt what we say and how we say it to a given audience. But *cultivating* a rhetorical mindset requires more intentional contemplation about how to develop a set of rhetorical strategies and habits of mind that will help us write flexibly and powerfully for diverse and shifting contexts. In what follows, we present a few rhetorical concepts to get started.

All writing is situated. Often represented as a rhetorical triangle, the **rhetorical situation** can help us understand the essential elements of a communicative situation:

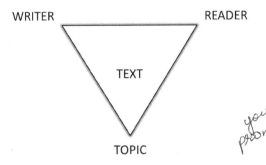

In short, a writer composes a text about a topic to readers. But *why?*

Rhetorician Lloyd Bitzer explains that "rhetorical discourse comes into existence as a response to situation, in the same sense that an answer comes into existence in response to a question, or a solution in response to a problem" (5). Writers compose texts in response to an **exigence,** a perceived need or desire that calls for a response. Put another way, we are often motivated to write when we care enough about the issue and when we believe that our writing can *do* something to address that question or problem. Exigences arise from our experiences in the world and can move us to write about these issues: e.g., proposed legislation, a cultural event (like a football game or lecture), an injustice, a blog about a social issue, etc. Exigences are invitations to write.

Writers in a particular rhetorical situation must determine their **purpose** and identify the most suitable **audience.** Who needs to read this text? What can readers do to address the question or remedy the problem? It makes sense to tailor our texts to readers who can help address the exigence—perhaps by changing their mindset or taking action in the world. In addition to identifying an appropriate audience, we need to make decisions about how to compose a **text** by drawing on symbolic resources, including writing traditions, languages, and rhetorical strategies. We consider options for content, form, style, language, and media, and we then compose, revise, and edit a text tailored to the intended readers.

The rhetorical triangle provides a useful start: the basic parts of a rhetorical situation are exigence, writer, reader, topic, and text. But as a static visual, the rhetorical triangle may be deceptively simple. First, the image may not adequately emphasize relationships among the parts of the rhetorical situation. What is the relationship between writer and topic, reader and topic, writer and reader? How do these relationships impact how we should compose a text? Second, a rhetorical situation is only a snapshot within an ongoing conversation; looking only at the situation, we might not see how the situation and its elements are part of wider social and historical contexts. That is, how is a given rhetorical situation part of an ongoing conversation? How has a particular topic been discussed in the past, and who was involved? What beliefs, past experiences, knowledge, and identities do writers bring to the situation? What do readers bring to the situation?

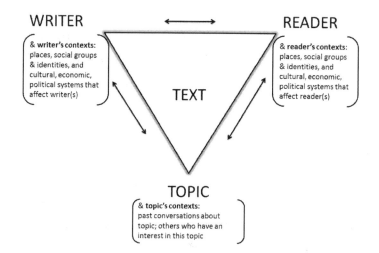

The concept of a rhetorical situation provides writers with a beginning. The next step is to examine how an interplay of contexts can affect a rhetorical situation.

A Writer's Contexts

All writers are shaped by our **contexts**. To each rhetorical situation, we bring our life experiences, our knowledge, and our identities and beliefs. Good writers, we propose, are thoughtful about how our contexts have shaped our sense of self and the perspectives that we bring to what, how, and why we write. For this reason, we might ask ourselves, *What social contexts am I a part of? How have these contexts shaped my outlook on the world?* These are admittedly big questions. As the essays in this collection suggest, contexts may include *places* like school, church, South Boston, Appalachia, India; *social groups* like family, athletic teams, political parties; *social identities* that are complex and changing like working class, African American, suburban, queer, multilingual, digital native; or *economic and political systems*. Writers carry the experiences and assumptions from these contexts into writing situations and so it's worth critically reflecting on where we've come from.

This idea of a writer's contexts may feel abstract but the concept is clearer when we look at the particulars of writers' texts. Several writers in this collection engage in critical self-reflection to varying degrees (read, for example, Ahuja, Anzaldúa, Fadiman, Hayes, hooks, Sedaris, Vargas, and Walker). Consider the introductions excerpted from two essays in this book, this first one from Jose Antonio Vargas's "My Life as an Undocumented Immigrant":

One August morning nearly two decades ago, my mother woke me and put me in a cab. She handed me a jacket. "*Baka malamig doon*" were among the few words she said. ("It might be cold there.") When I arrived at the Philippines' Ninoy Aquino International Airport with her, my aunt and a family friend, I was introduced to a man I'd never seen. They told me he was my uncle. He held my hand as I boarded an airplane for the first time. It was 1993, and I was 12.

And here is bell hooks's introduction to "A Place Where the Soul Can Rest":

Street corners have always been space that has belonged to men—patriarchal territory. The feminist movement did not change that. Just as it was not powerful enough to take back the night and make the dark a safe place for women to lurk, roam, and meander at will, it was not able to change the ethos of the street corner—gender equality in the workplace, yes, but the street corner turns every woman who dares lurk into a body selling herself, a lurking, lingering, lounging on a street corner is seen by everyone, looked at, observed. Whether she wants to be or not she is prey for the predator, for the Man, be he pimp, police, or just passerby. In cities women have no outdoor territory to occupy. They must be endlessly moving or enclosed. They must have a destination. They cannot loiter or linger.

Verandas and porches were made for females to have outdoor space to occupy. They are a common feature of southern living. Before air-conditioning cooled every hot space the porch was the summertime place, the place everyone flocked to in the early mornings and in the late nights [In our Kentucky world of poor southern black neighborhoods of shotgun houses and clapboard houses, a porch was a sign of living a life without shame.] ✓ *Black woman, southerner, Kentucky poor*

It's clear that Vargas's and hooks's contexts shape their writing: the exigence that each writer has identified, each writer's understanding of their respective topics, each writer's decisions about content, form, and style.

Further, all writers must decide on how to represent themselves. The rhetorical concept of **ethos**, or an appeal to the credibility or character of the writer or speaker, is instructive here. How do writers decide to represent themselves through content and style? What does each reveal about him/herself, and why? What does each withhold? How would we describe his/her character, and how does this fit with the writer's purpose in the text? For example, why does Vargas open with a first-person narration of his experiences as a child? Why does hooks begin with a third-person commentary on street corners and gender inequality and then shift to a first-person plural perspective? What message are they sending about their character? Even when writers are not narrating personal experience, ethos is always present. We imply our credibility and character through our writing choices. In responding to a text, readers will form an understanding of a writer's character and determine whether the writer is ethical, credible, trustworthy.

In a sense, when we reflect on our own contexts, we are also reflecting on our relationship to others in the parlor.

Listening to Others:
Critical Inquiry and Response

The parlor metaphor points to the fact that we are always in the company of others—others who bring their own contexts. As much as we should listen to our own experiences, it's equally important to listen, *truly listen*, to others in the parlor. Reading and writing (listening and speaking, too) depend on one another. As the parlor metaphor indicates, "others have long preceded" us in the conversation. Before we add our voices, we ought to listen to understand what others say and also to identify who is part of the conversation and how others bring their contexts to bear on the conversation.

Such listening is not always easy: a text may be difficult and complex, the topic may be unfamiliar, we may not connect with a given writer's experiences, and we may even be offended by a writer's worldview. Consider the challenges that Marjane Satrapi must face in her op-art piece reprinted in this collection. Some voices in the parlor are going to be louder than others, some silenced. Despite these difficulties, listening carefully and respectfully is important: it is not only ethical, but also this act helps writers comprehend the contours of a conversation and to begin to respond to that conversation. In practical terms, listening well can be cued by fair and accurate summary, paraphrase, and quoting of others in the conversation.

It's not surprising that writers in academic communities and beyond will often write in response to a text. Listening to others—or in this case, reading texts by others—can also be generative. If we approach a text with an open mind, with an attempt to understand others, we can also engage in critical inquiry: analyzing aspects of the text, making connections between different claims, extending the ideas presented, complicating an idea with our prior knowledge and experiences, and more. One's interaction with a text can lead to new meaning making. As writers, we may even feel compelled to **respond** where the point of responding isn't simply to arrive at a yes-no or agree-disagree position. Rather, the best responses will help us more fully understand the nuances of a conversation or re-imagine the conversation altogether. The best responses open up rather than close down conversations.

While more than a few essays in this collection might be read as a response to a text, event, or social issue, Nathan Jurgenson's essay "The IRL Fetish" provides a particularly good example of listening to others in the parlor *and* offering a complex response. Not only does he fairly represent an ongoing conversation (a lament that being online constantly is taking away from our "real" lives), but also he suggests a more complex view that moves beyond an either-or perspective on our "online" and "offline" lives. To be sure, Jurgenson's essay also *invites* response as do all others in this collection (in particular, Ahmed, Anzaldúa, Biss, Brooks, Carr, Crystal, Hitchings, Kalmar, Vargas, Zirin).

So far, we've discussed two corners of the triangle: writer and reader. Let's look at the whole again and then turn to the third corner: topic.

Entering a Conversation: What Can Writing Do?

In the end, as writers, we must repeatedly ask ourselves, *What conversations do I want to join? If exigence is an invitation to write, where do I find those motivations? What is my exigence, and what do I want my writing to do? What impact do I want my writing to make?* We can often find exigence all around us in the texts, events, and relationships that make up our everyday world. If we embrace curiosity, we can discover countless questions and problems, and we can use writing to impact those issues that matter to us.

For writers, preliminary and then more careful research offer a way to become familiar with a conversation and identify the stakeholders in that conversation. For those of us who have access to university libraries, we are fortunate to be able to search among huge volumes of sources, including peer-reviewed ones (i.e., sources that have been reviewed and selected for publication by researchers in the discipline). There's a widespread misconception that research is a passive activity (we let existing library research wash over us) and writing about research can be boring (we then pour this information on readers). Instead, we might see research as a kind of investigative listening: finding, evaluating, responding to, synthesizing, and using a variety of sources. Moreover, weaving multiple perspectives together becomes a kind of **invention**, a way of making meaning and generating new, compelling lines of inquiry.

Research is not only for academics. Indeed, research is important for many writers—including journalists, creative nonfiction writers, cultural critics, and activists. Moreover, even for academics, research does not only happen in university libraries and through online search engines. If research is about listening and seeking multiple perspectives and sources of information, then research may also include field observations, interviews with those who affect or are affected by the topic, surveys, and other methods of gathering knowledge and perspectives from our everyday lives. Even for personal narratives, a writer might engage in research by searching through old journals and other personal artifacts, interviewing family members and friends for their perspectives on a memory, and finding secondary sources about a particular time and place.

Research and writing are recursive and generative processes. As we attempt to analyze, synthesize, and respond to sources, we may discover new lines of inquiry, new exigencies, new audiences to reach. We may understand a conversation differently, change our minds, identify new questions. These processes can help us crystallize the most pressing exigence and our purpose in writing.

When we write to enter a conversation, the goal is not simply to parrot what we've learned. Rather, we *use* research for a purpose—e.g., to invite empathy, to create change in our society, to argue for a particular position. **Kairos** is a useful rhetorical concept here: *Why is this an opportune moment to add one's voice to a conversation?* Our purpose in writing can become a guide as we make decisions about how to make our texts *do* something in the world: *Who needs to read this text at this moment? What genre, medium, and style makes sense in light of purpose and intended readers? What publications would reach these intended readers? How can the text circulate?*

Writing, after all, is meant to engage others and create an impact on our worlds. In this collection, Eula Biss addresses the divisive contemporary issue of vaccination and invites readers to see the nuances of the conversation. Leslie Feinberg's essay is a speech on inequalities in the U.S. health care system and was delivered to a national transgender health conference. Other essays in this collection also draw on research and add to a conversation (see also Almond, Brooks, Crystal, Hitchings, Kalmar, Useem, and Zirin). These texts have power. Through their essays, these writers affect the ways in which many of us see the world and act in the world.

We Are All Writers

Our hope is that this book opens up conversations about writing and helps you on your own writing journey. In this collection, there are writers who are academic researchers, journalists, cultural critics, creative nonfiction writers, graphic essayists, and novelists. They use humor, passion, measured distance, emotion, and contemplation, and draw on personal experiences, current events, primary and secondary sources. They include visual images, multiple dialects and languages, genres within genres, and various points of view. As you read these essays and continue to cultivate a rhetorical mindset, we invite you

+ to reread this introduction alongside the essays,

+ to use the glossary terms at the end of this book to examine each writer's choices,

+ to use the essays to broaden the definitions of glossary terms, and

+ to analyze each writer's choices in relation to the writer's publication contexts described in the brief prefaces to each essay.

That is, take note of each writer's choices, and build a repository of rhetorical strategies to employ in your own writing.

Finally, it's not enough to cultivate a rhetorical mindset and critically reflect on others' choices. Learning to write well—with purpose, intelligence, and power—requires practice. It's only by writing regularly that you will develop fluency and an ability to add your voice to conversations that matter. So yes, cultivate a rhetorical mindset, but remember also to write and write often.

Works Cited

Bitzer, Lloyd. "The Rhetorical Situation." *Philosophy and Rhetoric* 1.1 (1968): 1–14 *EBSCO Host.* Web. 29 May 2015..

Brandt, Deborah. *The Rise of Writing: Redefining Mass Literacy.* Cambridge: Cambridge UP, 2015. Print.

Burke, Kenneth. *The Philosophy of Literary Form.* Baton Rouge: Louisiana State UP, 1967. Print.

Thompson, Clive. "On the New Literacy." *Wired Magazine* 24 Aug. 2009. Web. 29 May 2015.

Why Happiness, Why Now?

SARA AHMED

Sara Ahmed, whose books include The Cultural Politics of Emotion, Queer Phenomenology, *and* Willful Subjects, *is a Professor of Race and Cultural Studies at Goldsmiths College, University of London. The* Promise of Happiness, *from which this introduction has been excerpted, was published in 2010. Here, Ahmed casts doubt on moral philosophy's stance towards happiness as an unquestionable object of desire, instead showcasing the various ways in which "happiness" has been used for oppressive ends. This excerpt is rhetorically significant for its theoretical complexity and insight on an everyday feeling, as well as for the way it elegantly maps existing conversations.*

Happiness is consistently described as the object of human desire, as being what we aim for, as being what gives purpose, meaning and order to human life. As Bruno S. Frey and Alois Stutzer argue, "Everybody wants to be happy. There is probably no other goal in life that commands such a high degree of consensus" (2002: vii).[1] What they are describing is perhaps a consensus that happiness is the consensus. Do we consent to happiness? And what are we consenting to, if or when we consent to happiness?

Even a philosopher such as Immanuel Kant, who places the individual's own happiness outside the domain of ethics, argues that "to be happy is necessarily the wish of every finite rational being, and this, therefore, is inevitably a determining principle of its faculty of desire" ([1788] 2004: 24). And yet Kant himself suggests rather mournfully that "unfortunately, the notion of happiness is so indeterminate that although every human being wishes to attain it, yet he can never say definitely and consistently what it is that he really wishes and wills" ([1785] 2005: 78). If happiness is what we wish for, it does not mean we know what we wish for in wishing for happiness. Happiness might even conjure its own wish. Or happiness might keep its place as a wish by its failure to be given.

Happiness: a wish, a will, a want. In this book, I wonder what it means for happiness to be thought in such terms. The question that guides the book is thus not so much "what is happiness?" but rather "what does happiness do?" I do not offer a definition of happiness, or a model of authentic happiness. Nor do I offer a set of instructions on how to achieve happiness: I do not have one to offer, and if anything, I write from a position of skeptical disbelief in happiness as a technique for living well. I am interested in how happiness is associated with some life choices and not others, how happiness is imagined as being what follows being a certain kind of being. The history of happiness can be thought of as a history of associations. In wishing for happiness we wish to be associated with happiness, which means to be associated with its associations. The very promise that happiness is what you get for having the right associations might be how we are directed toward certain things.

Happiness shapes what coheres as a world. In describing happiness as a form of world making, I am indebted to the work of feminist, black, and queer scholars who have shown in different ways how happiness is used to justify oppression. Feminist critiques of the figure of "the happy housewife," black critiques of the myth of "the happy slave," and queer critiques of the sentimentalization of heterosexuality as "domestic bliss" have taught me most about happiness and the very terms of its appeal. Around these specific critiques are long histories of scholarship and activism which expose the unhappy effects of happiness, teaching us how happiness is used to redescribe social norms as social goods. We might even say that such political move-ments have struggled *against* rather than *for* happiness. Simone de Beauvoir shows so well how happiness translates its wish into a politics, a wishful politics, a politics that demands that others live according to a wish. As she argued: "It is not too clear just what the word *happy* really means and still less what true values it may mask. There is no possibility of measuring the hap-piness of others, and *it is always easy to describe as happy the situation in which one wishes to place them*" ([1949] 1997: 28; second emphasis added). I draw on such critiques of happiness as a way of asking questions about the hap-piness wish. We need to draw on such critiques *now*, as a way of responding to the worldliness of this *now*. Why happiness, why now? We could certainly describe this *now* as a "happiness turn." *The Promise of Happiness* is written in part as a response to this turn.

The Happiness Turn

What do I mean by "the happiness turn"? It is certainly the case that numer-ous books have been published on the science and economics of happiness, especially from 2005 onward.[2] The popularity of therapeutic cultures and discourses of self-help have also meant a turn to happiness: many books and courses now exist that provide instructions on how to be happy, drawing on a variety of knowledges, including the field of positive psychology, as well as on (often Orientalist) readings of Eastern traditions, especially Buddhism.[3] It is now common to refer to "the happiness industry": happiness is both produced and consumed through these books, accumulating value as a form of capital. Barbara Gunnell (2004) describes how "the search for happiness is certainly enriching a lot of people. The feel-good industry is flourishing. Sales of self-help books and CDs that promise a more fulfilling life have never been higher."

The media are saturated with images and stories of happiness. In the UK, many broadsheet newspapers have included "specials" on happiness and a BBC program, *The Happiness Formula*, was aired in 2006.[4] This happiness turn can be described as international; you can visit the "happy plant index" on the World Wide Web and a number of global happiness surveys and reports that measure happiness within and between nation states have been published.[5] These reports are often cited in the media when research findings do not correspond to social expectations, that is, when developing countries are shown to be happier than overdeveloped ones. Take the opening sentence of one article: "Would you believe it, Bangladesh is the happiest nation in the world! The United States, on the other hand, is a sad story: it ranks only 46th in the World Happiness Survey."[6] Happiness and unhappiness become newsworthy when they challenge ideas about the social status of specific individuals, groups, and nations, often confirming status through the language of disbelief.

The happiness turn can also be witnessed in changing policy and governance frameworks. The government of Bhutan has measured the happiness of its population since 1972, represented as Gross National Happiness (GNH). In the UK, David Cameron, the leader of the Conservative party, talked about happiness as a value for government, leading to a debate in the media about New Labour and its happiness and "social well-being" agenda.[7] A number of governments have been reported to be introducing happiness and well-being as measurable assets and explicit goals, supplementing the Gross Domestic Product (GDP) with what has become known as the Genuine Progress Indicator (GPI).[8] Happiness becomes a more genuine way of measuring progress; happiness, we might say is, the ultimate performance indicator.

Unsurprisingly, then, happiness studies has become an academic field in its own right: the academic journal *Happiness Studies* is well established and a number of professorships in happiness studies now exist. Within academic scholarship, we have witnessed a turn to happiness within a range of disciplines, including history, psychology, architecture, social policy, and

3

economics. It is important to witness this turn, reflecting not simply on happiness as a form of consensus but on the consensus to use the word *happiness* to describe something.

Some of this work has been described under the rubric of "the new science of happiness." This is not to say that the science of happiness is itself new; many of the key texts in this area offer revivals of classical English utilitarianism, in particular, the work of Jeremy Bentham with his famous maxim of "the greatest happiness for the greatest number." As Bentham explains in *A Fragment of Government*, "it is the greatest happiness of the greater number that is the measure of right and wrong" ([1776] 1988: 3). Bentham is himself drawing on an earlier tradition, including the work of David Hume as well as Cesare Beccaria and Claude Adrien Helvétius. The science of happiness shares a history with political economy: just recall Adam Smith's argument in *The Wealth of Nations* that capitalism advances us from what he might call "miserable equality" to what we could call "happy inequality" such that "a workman, even of the lowest and poorest order, if he is frugal and industrious, may enjoy a greater share of the necessaries and conveniences of life than it is possible for any savage to acquire" ([1776] 1999: 105).

Of course, nineteenth-century utilitarianism involves an explicit refutation of such a narrative, in which inequality becomes the measure of advancement and happiness. Bentham, following Alexander Wedderburn, describes the principle of utility as dangerous for government: "a principle, which lays down, as the only *right* and justifiable end of Government, the greatest happiness of the greatest number—how can it be denied to be a dangerous one? dangerous to every Government, which has for its *actual* end or object the greatest happiness of a certain *one*" ([1776] 1988: 59). Despite this belief that every person's happiness should count equally (the happiness of many refuses to elevate the happiness of any one), the utilitarian tradition did uphold the principle that increased levels of happiness function as a measure of human progress. Émile Durkheim offered a forceful critique of this principle "But in fact, is it true that the happiness of the individual increases as man advances? Nothing is more doubtful" ([1893] 1960: 241).

One of the key figures in the recent science of happiness is Richard Layard, often referred to as "the happiness tsar" by the British media. Layard's important book *Happiness: Lessons from a New Science*, first published in 2005, begins as a critique of the discipline of economics for how it measures human growth: "economics equates changes in the happiness of a society with changes in its purchasing power" (ix). Layard argues that happiness is the only way of measuring growth and advancement: "the best society is the happiest society." One of the fundamental presumptions of this science is that happiness is good, and thus that nothing can be better than to maximize happiness. The science of happiness presumes that happiness is "out there," that you can measure happiness and that these measurements are objective: they have even been called "hedonimeters" (Nettle 2006: 3).

If the science of happiness presumes happiness as being "out there," then how does it define happiness? Richard Layard again provides us with a useful reference point. He argues that "happiness is feeling good, and misery is feeling bad" (6). Happiness is "feeling good," which means we can measure happiness because we can measure how good people feel. So "out there" is really "in here." The belief that you can measure happiness is a belief that you can measure feelings. Layard argues that "most people find it easy to say how good they are feeling" (13). Happiness research is primarily based on self-reporting: studies measure how happy people say they are, presuming that if people say they are happy, they are happy. This model both presumes the transparency of self-feeling (that we can say and know how we feel), as well as the unmotivated and uncomplicated nature of self-reporting. If happiness is already understood to be what you want to have, then to be asked how happy you are is not to be asked a neutral question. It is not just that people are being asked to evaluate their life situations but that they are being asked to evaluate their life situations through categories that are value laden.[9] Measurements could be measuring the relative desire to be proximate to happiness, or even the relative desire to report on one's life well (to oneself or others), rather than simply how people feel about their life as such.

It matters how we think about feeling. Much of the new science of happiness is premised on the model of feelings as transparent, as well as the foundation for moral life. If something is good, we feel good. If something is bad, we feel bad.[10] The science of happiness thus relies on a very specific model of subjectivity, where one knows how one feels, and where the distinction between good and bad feeling is secure, forming the basis of subjective as well as social well-being. Cultural studies, as well as psychoanalysis, may have an important role to play in these debates by offering alternative theories of emotion that are *not* based on a subject that is fully present to itself, on a subject that always knows how it feels (see Terada 2001). Cultural and psychoanalytic approaches can explore how ordinary attachments to the very idea of the good life are also sites of ambivalence, involving the confusion rather than separation of good and bad feelings. Reading happiness would then become a matter of reading the grammar of this ambivalence.

Happiness research does not simply measure feelings; it also interprets what it measures. Measuring happiness primarily generates knowledge about the distribution of happiness. Happiness research has produced databases that show where happiness is located, which are largely predicated on a comparative model. Happiness databases show us which individuals are happier than others, as well as which groups, or nation-states are happier than others. The science of happiness makes correlations between happiness levels and social indicators, creating what are called "happiness indicators." Happiness indicators tell us which kinds of people have more happiness; they function not only as measures of happiness but also as predictors of happiness. As Frey and Stutzer argue in *Happiness and Economics*, social indicators can predict how happy different kinds of persons will be, creating what they call "happiness psychograms" (2002: 7). *discuss.*

One of the primary happiness indicators is marriage. Marriage would be defined as "the best of all possible worlds" as it maximizes happiness. The argument is simple: if you are married, then we can predict that you are more likely to be happier than if you are not married. The finding is also a recommendation: get married and you will be happier! This intimacy of measurement and prediction is powerful. The science of happiness could be described as performative: by finding happiness in certain places, it generates those places as being good, as being what should be promoted *as* goods. Correlations are read as causalities, which then become the basis of promotion. We promote what I call in the first chapter "happiness-causes," which might even cause happiness to be reported. The science of happiness hence redescribes what is already evaluated as being good as good. If we have a duty to promote what causes happiness, then happiness itself becomes a duty. I will explore the significance of "the happiness duty" throughout this book.

The pursuit of happiness?!

This is not to say that happiness is always found. Indeed, we might even say that happiness becomes more powerful through being perceived as in crisis. The crisis in happiness works primarily as a narrative of disappointment: the accumulation of wealth has not meant the accumulation of happiness. What makes this crisis "a crisis" in the first place is of course the regulatory effect of a social belief: that more wealth "should" make people happier. Richard Layard begins his science of happiness with what he describes as a paradox: "As Western societies have got richer, their people have become no happier" (2005: 3). If the new science of happiness uncouples happiness from wealth accumulation, it still locates happiness in certain places, especially marriage, widely regarded as the primary "happiness indicator" (see chapter 2), as well as in stable families and communities (see chapter 4). Happiness is looked for where it is expected to be found, even when happiness is reported as missing. What is striking is that the crisis in happiness has not put social ideals into question and, if anything, has reinvigorated their hold over both psychic and political life. The demand for happiness is increasingly articulated as a demand to return to social ideals, as if what explains the crisis of happiness is not the failure of these ideals but our failure to follow them. And arguably, at times of crisis the language of happiness acquires an even more powerful hold.[11]

Notes

1. There are so many articulations of this belief that it is difficult to choose whom to quote. I open with this quote as it uses everyday language to describe an idea that is both everyday and philosophical: that happiness is what we aim for. Probably one of the most dramatic philosophical articulations of the principle was offered in the seventeenth century by Blaise Pascal, who argued: "All men seek happiness. This is without exception. Whatever different means they employ, they all tend to this end. The cause of some going to war, and of others avoiding it, is the same desire in both, attended with different views. The will never takes the least step but to this object. This is the motive of every action, of every man, even of those who hang themselves" ([1669] 1910: 138). This rather extraordinary insistence on the universality of happiness as a motive of the will involves an equally extraordinary discussion of the necessary failure of happiness, which clearly anticipated the psychoanalytic enterprise: "What is it then this desire and this inability proclaim to us, but that there was once in man a true happiness of which there now remain to him only the mark and empty trace, which he in vain tries to fill from all his surroundings, seeking from things absent to help he does not obtain in things present? But these are all inadequate, because the infinite abyss can only be filled by an infinite and immutable object, that is to say, only by God Himself" (138–39).

2. The following are some of the key books published in the last few years: Layard 2005; McMahon 2006; Nettle 2006; Gilbert 2006; Haidt 2006; Schoch 2006; de Botton 2006. See the collection of essays on happiness that I edited in *New Formations* (2008) for some perspectives from cultural studies, as well as the humanities more broadly.

3. Examples of recent books on happiness that we could describe as popular psychology or "how-to" manuals include Summers and Watson 2006, Seligman 2003, Holden 1998, Ricard 2007. One of the most popular books on happiness is based on a series of interviews between the Dalai Lama and Howard C. Cutler (1998).

4. For example, the *Independent on Sunday* had a special, "The Secrets of Happiness: Why the Ancients Hold the Key," March 17, 2006. Information about the BBC program *The Happiness Formula* can be accessed at http://news.bbc.co.uk. Last visited February 11, 2009.

5. See: http://www.happyplanetindex.org. The results of global surveys of happiness are debated in the journal *Happiness Studies*. Last visited February 11, 2009.

6. See http://www.nriol.com. Last visited February 11, 2009.

7. For details of David Cameron's speech about happiness, see http://news.bbc.co.uk. Last visited February 11, 2009.

8. GPI was first coined by three Californian researchers in 1995. Along with 400 leading economists, business leaders, and professionals, they stated: "Since the GDP measures only the quantity of market activity without accounting for the social and ecological costs involved, it is both inadequate and misleading as a

measure of true prosperity. Policy-makers, economists, the media, and international agencies should cease using the GDP as a measure of progress and publicly acknowledge its shortcomings. New indicators of progress are urgently needed to guide our society...The GPI is an important step in this direction." For further information about GPI and the genealogy of the term, see http://www.gpiatlantic.org. Last visited February 11, 2009.

9. One study reveals what should be obvious: if you ask subjects how happy they are after asking them about positive topics, you are more likely to get higher happiness levels reported than if you ask them how happy they are after asking them questions about negative topics: "Subjects who had previously been induced to think about positive aspects of their present life described themselves as happier and more satisfied with their life-as-a-whole than subjects who had been induced to think about negative aspects" (Schwarz and Strack 1991: 28).

10. We can see the problems with such an approach when feelings become measures of rights and wrongs. Richard Layard, for example, argues that what makes something wrong is that it makes people unhappy, or even offends peoples' feelings. For Layard, the science of happiness is "inherently" pro-poor and for the redistribution of wealth as inequalities increase unhappiness (2005: 120-21): though the unfortunate implication of his argument is that if inequalities did not increase unhappiness, then he would not be against them, As he describes: "American slaves wanted their freedom, not because it would give them higher incomes, but because of the humiliation of being a slave. Slavery offended their feelings, and that is why slavery is wrong" (121). The idea that slavery was wrong because it hurt people's feelings shows us what is wrong with this model of wrong. It individuates and psychologizes social wrongs. See Lauren Berlant's (2000) important critique of the conflation of pain and in justice, as well as my conclusion to *The Cultural Politics of Emotion* (2004) for a reflection on the relationship between social wrongs and hurt. Note in particular that one of the problems of the conflation of injustice with hurt is that it presumes access to the other's feelings. Any forms of wrong that are not accompanied by consciously felt suffering that can be spoken about to others would become invisible in such a model.

11. The implication of my suggestion here is that the contemporary moment of the "financial crisis" in which I have completed this book will not mean a withdrawal of public or private concern with happiness but if anything may heighten the cultural preoccupation with happiness (perhaps as an uneasiness in the want of the good life for those who feel they did have and should still have a good life).

Death Metal and the Indian Identity

AKSHAY AHUJA

"Death Metal and the Indian Identity" originally appeared in 2008 in Guernica: A Magazine of Art & Politics, which publishes interviews, poetry, fiction, art, and "features" such as Akshay Ahuja's piece. As the movement toward online-only literary magazines has grown in the past ten years, Guernica has become a competitive place of publication for artists, writers, and activists. In this nonfiction essay, Ahuja recalls a trip from the U.S. to Bangalore, India, in which he gets to know musicians in a metal band. Ahuja is a Boston-based writer who currently works at Ploughshares, *a literary journal; he is also an Assistant Professor of Liberal Arts at the Berklee College of Music.*

It was near midnight on the eve of India's independence, and I was at a concert called Freedom Jam, held at a club on the outskirts of Bangalore called only The Club. Watching the band perform from beside the stage, I noticed a girl with a nose ring. My grandmother's nose was pierced when she married at thirteen; her nose ring was a sign that she adhered to a certain traditional image of Indian womanhood. For this girl, however, the ring indicated that she was not just westernized (such girls simply chose not to get their noses pierced) but a member of an alternative community that existed outside the mainstream of westernized Indian youth.

Essentially, the nose ring had traveled to the other side of the world, assumed a fringe rather than traditional meaning, and then come back to India, where it now has two different meanings. Such dual gestures exist in America, but they usually have one sincere and one ironic meaning—trucker hats on truckers, for example, as opposed to everyone else. In India, however, both meanings are perfectly sincere, both carry conviction.

Our group had left late for the show, stopping at a store on the side of the highway for a few bottles of whiskey. When we finally pushed through the turnstiles and found the promoter, all they could get was the 4 a.m. slot.

Pradyum was the band's guitarist, and my friend. He had only slept a few hours over the past several days and I had been following my parents' schedule, which involved getting up at 5 a.m, so we were both exhausted. The band on stage was playing a less-than-thrilling version of Roadhouse Blues, which had already been covered twice by two of the other bands. Pradyum and I decided on a nap before the show. Leaving the side of the main stage, we pushed through the immense crowd—ten thousand people all told—and made our way to a tiny red hatchback parked at the edge of the immense field surrounding The Club.

Pradyum fell asleep immediately in the backseat while I slapped at the mosquitoes. It was extremely humid. The bass from the concert faintly vibrated the car, and I could swear someone was playing Roadhouse Blues again.

~

I met Pradyum through my father. One summer, just before I was to go to Bangalore to visit my parents, my Dad asked if I was willing to bring something with me—a guitar, for a colleague's son. I was out of college and could only visit them for a few weeks, so I had space for another piece of luggage. I agreed to bring the guitar.

A week later, I got an email from Pradyum: "With regard to customs," he wrote, "if I could only get one of your recent photographs, which your father said would not be a problem, I could arrange for a customs officer to have you escorted from the plane. Also, my band is called 'Cremated Souls', may sound very morbid. We are a semi-pro death metal band." He directed me to a website where I could check out his music.

The website was, mysteriously, in French. I muddled through it with the aid of a dictionary. The band was looking for a label and offered to send its demo to anyone who liked the mp3s they heard on the website. Par notre musique, they wrote, nous esperons capturer vos Ames...vos Ames incendiees. With our music, we hope to capture your souls...your cremated souls. There was a picture of four very serious-looking Indian boys dressed in black and posed in front of a cross in a graveyard.

The rest of the website was about the lack of appreciation for death metal in India—Nous avons souffert beaucoup, they wrote—which had forced the band to turn to the west for recognition. On the mp3 page, the band said that they wished to compose pieces that combined "melody and brutality." The three songs on the website were named "Shattered Shield," "Perceiving Resurrection," and "Removal of the Fetus." I tried "Shattered Shield," which was identified as being about police and government corruption.

11

The song loaded. A single guitar played arpeggios on a slow, dark three-chord progression. The drums came in, and then some fairly complicated ornamentation from a second guitar. Wow, I thought, they're pretty good. Then the drums started pounding bapbapbapbap, the guitars raged, and the vocals came in—grunts, growls, screams, all emerging from some place deep in the back of the throat. I couldn't imagine what connection the words had to the Indian police force.

A few days later the guitar arrived; it was beautiful and black and, strangely, had seven strings. Remembering what Pradyum had said about the customs officer, I opened it to make sure it wasn't stuffed with cocaine.

When I arrived at the Bangalore airport at two in the morning—my flight was hours late—all the Cremated Souls were there, waiting in the damp heat next to my tired parents. Pradyum was beaming. I handed him the guitar, and he gave me a box of Indian sweets with an invitation to come hear the band play.

A few days later Pradyum came to my parents' house on a black Royal Enfield motorcycle, wearing a leather jacket. He was strong and well-built. I found out later that until a few years ago, he had been serious about track and field before a scooter accident had crushed his leg.

Pradyum would drop me off several times after this, but this was the only time he came inside. He was always afraid that he smelled like cigarettes (he smoked constantly) and that this would offend my parents. Once in the house, he complimented my mother on her beautiful home—and such a nice garden! This immense politeness was strangely incongruous. Looking just like James Dean, he had all the American gestures of rebelliousness, but without the appropriate American attitude.

After Pradyum had charmed my mother, we jumped on the bike and headed to his house to pick up some equipment for rehearsal. Pradyum wove around potholes while I hung on nervously to the back of the seat. I asked him why the website was in French, and he said that the Cremated Souls had sent their demo tape to a label in France. They hadn't been signed, but another metal band had picked up the tape and liked it. It was this French band that set up the site for them.

"What does it say about us?" he asked.

I gave him the highlights.

Pradyum didn't disagree with the site's claims, although the band's level of suffering and isolation had apparently been exaggerated. "We play all the time for many thousands of people. Delhi, Bombay. In the universities," he said.

I asked him if there were many death metal fans in India, and he told me that most people in India were willing to listen to anything, that they didn't believe in "identity music"—that is, they didn't care enough about any one genre to build their identity around it. To Pradyum this wasn't evidence of having an open mind, or enjoying as much as you could from a necessarily hybrid culture; instead he thought this Indian willingness to embrace everything was a variety of shallowness. The west was better in this way. Even playing to such large groups in India, he knew that he would eventually have to go to Europe or America to find a real audience. Pradyum bent the motorcycle into a turn; signs flashed by in four different languages.

When we arrived at his house, I discovered that he had painted his room black. "Don't be scared," he told me. His mother insisted that I sit down and immediately began bringing out plates of food. Pradyum, like every unmarried person around my age that I knew in India, still lived with his parents. A pretty, round-faced girl also started bringing me snacks. She introduced herself as Anitha and turned out to be Pradyum's fiancée. Anitha said that she would come with us to the rehearsal but had to go to work later. She managed a call center for Alamo car rental at night, and then slept during the day. She was basically living on American hours. A couple of my cousins in Bangalore did this too, and they told me that entire malls and restaurants had sprung up in certain areas of the city to cater to people who followed these vampire schedules. One cousin told me that he went to such places after work to "freak out." After much confusion, I discovered that this term has, like the nose ring, crossed the oceans to mean its exact opposite—in India, it means to relax or hang out.

I asked Anitha when she and Pradyum saw each other. She told me that there were always weekends and afternoons.

Pradyum called me into his room. "Do you want to see the guitar?" he asked. He opened up the case. "Look at these," he said, pointing to the base of the strings. "These are Steve Vai's pickups."

I admired them with an expression of discernment.

"The pickups are the most important part of the guitar," Pradyum explained. "I could not afford this guitar new. It was almost a thousand dollars even used."

Pradyum, it turned out, was making some money from an Internet marketing business whose particulars I never quite understood. For a while he had done the call center thing too, which was how he and Anitha had met. But while Anitha stayed on at Alamo and became a manager, Pradyum had gotten sick of it and quit.

"Do they still make you change your names?" I asked Anitha.

"No," she said. "We can be ourselves now."

Almost all of Pradyum's friends, most of whom were musicians, said that they had worked occasionally in call centers as well, taking jobs when they needed a little money and then quitting when they got tired. They all lived at home and didn't need much. Generally, it seemed, it was no longer necessary to slowly build a career through extensive education and continuous professional diligence. A decent livelihood was available at any point, as long as one spoke English. This easy money allowed for a semi-bohemian lifestyle that hadn't been possible or acceptable in India before. Until keeping a serious job was absolutely necessary, you could do anything you wanted with your time. This withdrawal of obligations was perhaps the first step in creating an artistic class outside the mainstream of a culture.

~

We piled the guitars and a few other pieces of equipment—amplifiers, pedals—into the car and drove to the band's rehearsal site, a room on the roof of one of Pradyum's relatives' houses. There, I met the other members of the band: Ali, the drummer; Charlie, the vocalist; and Ganesh, the second guitarist. They were all standing outside smoking. Pradyum and Anitha went inside to greet the family.

The rest of the band wasn't very talkative. Charlie was wearing a black shirt with something silver painted on it in jagged gothic letters. I looked at it: "Cytos..."

"Cryptopsy," he said. Then he explained that it was a band he liked. He couldn't find a t-shirt of theirs in India so he made it himself with red and silver puffy paint. Pradyum was wearing a History Channel t-shirt. I wondered if members of any American band would have worn these two items of clothing—a homemade shirt, and one that advertised for a television channel—without being enormously conscious of what they were doing, of aiming to produce some sort of effect. Things that have been weighted down in the west with ironic associations—Scooby Doo T-shirts, hair metal, huge striped V-shaped guitars like the one Ganesh had—had regained their innocence on the other side of the world. In India, they mean nothing more than what they are, and people either like them or don't, but they never "like" them.

We went up to the roof and entered the band room—a dirty mattress, a busted-up acoustic guitar, and wires all over the ground. There was also an adjoining room I couldn't see into, where the instruments were. The pedals for Ali's two-bass drum kit were already set up, so the two of us talked while the other guys plugged in. He explained the world of metal to me. Like any fringe movement, it was prone to subdivision. There were different guitar and drum styles, every level of violence from low to horrifying, and various sets of subject matter—each one had its own genre. If you wanted to include dragons and castles in your lyrics, for example, that was its own genre.

All of the band members had their favorites—musicians, books, movies— and were excited to tell me about them: Pantera, Slayer, the novel *Lost Horizon*. This surprised me; most of the people I had met in India didn't bother ranking the things that gave them pleasure. In fact, they were surprised and a little confused when I asked them to tell me their favorite anything. But Pradyum's friends were like me; they naturally created hierarchies of value, building identities around pieces of culture, which necessitated ranking and exclusion.

In the other room, I could hear Charlie growling a few times to warm up his throat. "Ghraagh," he said. "Bregkk."

The band was ready. I walked over to the room with the drum set and realized from the pictures and statues that they were playing in the devramane—a small shrine that all reasonably devout Hindu families have somewhere in their house. There was a brightly colored picture of Parvati and statues of Shiva and Ganesha, along with oil lamps and other implements of devotion.

I looked around. "You're going to play in here?" I asked.

Pradyum laughed. "Don't worry," he said. "The gods don't mind."

I was strangely bothered by this; they all found the old strictures rather silly and considered ignoring them a constructive, radical gesture. This seemed backward to me, since actually following them is a similarly radical gesture for an Indian in America.

Anitha took a brief drag from Pradyum's cigarette, something I had never seen an Indian girl do before. "Can I ask you something?" she said. "My friend and I have a bet."

"Sure," I said.

"How do you pronounce this word? T-U-L-S-A."

"Tulsa," I said.

"I knew it," Anitha said, smiling. "I was right."

The band plugged in and started to rage. It was strange to see these quiet, polite boys pounding out music of such incandescent fury. But I envied the way Pradyum brought this intensity to everything he did, the way he committed entirely to whatever he was doing at the time. Before his injury, he had been devoted to competing professionally as a runner; music only became his passion after that.

Pradyum stopped them several times. He wasn't happy with how the guitar runs were lining up. Once the practice was over, Pradyum picked up the cigarette butts littering the roof. "Let's not make a mess," he said.

~

Having barely slept, I woke up in the car, at Freedom Jam. Levis sponsored the concert, and the huge banners that surrounded The Club flapped softly in the wind, showing glimpses of female midsections of indeterminate race.

Pradyum was up too. There was still an hour until the performance, and we made our way back to the gate. On the list of acts just inside the entrance, I noticed for the first time that the Cremated Souls were no more. At the insistence of a label abroad that was interested in releasing some of their material, they had changed their name to Gorified—probably to ratchet up the level of brutality—and also switched to a new genre. Instead of "Death Metal," they were now a "Grind Band," but whoever made the board had listed them instead, in parentheses after their name, as a Grime band.

We walked through the crowd. Even at this hour the place was packed. Pradyum was meeting friends everywhere, speaking mostly English with slangy Tamil, Telugu, and Kannada thrown in. A tall, thin boy drifted by, face completely ashen, walking shakily with a strangely beatific smile until he fell hard, face down, on the concrete steps. His friends rushed around him and carried him away. "Ketamine," Pradyum said by way of explanation.

We made our way to the main stage. A sizable portion of the crowd was chanting "Ozzy! Ozzy!" The band on stage obliged them by playing Judas Priest's "Breakin' the Law." The Ozzy chants meant only, "play another song." Two tall Indian guys dressed in black trench coats and holding guitars came on stage. It was the first sign of theatricality I had seen from any of the Indian bands, whose members had all worn ordinary clothes and shown no flair for the dramatic. "Alright," the lead singer screamed, in a perfect American accent. "It's time to wake the fuck up!" I felt a strange sense of vertigo at hearing him, as if I had flown around the world and returned to the same spot. To steady myself, I thought about something I had seen earlier. After a rather sloppy cover of Whole Lotta Love, the lead singer of a band had apologized to the audience for not playing the song better. They would try harder, he said. Nowhere but in India, I thought, would you get such courtesy from a rock band.

The two guys started to play; they were terrible. The promoter decided when each band's time was up, and he gave vastly different amounts of time to various acts. The trench coats were removed from the stage after only three songs. I sat next to Anitha, who was incredibly lively since these were her usual hours.

Soon Gorified was up. While they set up, a few people chanted "Ozzy" again. Out came the replacement bass player, leaving his friend with the nose ring by the side of the stage. I thought about the original bass player, whom I had met with Pradyum one evening. An immensely shy, quiet person, he kept smiling and smiling. What was it that drew him to this music?

Gorified started with "Shattered Shield," the crowd favorite. The loud screaming part of the song began. A few people were head-banging in the audience, but quite peacefully; there was no one jumping around hoping to slam into someone else. In fact, most people stood stock still. After two songs, Gorified was pulled. We had waited most of the night for ten minutes.

We got back in the car and drove through the empty streets, the blue coming into the sky. We reached my home just as dawn was breaking on Independence Day. I gave Pradyum a hug, and we promised to see each other again soon.

When we did, more than a year later, Gorified had broken up—the others weren't serious enough about it, Pradyum said—and Pradyum had formed a new band called Infinite Dreams; their music was softer, more melodic. His band mate was headed to London for a six-month course in audio recording, and Pradyum would hopefully follow him there. Then they would try to really make it abroad. He and Anitha were married now, and she was moving up the Alamo chain. Pradyum was making good money too; he had started a real estate company that, he told me in an email, dealt in "total real estate solutions." The rural land around the city was being bought up for office buildings, and Pradyum brokered deals with the farmers and secured the land for the companies, making sure, he assured me, that no one was cheated.

From the calls he took on his cell phone, I could already tell that he had the necessary combination of forcefulness and charm. I told him that he must be good at his job and he seemed offended. Music was his life, he said; this was just temporary.

We drove in his new car around this stretch of land, beautiful and green after the monsoon. We were heading towards the Nandi Hills, an hour outside Bangalore. There were buildings going up everywhere.

I asked him about the guitar, and he told me, half sheepishly and then with a smile when he saw that I didn't mind, that he had sold it. It wasn't right for his new band, he said. He had made a rather sizable profit on its sale.

I remembered what he had said about identity music, and wondered how much of your life you had to give to something before you could claim it as identity, and how you could measure the level of that allegiance. Was it in clothes and nose rings and how many hours a day you spent doing each thing? Or maybe all of that was irrelevant, and it was purely how you looked at your life, even while selling real estate or being an engineer or taking midnights calls from Americans.

Pradyum turned the stereo up—it was Judas Priest—and we headed towards the mountains.

You Knock My Brains Out This Sunday and I Knock Your Brains Out the Next Time We Meet

STEVE ALMOND

Steve Almond is an American short story writer and essayist. In this chapter from his book, Against Football *(2014), Almond (a self-described football fan) considers the ethical implications of watching NFL football in light of growing research on Chronic Traumatic Encephalopathy and the rising number of concussions reported by players. Writing persuasively to football fans, he maps out a rather large discussion concerning concussions in football in a concise and careful manner, considering various viewpoints, gathering research from both primary and secondary sources, and integrating relevant personal experience and opinion.*

And if that's all there was to football, well, we could stop right here and go stock up on snacks for this weekend's games. But of course I've left the ugly parts out of this highlight reel. I've failed to mention, for instance, the single most haunting memory of my childhood fandom.

In the summer of 1978, during a pre-season game, a wide receiver for the New England Patriots named Darryl Stingley lunged for a pass just out of his reach. Before he could regain his balance he was leveled by Raiders defensive back Jack Tatum. It was clear at once that Stingley was, in the gentle parlance of the broadcast booth, "shaken up on the play." Team doctors rushed to his side.

I was eleven years old. I knew I was supposed to feel bad for Stingley, and I did in some minor, dutiful way. Mostly I was proud of Tatum, of the destructive capacities central to his identity. The whole point of being Jack "The Assassin" Tatum was to poleax wide receivers in this manner.

The problem was that Stingley wasn't moving. The doctors kept tapping at his knees with reflex hammers and I remember this because my dad had pulled a reflex hammer from his old medical kit and done the same thing to us. The longer Stingley lay on the chalked grass, the more ashamed I grew. I knew, even then, that part of my attraction to football was the thrill of such violent transactions.

I can still see that hit. Stingley lowers his head just before impact. Tatum's shoulder pad strikes his helmet. What you don't see, what's safely hidden away under the armor, is how this impact compresses Stingley's spinal cord and fractures his fourth and fifth cervical vertebrae. Tatum and his teammates stride away from Stingley's grotesquely bent body with no apparent remorse.

What I remember most of all is the fear that dogged me in the days afterward as it became clear that a star player had been rendered a quadriplegic on national TV: surely the game of football would now be outlawed.

Two years later, a congressional sub-committee did call Stingley to testify about a proposed bill to limit excessive violence in pro sports. But that measure, like other previous efforts, proved ceremonial. Instead, the Patriots gave Stingley a desk job and honored him in the manner of a war hero. Tatum, who was neither flagged nor fined for the hit, continued to terrorize opposing players. The NFL juggernaut rolled on. And I kept right on watching.

~

I spent most of my youth playing soccer. I was lucky enough to witness the first heyday of the pro game in this country. We lived twenty minutes from one of its marquee franchises, the San Jose Earthquakes. So why didn't I watch soccer instead? Why did I gravitate towards football? Why did I take up with the Raiders and remain loyal to them even after their rebel mystique had curdled?

I've argued above that the game of football is simply more gripping as a spectacle, a more faithful reenactment of our fundamental athletic impulses. But if we're going to be honest about all this, then we should specify what we mean when we say "impulses," we're not just talking about the frolicking verbs—run, leap, catch—but the delight that boys (and later men) take in tackling and pounding and hurting.

And I should talk, too, a little more about the family in which I grew up. My parents met in medical school and later established private practices. They were politically active on the left. They made homemade jam and bread and candles. They read novels and performed Lieder as a duet, my father singing in German while my mother accompanied him on piano. They were gentle souls with three well-behaved sons who earned good grades. That was the public version of our family.

The private version was troubled. There was a lot of anger in our home and very little corresponding mercy. As I see it now, my folks had too many children too quickly—Dave was barely two when my twin Mike and I arrived.

They felt overrun in ways that I, as a parent of three young children, am only beginning to comprehend.

My folks worked hard to connect with us individually. My dad, for example, coached my soccer team for years. But he and Mom also had ambitions of their own. And none of us boys, to be blunt, felt entirely secure in their love. We desperately wanted more attention, but this desperation frightened us, so we strangled it into silence. Rather than entreat our parents, we froze them out. It was how we punished them. We turned our brotherhood into a furious little fortress.

We sought to humiliate and injure one another constantly. I took a perverse pride in the fact that both of my brothers broke their hands in fights with me. One afternoon in high school, I arrived home to find my brother Mike stomping around with a carving knife. Dave had stabbed him in the thigh with a fork and now he wanted revenge.

Beneath all the fury, we felt tremendous fear and despair. Later in life, these emotions would bubble up through the cracks and swallow each of us, but back then we remained loyal to our chosen omertà. To reveal any weakness, to ask for comfort or love, was forbidden.

We all dealt with the pressure in different ways. My older brother maniacally pursued hobbies. My twin brother withdrew into himself. I watched football. In a home swirling with chaotic rage, it soothed me to see aggression granted a coherent, even heroic, context.

~

I'm setting all this out to explain why, even after watching a man get crippled, my devotion to the sport never wavered. My dad may have felt the same way, because I don't recall that we ever talked about the Stingley incident. We must have been content to write it off as a freak accident. We had that luxury back then.

We don't anymore.

Over the past few years, a growing body of medical research has confirmed that football can cause traumatic injury to the brain, not as a rare and unintended consequence, but as a routine byproduct of how the game is played. The central concern among doctors is no longer catastrophic injuries—concussions that result from big collisions—but the incremental (and therefore largely invisible) damage done by numerous sub-concussive hits.

A study commissioned by the NFL Players Association determined that recently retired pros (ages thirty to forty-nine) are nineteen times more likely to suffer from brain-trauma-related illness than—what's the right word here?—noncombatants. Given that aging stars don't want to be seen as disabled, they tend to downplay or even hide their infirmities. The numbers are likely higher.

Players may die younger, too. "Whereas white males live to 78 years and African-American males live to approximately 70 years, it appears that professional football players in both the United States and Canada have life expectancies in the mid to late 50s," according to Dr. Lee Nadler, a neurologist at Harvard. A 2011 study conducted by the Sport-Related Traumatic Brain Injury Research Center at the University of North Carolina put life expectancy for players at fifty-five.

NFL officials have sought to rebut these claims by trumpeting a 2012 study conducted by the National Institute for Occupational Safety and Health. It tallied death rates among more than 3,400 former players and concluded that they enjoy greater longevity.

But this approach, as any actuary would tell you, is inherently flawed because the average age of death among men in the general population factors in those who die as children or young adults, as well as the poor, sickly, and undernourished. Oh, and smokers. The proper control for NFL players would be a cohort of super-fit, affluent, college-educated men. The study also tracked subjects who turned pro between 1959 and 1988, an era when players were much smaller. Until a sound longitudinal study is conducted, no one can say for sure how playing football affects mortality.

What has become increasingly obvious is that numerous NFL players incur brain damage. Doctors have autopsied the brains of dozens of former pros, such as Junior Seau, Mike Webster, and Dave Duerson, and confirmed that they suffered from a form of dementia called Chronic Traumatic Encephalopathy (CTE). Like Seau, Duerson, an All-Pro safety, shot himself in the chest. Before taking his life, he sent his family a text message requesting that his brain be used for research.

A new crop of retired stars is just beginning to report symptoms. Brett Favre, among the most heralded quarterbacks of the past two decades, shocked fans when he confessed to memory lapses last year. "I don't remember my daughter playing soccer one summer," Favre said. "So that's a little bit scary to me. For the first time in forty-four years, that put a little fear in me."

Terry Bradshaw was so concerned about his faculties that he sought diagnostic help five years ago. "I couldn't focus and remember things, and I was dealing with depression," the sixty-five-year-old Hall of Famer recounted. "I got tested to see what condition my brain is in. And it's not in real good shape."

Running back Tony Dorsett received the same news last year. At fifty-nine, he had been living with bouts of depression and memory loss. In a tearful television interview, he admitted he gets lost driving his daughters to their sports games. "It's painful, man, for my daughters to say they're scared of me…I've thought about crazy stuff, sort of like, 'Why do I need to continue going through this?' I'm too smart of a person, I like to think, to take my life, but it's crossed my mind."

Once again, nobody can say for sure what the prevalence rate of CTE is in active NFL players. The diagnostic tools don't exist yet. Doctors have yet to determine how factors such as drug use or genetic disposition might contribute to the brain damage they're seeing. And the sample group is admittedly skewed—former players whose families have submitted their brains for examination. But the numbers are stark. As of March, neuropathologists at the NFL's designated brain bank had examined fifty-five former football players. All but one showed signs of CTE. Already, the disease has been identified in the brains of deceased college players and even one high schooler.

The first wave of media coverage, two decades ago, focused narrowly on the impact of concussions. As doctors gathered more data and shifted focus to the risks posed by the smaller collisions that occur every single play, the story evolved from a practical question—how to minimize big hits?—to an existential crisis.

It's useful to recall here the manner in which the public outcry over violence reshaped football a century ago. Back then, the President of the United States felt duty-bound to help speed reforms. The game was killing and maiming college and high school players. It was a moral problem.

The moment football became a business, violence was no longer just a moral problem. It was a money problem.

This, of course, is the big dance of capitalism: how to keep morality from gumming up the gears of profit, how to convince people to make bad decisions without seeing them as bad. We have whole industries devoted to this voodoo, the dark arts of advertising, marketing, public relations, lobbying. Every day, an army of clever men and women are devising new ways to get us to enjoy tobacco and animal flesh and petroleum and corn syrup without suffering the harsh aftertaste of guilt, without dwelling on the ethical costs of these pleasures. Oftentimes, you will hear some academic type marvel at the American capacity for self-delusion. Here's our secret: we're soaking in it.

I mention all this not just to get my socialist jollies, but to emphasize the larger system within which modern football operates. From the perspective of its governing body, the NFL, the game is a multi-billion-dollar product. And those of us who love it are not innocent fans rooting for our teams to prevail. We're consumers. Our money and attention are what subsidize the game.

This is true of all pro sports. But it's especially true of football. Consider this factoid. In 1948, nearly nine-tenths of the revenue earned by the NFL's best team, the Philadelphia Eagles, came from ticket sales. The share from radio and TV rights was 3 percent. Hardcore fans kept the league afloat, the ones who braved stadiums so cold that players sat bundled in hay to keep warm on the sidelines.

This season, the NFL will receive $5 billion in TV rights alone, nearly half its total revenue, and three times more than Major League Baseball earns. This money is generated by the tens of millions of casual fans engaged in what we might call "passive consumption" (i.e., watching a game on your couch while inhaling Cheetos).

But the league's ascendance has had unintended consequences. Stars now qualify as national celebrities, and their physical deterioration is front-page news. Television coverage renders each game as both epic and personal. Back in the seventies, the camera angles were limited and the images often grainy. The players remained obscure under their bulky exoskeletons, more like superheroes than human beings. Today, we see the game in high-def. Slow motion replays show us the unnatural angle of a broken ankle and a quarterback's contorted face at the precise moment he is concussed. We hear the impact thanks to tiny microphones affixed to player's uniforms. It's gotten harder and harder for even casual fans to deny the cruelty of the game.

The standard rationalization hauled out at this point is that the NFL will clean up the game. As fans, we want to believe that league officials will choose the righteous path over the profitable one. This is nonsense and always has been.

From the beginning, the NFL has sought to obscure the most disturbing aspects of the game. This is why Bertie Bell, the first great commissioner of the NFL, wrote a stipulation into the contracts the league signed with TV networks prohibiting them from showing injuries or fights. "In the matter of television and radio we are doing a job for the public," he explained, "a job of showing them the best football in the world." In a more candid moment, Bell explained the appeal of the sport this way: "You knock my brains out this Sunday and I knock your brains out the next time we meet."

So football's guardians have always tried to walk this absurd line, between selling violence and disavowing it. The best way to gauge how league officials will respond to safety concerns is to consider what they have done thus far.

The first commissioner to issue a public statement on concussions was Paul Tagliabue, who succeeded Pete Rozelle in 1989. His statement: "On concussions, I think this is one of those pack journalism issues, frankly. The problem is a journalist issue." He cited steroids, drinking, and other injuries as more pressing matters.

Having served as the league's lead counsel before becoming commissioner, Tagliabue eventually adopted the same activist strategy employed by the tobacco industry. He sought to shape public debate by flooding the market with junk science. The NFL created a "research body" called the Mild Traumatic Brain Injury Committee. (If you believe, as I do, that language is essentially an instrument of truth, we might pause here a moment to linger upon the spooky propagandistic frisson produced by the juxtaposition of those two words: *mild, traumatic.*)

Tagliabue chose a man named Elliot Pellman to chair the committee. Pellman was a rheumatologist with no experience in brain research. He worked for the New York Jets and was Tagliabue's personal physician.

Members of the committee published sixteen papers in a medical journal called *Neurosurgery*, whose editor-in-chief was a consultant to the New York Giants. These papers invariably reached the same conclusion: NFL players were, if not impervious to brain injury, unlikely to suffer long-term effects. The authors, many of whom had worked in and around football for years, seemed at times almost touchingly naive about the fundamental nature of the game. ("Professional football players do not sustain frequent repetitive blows to the brain on a regular basis.") A number of these papers found a home in *Neurosurgery* only after being rejected by other editors and peer reviewers. Some were later repudiated by their own authors. Still, the committee provided crucial cover for Tagliabue. Every time some pesky reporter brought up concussions, he could point to the MBTI and its reams of exculpatory data.

The problem was that the number of former players showing signs of cognitive damage kept growing. They also began committing suicide in rather flamboyant ways. Steelers lineman Terry Long drank anti-freeze. His teammate Justin Strzelczyk led police on a high-speed chase before crashing into a tank truck at 90 mph. Long was forty-five, Strzelczyk thirty-six.

By the mid-2000s, a group of neurologists unaffiliated with the NFL had begun examining deceased players and finding incontrovertible evidence of brain damage that explained the disturbing symptoms of dementia reported by family members. In 2007, new commissioner Roger Goodell listened to a number of these doctors present their findings at a conference he convened on brain injuries.

His public response subtly undermined the link between football and brain damage. "I'm not a doctor, but you have to look at their entire medical history," he said. "To look at something that is isolated without looking at their entire medical history I think is irresponsible." The league also released a carefully worded pamphlet whose ostensible purpose was to inform players of the risks associated with concussions: "Current research with professional athletes has not shown that having more than one or two concussions leads to permanent problems if each injury is managed properly…Research is currently underway to determine if there are any long-term effects of concussions in NFL athletes."

The league had entered its official Obfuscation Phase.

It didn't last long. Two years later, an NFL spokesman told a reporter this: "It's quite obvious from the medical research that's been done that concussions can lead to long-term problems." By this time, larger media outlets— *The New York Times* and *PBS* in particular—had begun piecing together the NFL's systematic cover-up. Players had begun to speak out and to consider legal remedy.

In 2011, a former Atlanta Falcons safety named Ray Easterling sued the NFL, an action eventually joined by more than 4,500 other former players. The suit accuses the NFL not only of negligence but fraud, a "concerted effort of deception and denial" that includes "industry-funded and falsified research."

In 2013, the NFL agreed to pay a settlement of $765 million, along with an estimated $200 million in legal fees. The presiding judge deemed this sum insufficient to cover the anticipated medical costs of the 20,000 players who eventually may qualify for payment.

Anybody with even a rudimentary sense of how corporations regard liability will understand why the NFL is so eager to make a deal. First, a settlement would guarantee that league officials never have to answer questions under oath regarding what they knew, and when, about the link between football and brain damage. Second, they would avoid the discovery phase, which would make public the grisly medical histories of former players. Presumably, some of these players and their family members would testify. It would be a public relations disaster.

And that's what matters, in the end, to NFL officials and what makes their conduct so transparent. Roger Goodell and the men who work for him are not stupid. They've looked at the mountain of medical data and come to the same reluctant conclusion that Big Coal and Big Meat did decades ago. The business they run is unsafe for their workers.

The moral decision in this situation isn't very complicated: you stop playing the game until you learn more. You explain the dangers to your players (and the public) and you apologize for gambling with their health.

Goodell has made business decisions. He's done just enough—purged the deniers, tweaked the rules, funded research—to allow us fans to pretend that the league gives a damn. He's placed his faith in our capacity for self-delusion.

The second big rationalization in the NFL Fan Survival Kit is that players knowingly choose to incur the game's risks and are paid for doing so. You hear this line all the time on sports talk radio, often in that pitched, contemptuous tone characteristic of men who resent moral contemplation.

Okay. Let's start with the issue of what constitutes informed consent. Here's what seems fair: On NFL Draft Day, Roger Goodell can call the number one draft pick to the stage and give him his jersey and hat. But the commish will also have to hand the kid a waiver, the text of which would be printed on-screen:

> *I, _____, the undersigned, am aware that the average age of death of an NFL player is, according to the Players Union, up to two decades shorter than normal life expectancy. Furthermore, I recognize that playing in*

27

the League, even in the absence of formally diagnosed concussions, may cause brain damage leading to the loss of cognitive function, depression, disorienta-tion, and suicidal ideation.

A copy of this waiver will be distributed to the draftee's family. They will then be required to watch a brief video of former players, such as the late Pittsburgh Steeler Mike Webster, describing—or attempting to describe—what life is like with CTE. Then the player and his family will be given a week to consider the matter.

That would be informed consent.

Most of those kids would sign. They would sign not just because they're twenty years old and believe they're bulletproof, but because their talent for football is the single attribute upon which they have been judged for most of their lives. Football isn't just what they do. It's who they are.

NFL players are members of an elite fraternity that knowingly places self-sacrifice, valor, and machismo above medical commonsense. Football is the one major American sport that selects specifically for the ability to inflict and absorb physical pain. (We don't judge baseball or basketball players on how well they can take a hit.) The ultimate badge of honor for a pro football player is not that he play *fair* or that he play *hard* but that he play *hurt*.

In January of 2014, ESPN asked 320 NFL players, anonymously, if they would play in the Super Bowl with a concussion. Eighty-five percent said yes. More recently, a linebacker for the Jacksonville Jaguars named Russell Allen revealed the reason for his unexpected retirement: he suffered a stroke after being hit during a game last year. Allen refused to leave the game or inform medical personnel because he feared he might lose his starting job.

One of the more despicable arguments put forward by the MBTI committee was that the rigors of football weeded out the weak. Those who made it to the pro level were less susceptible to concussions and quicker to recover from them. The proof of this claim was that so many players returned to the playing field so quickly after suffering concussions, which was a little like claiming that the dangers of black lung weren't that serious because so many coal miners returned to work after bouts of respiratory illness.

What an unbiased examination of the data suggests is that concussions have been under-reported, under-diagnosed, and under-treated for decades. When doctors describe symptoms to an older player—dizziness, seeing stars—they often identify these as routine. The linebacker Bill Romanowski, by all accounts one of the nastiest players in league history, estimated that by these standards he'd suffered five hundred or more concussions during his career. "I saw stars every day for sixteen years. I saw stars in college." He was diagnosed with twenty concussions.

The NFL's research wasn't gauging the resilience of players' brains, but the toxic convergence of its own reckless cupidity with the macho culture that prevails among its employees.

What happens to a player who rejects this culture?

Consider the case of Ted Johnson. During his ten-year career, the hard-hitting linebacker helped the Patriots win three Super Bowls. In 2002, he suffered a concussion and briefly blacked out during a pre-season game. He returned to practice four days later, expecting he would wear a red jersey for "minimal contact." A blue "full contact" jersey was hanging in his locker. Johnson confronted a trainer, who told him there had been a mistake, that he wasn't cleared for contact. Johnson put on the red jersey. Out on the practice field, as the team prepared for a contact drill, an assistant trainer brought him a blue jersey. Coach Bill Belichick had directed him to do so. Johnson was incensed.

Here's where things get truly messed up.

Johnson put the jersey on anyway. Almost immediately, he suffered a second concussion and was rushed to the hospital. When he confronted Belichick privately, Johnson says the coach admitted that he'd screwed up and apologized to him.

Belichick's public response to the incident was considerably different: "If Ted felt so strongly that he didn't feel he was ready to practice with us, he should have told me."

This is part of what makes Bill Belichick a great coach. He knows how to "get the most out of his players," which is a kinder way of saying that he knows how to manipulate them. He knows that a tough guy like Johnson would rather risk his health than risk losing face by refusing to put on that blue jersey. "They weren't going to beat me," is how Johnson put it.

Instead, Belichick got Johnson to beat himself.

Johnson played three more seasons for the Patriots. He estimates that he suffered half a dozen more concussions, though he reported only one of them because he wanted to avoid being labeled soft. He was already suffering from symptoms of neurological damage, which have worsened.

If you follow football, especially in New England, you hear a lot of talk about the so-called "Patriot way," a dignified, stoic approach to the game. One of its central tenets is extreme secrecy when it comes to injuries. And yet here is how one team official summed up Johnson's medical condition to a *Boston Globe* reporter: "Ted Johnson is a very sick young man. We've been aware of the emotional issues he's had for years. You can't blame all of his behavior on concussions."

The Patriot Way: When a player receives serial brain traumas trying to honor your code, suggest in print that he is mentally ill.

Of course, it's easy to blame ruthless coaches and venal owners and foolhardy players, and much harder for us to see our own role in all this.

Most football players begin life with limited socioeconomic options. They may love football for its inherent virtues. But they also quickly come to see the game as a path to glory and riches. These rewards aren't inherent. They arise from a culture of fandom that views players as valuable only so long as they can perform.

We might pay lip service to health issues, but we're much less forgiving when the injury report comes out. Scroll through the Internet message boards, or listen to the provocateurs on sports talk radio. A frequently hurt player is not to be pitied, but suspected. In these kangaroo courts, "injury prone" has become synonymous with cowardly or weak-willed. The explosion in steroid use is partly a response to this mindset. The drugs help speed recovery from injuries.

Then again, according to a lawsuit filed in May, scores of ex-players were fed pain pills by team doctors and trainers—the pills were "handed out to us like candy," in the words of one retired lineman—and pressured to soldier on despite severe injuries. One of the named plaintiffs (there are more than five hundred in all), former Pro Bowl quarterback Jim McMahon, claims he incurred a broken neck and ankle during his career, never received proper diagnoses, and played through both. Like other former players, McMahon wound up addicted to painkillers and now suffers from the early stages of dementia.

We worship players for bravery and excoriate them for vulnerability because we wish to see masculine ideals on display. But I think here also of Cicero, who speculated that the loathing for timid gladiators wasn't a function of their diminished entertainment value but the fact that they forced spectators to confront the profound heartlessness of the games.

If you want to know what the current state of the research is on NFL players and brain damage, one of the best people on earth to consult is Dr. Ann McKee, co-director of the Center for the Study of Traumatic Encephalopathy at Boston University and chief neuropathologist for the National Veterans Affairs ALS Brain Bank in Bedford, MA. McKee is the person who cuts up the brains of former players and determines if they have CTE. Because so many brains have been coming in recently, and because (as her titles suggest) she is a very busy person, she is perpetually "about thirty brains behind."

She believes the gravest threat to players comes from sub-concussive hits, which the NFL's safety rules and concussion protocols won't prevent. The next milestone, McKee predicts, will be when doctors can measure brain injuries incurred during play and brain disease in living players. "That will be the defining moment, the one that rewrites the book," she says. "I don't think we're that far away." She foresees a day when players entering the NFL will receive a risk assessment for brain damage based on factors such as genetic disposition, the number of years played, position, etc.

The introduction of such innovations would erode the haze of medical uncertainty that has long insulated the league and us fans. Imagine what would happen if word leaked that the top draft choice in 2017 stood a 25 percent chance of incurring brain damage five years into his career? Or if he was revealed to have incipient CTE? Or if fans had to confront not just replays of a superstar being knocked insensate, but a CAT scan showing the damage to his frontal lobes?

McKee is sometimes miscast as the bête noir of the NFL because she was among the most visible early authorities on CTE. In fact, league executives dismissed her research for years. They've since adopted a kind of keep-your-enemies closer approach by designating her lab as the league's "preferred" brain bank and granting her millions in funding.

McKee is also, helpfully, an outspoken fan of the game. Her desk is surrounded by hundreds of slides of brain slices dyed to show areas with a buildup of tau, the cell-strangling protein symptomatic of CTE. Precariously balanced atop one stack of slides is a bobblehead doll of Aaron Rodgers, the quarterback of her Green Bay Packers.

McKee told me if she were a boy she would have played football, and that she wanted her son to play. "When he got to high school, his dad didn't want him to play because it was too dangerous. I said, 'You've got to be kidding me.' It was horrifying to me!" McKee laughed. "So he played soccer."

I asked McKee how she justifies watching the game, knowing its dangers so intimately. "I don't know," she said. "I don't know where I am. I think it's a really important question. I have, like, these two faces. Right now they're pretty separate. I do watch a lot of football on Sunday."

In the morgue, a small, frigid room thick with the smell of preserving fluid, McKee lifted the lid of a white plastic bucket. Inside was a brain covered with splotches of dark crimson. "That's a suicide," explained her colleague, Dr. Victor Alvarez. McKee selected another brain and set it down on her cutting board. It looked like a small, discolored ham. She began slicing it up with a long scalpel.

Most of the brains McKee examines belong to veterans, not athletes. But the second brain she chose was a young female rugby player who had suffered a concussion, then continued to play. After a second impact, she suffered massive swelling of the brain and died. High school athletes are especially susceptible to so-called "second-impact syndrome."

I was there to talk to McKee about CTE, but the conversation between her and Alvarez and a young assistant named Brian quickly turned to the Super Bowl, which had been played a few weeks earlier.

Brian was a fan of the Denver Broncos, who had been routed. "After the first quarter, I just wanted it to be an entertaining game!" he said, carefully sliding brain slices into small plastic cases.

"After the first series!" said Alvarez, a Buffalo Bills fan.

At a certain point, I outed myself as a Raiders partisan, and we were off to the races.

It was an odd situation—actually *surreal* is closer to the mark. Even as McKee was dissecting this girl's hippocampus and amygdala and her delicate spinal cord, we were gabbing about football.

Before I left, McKee showed me two large color prints that hung in the hallway outside her office. One showed the brain of an eighteen-year-old football player with the brown spotting that signifies the onset of CTE. The other was a photo of a brain with two ghastly gouges in its frontal lobes, a lobotomy as they were conducted in the years after World War I.

A psychiatrist named Walter Freeman performed nearly 3,500 lobotomies, many of them by pressing an icepick through the corner of the eye socket and into the patient's brain. The procedure was sometimes used to treat victims of shell shock. The press hailed Freeman as a miracle worker. Only years later were his methods debunked. McKee marveled at the public acceptance of such barbarism, and I said, only half joking, that maybe decades from now the public will recoil at the thought that we ever watched a game that could permanently harm a teenager's brain.

"I've started to think it's impossible to change the NFL," McKee said. "People think none of this work will change the NFL."

She seemed completely blind to the irony hanging right in front of her. The ultimate agents of social change aren't researchers like her, but individual fans (like her) who confront the moral meaning of the research, who make the connection between the damaged brains—such as those McKee dissects— and their own behavior.

How to Tame a Wild Tongue

GLORIA ANZALDÚA

A poet and an essayist, Gloria Anzaldúa published widely on feminist theory, queer theory, Chicano studies, and issues related to "borderlands" during her career. In "How to Tame a Wild Tongue," she contends that language is central to ethnic identity, and she offers an impassioned response to the violence of restricting one's dialects and languages by incorporating her own languages and dialects into the text. "How to Tame a Wild Tongue" is perhaps the most widely circulating essay among her many award-winning publications. Here, her play with essay conventions raises compelling questions about how a text's purpose can be conveyed through rhetorical choices: she blurs the boundaries between essay writing and poetry, emotion and logic, spirituality and rationality.

"We're going to have to control your tongue," the dentist says, pulling out all the metal from my mouth. Silver bits plop and tinkle into the basin. My mouth is a motherlode.

The dentist is cleaning out my roots. I get a whiff of the stench when I gasp. "I can't cap that tooth yet, you're still draining," he says.

"We're going to have to do something about your tongue," I hear the anger rising in his voice. My tongue keeps pushing out the wads of cotton, pushing back the drills, the long thin needles. "I've never seen anything as strong or as stubborn," he says. And I think, how do you tame a wild tongue, train it to be quiet, how do you bridle and saddle it? How do you make it lie down?

"Who is to say that robbing a people of
its language is less violent than war?"
—Ray Gwyn Smith[1]

I remember being caught speaking Spanish at recess—that was good for three licks on the knuckles with a sharp ruler. I remember being sent to the corner of the classroom for "talking back" to the Anglo teacher when all I was trying to do was tell her how to pronounce my name. "If you want to be American, speak 'American.' If you don't like it, go back to Mexico where you belong."

"I want you to speak English. *Pa' hallar buen trabajo tienes que saber hablar el inglés bien. Qué vale toda tu educación si todavía hablas inglés con un* 'accent,'" my mother would say, mortified that I spoke English like a Mexican. At Pan American University, I, and all Chicano students were required to take two speech classes. Their purpose: to get rid of our accents.

Attacks on one's form of expression with the intent to censor are a violation of the First Amendment. *El Anglo con cara de inocente nos arrancó la lengua.* Wild tongues can't be tamed, they can only be cut out.

Overcoming the Tradition of Silence

> *Ahogadas, escupimos el oscuro.*
> *Peleando con nuestra propia sombra*
> *el silencio nos sepulta.*

En boca cerrada no entran moscas. "Flies don't enter a closed mouth" is a saying I kept hearing when I was a child. *Ser habladora* was to be a gossip and a liar, to talk too much. *Muchachitas bien criadas,* well-bred girls don't answer back. *Es una falta de respeto* to talk back to one's mother or father. I remember one of the sins I'd recite to the priest in the confession box the few times I went to confession: talking back to my mother, *hablar pa' 'trás, repelar. Hocicona, repelona, chismosa,* having a big mouth, questioning, carrying tales are all signs of being *mal criada.* In my culture they are all words that are derogatory if applied to women—I've never heard them applied to men.

The first time I heard two women, a Puerto Rican and a Cuban, say the word "*nosotras,*" I was shocked. I had not known the word existed. Chicanas use *nosotros* whether we're male or female. We are robbed of our female being by the masculine plural. Language is a male discourse.

> And our tongues have become
> dry   the wilderness has
> dried out our tongues   and
> we have forgotten speech.
> —Irena Klepfisz[2]

Even our own people, other Spanish speakers *nos quieren poner candados en la boca.* They would hold us back with their bag of *reglas de academia.*

Oyé como ladra: el lenguaje de la frontera

Quien tiene boca se equivoca.

—Mexican saying

"*Pocho*, cultural traitor, you're speaking the oppressor's language by speaking English, you're ruining the Spanish language," I have been accused by various Latinos and Latinas. Chicano Spanish is considered by the purist and by most Latinos deficient, a mutilation of Spanish.

But Chicano Spanish is a border tongue which developed naturally. Change, *evolución, enriquecimiento de palabras nuevas por invención o adopción* have created variants of Chicano Spanish, *un nuevo lenguaje. Un lenguaje que corresponde a un modo de vivir.* Chicano Spanish is not incorrect, it is a living language.

For a people who are neither Spanish nor live in a country in which Spanish is the first language; for a people who live in a country in which English is the reigning tongue but who are not Anglo; for a people who cannot entirely identify with either standard (formal, Castillian) Spanish nor standard English, what recourse is left to them but to create their own language? A language which they can connect their identity to, one capable of communicating the realities and values true to themselves—a language with terms that are neither *español ni inglés*, but both. We speak a patois, a forked tongue, a variation of two languages.

Chicano Spanish sprang out of the Chicanos' need to identify ourselves as a distinct people. We needed a language with which we could communicate with ourselves, a secret language. For some of us, language is a homeland closer than the Southwest—for many Chicanos today live in the Midwest and the East. And because we are a complex, heterogeneous people, we speak many languages. Some of the languages we speak are:

1. Standard English
2. Working class and slang English
3. Standard Spanish
4. Standard Mexican Spanish
5. North Mexican Spanish dialect
6. Chicano Spanish (Texas, New Mexico, Arizona and California have regional variations)
7. Tex-Mex
8. *Pachuco* (called *caló*)

My "home" tongues are the languages I speak with my sister and brothers, with my friends. They are the last five listed, with 6 and 7 being closest to my heart. From school, the media, and job situations, I've picked up standard and working class English. From Mamagrande Locha and from reading Spanish and Mexican literature, I've picked up Standard Spanish and Standard Mexican Spanish. From *los recién llegados*, Mexican immigrants, and *braceros*, I learned the North Mexican dialect. With Mexicans I'll try to speak either Standard Mexican Spanish or the North Mexican dialect. From my parents and Chicanos living in the Valley, I picked up Chicano Texas Spanish, and I speak it with my mom, younger brother (who married a Mexican and who rarely mixes Spanish with English), aunts and older relatives.

With Chicanas from *Nuevo México* or *Arizona* I will speak Chicano Spanish a little, but often they don't understand what I'm saying. With most California Chicanas I speak entirely in English (unless I forget). When I first moved to San Francisco, I'd rattle off something in Spanish, unintentionally embarrassing them. Often it is only with another Chicana *tejana* that I can talk freely.

Words distorted by English are known as anglicisms or *pochismos*. The *pocho* is an anglicized Mexican or American of Mexican origin who speaks Spanish with an accent characteristic of North Americans and who distorts and reconstructs the language according to the influence of English.[3] Tex-Mex, or Spanglish, comes most naturally to me. I may switch back and forth from English to Spanish in the same sentence or in the same word. With my sister and my brother Nune and with Chicano *tejano* contemporaries I speak in Tex-Mex.

From kids and people my own age I picked up Pachuco. Pachuco (the language of the zoot suiters) is a language of rebellion, both against Standard Spanish and Standard English. It is a secret language. Adults of the culture and outsiders cannot understand it. It is made up of slang words from both English and Spanish. *Ruca* means girl or woman, *vato* means guy or dude, *chale* means no, *simón* means yes, *churro* is sure, talk is *periquiar*, *pigionear* means petting, *que gacho* means how nerdy, *ponte águila* means watch out, death is called *la pelona*. Through lack of practice and not having others who can speak it, I've lost most of the *Pachuco* tongue.

Chicano Spanish

Chicanos, after 250 years of Spanish/Anglo colonization, have developed significant differences in the Spanish we speak. We collapse two adjacent vowels into a single syllable and sometimes shift the stress in certain words such as *maíz/maiz, cohete/cuete.* We leave out certain consonants when they appear between vowels: *lado/lao, mojado/mojao.* Chicanos from South Texas pronounced *f* as *j* as in *jue (fue).* Chicanos use "archaisms," words that are no longer in the Spanish language, words that have been evolved out. We say *semos, truje, haiga, ansina,* and *naiden.* We retain the "archaic" *j,* as in *jalar,* that derives from an earlier *h,* (the French *halar* or the Germanic *halon* which was lost to standard Spanish in the 16th century), but which is still found in several regional dialects such as the one spoken in South Texas. (Due to geography, Chicanos from the Valley of South Texas were cut off linguistically from other Spanish speakers. We tend to use words that the Spaniards brought over from Medieval Spain. The majority of the Spanish colonizers in Mexico and the Southwest came from Extremadura—Hernán Cortés was one of them—and Andalucía. Andalucians pronounce *ll* like a *y,* and their *d*'s tend to be absorbed by adjacent vowels: *tirado* becomes *tirao.* They brought *el lenguaje popular, dialectos y regionalismos.*[4])

Chicanos and other Spanish speakers also shift *ll* to *y* and *z* to *s.*[5] We leave out initial syllables, saying *tar* for *estar, toy* for *estoy, hora* for *ahora (cubanos* and *puertorriqueños* also leave out initial letters of some words.) We also leave out the final syllable such as *pa* for *para.* The intervocalic *y,* the *ll* as in *tortilla, ella, botella,* gets replaced by *tortia* or *tortiya, ea, botea.* We add an additional syllable at the beginning of certain words: *atocar* for *tocar, agastar* for *gastar.* Sometimes we'll say *lavaste las vacijas,* other times *lavates* (substituting the *ates* verb endings for the *aste*).

We use anglicisms, words borrowed from English: *bola* from ball, *carpeta* from carpet, *máchina de lavar* (instead of *lavadora*) from washing machine. Tex-Mex argot, created by adding a Spanish sound at the beginning or end of an English word such as *cookiar* for cook, *watchar* for watch, *parkiar* for park, and *rapiar* for rape, is the result of the pressures on Spanish speakers to adapt to English.

We don't use the word *vosotros/as* or its accompanying verb form. We don't say *claro* (to mean yes), *imagínate,* or *me emociona,* unless we picked up Spanish from Latinas, out of a book, or in a classroom. Other Spanish speaking groups are going through the same, or similar, development in their Spanish.

Linguistic Terrorism

Deslenguadas. Somos los del español deficiente. We are your linguistic nightmare, your linguistic aberration, your linguistic *mestisaje,* the subject of

your *burla*. Because we speak with tongues of fire we are culturally cruci-
fied. Racially, culturally, and linguistically *somos huérfanos*—we speak an
orphan tongue.

Chicanas who grew up speaking Chicano Spanish have internalized the belief
that we speak poor Spanish. It is illegitimate, a bastard language. And because
we internalize how our language has been used against us by the dominant
culture, we use our language differences against each other.

Chicana feminists often skirt around each other with suspicion and hesita-
tion. For the longest time I couldn't figure it out. Then it dawned on me. To be
close to another Chicana is like looking into the mirror. We are afraid of what
we'll see there. *Pena*. Shame. Low estimation of self. In childhood we are told
that our language is wrong. Repeated attacks on our native tongue diminish
our sense of self. The attacks continue throughout our lives.

Chicanas feel uncomfortable talking in Spanish to Latinas, afraid of their cen-
sure. Their language was not outlawed in their countries. They had a whole
lifetime of being immersed in their native tongue; generations, centuries in
which Spanish was a first language, taught in school, heard on radio and TV,
and read in the newspaper.

If a person, Chicana or Latina, has a low estimation of my native tongue, she
also has a low estimation of me. Often with *mexicanas y latinas* we'll speak
English as a neutral language. Even among Chicanas we tend to speak English at parties or conferences. Yet, at the same time, we're afraid the other will
think we're *agringadas* because we don't speak Chicano Spanish. We oppress
each other trying to out-Chicano each other, vying to be the "real" Chicanas, to speak like Chicanos. There is no one Chicano language just as there
is no one Chicano experience. A monolingual Chicana whose first language
is English or Spanish is just as much a Chicana as one who speaks several
variants of Spanish. A Chicana from Michigan or Chicago or Detroit is just
as much a Chicana as one from the Southwest. Chicano Spanish is as diverse
linguistically as it is regionally.

By the end of this century, Spanish speakers will comprise the biggest minority group in the U.S., a country where students in high schools and colleges
are encouraged to take French classes because French is considered more
"cultured." But for a language to remain alive it must be used.[6] By the end
of this century English, and not Spanish, will be the mother tongue of most
Chicanos and Latinos.

~

So, if you want to really hurt me, talk badly about my language. Ethnic identity is twin skin to linguistic identity—I am my language. Until I can take pride in my language, I cannot take pride in myself. Until I can accept as legitimate Chicano Texas Spanish, Tex-Mex and all the other languages I speak, I cannot accept the legitimacy of myself. Until I am free to write bilingually and to switch codes without having always to translate, while I still have to speak English or Spanish when I would rather speak Spanglish, and as long as I have to accommodate the English speakers rather than having them accommodate me, my tongue will be illegitimate.

I will no longer be made to feel ashamed of existing. I will have my voice: Indian, Spanish, white. I will have my serpent's tongue—my woman's voice, my sexual voice, my poet's voice. I will overcome the tradition of silence.

> My fingers
> move sly against your palm
> Like women everywhere, we speak in code....
> —Melanie Kaye/Kantrowitz[7]

"Vistas," corridos, y comida: My Native Tongue

In the 1960s, I read my first Chicano novel. It was *City of Night* by John Rechy a gay Texan, son of a Scottish father and a Mexican mother. For days I walked around in stunned amazement that a Chicano could write and could get published. When I read *I Am Joaquín*[8] I was surprised to see a bilingual book by a Chicano in print. When I saw poetry written in Tex-Mex for the first time, a feeling of pure joy flashed through me. I felt like we really existed as a people. In 1971, when I started teaching High School English to Chicano students, I tried to supplement the required texts with works by Chicanos, only to be reprimanded and forbidden to do so by the principal. He claimed that I was supposed to teach "American" and English literature. At the risk of being fired, I swore my students to secrecy and slipped in Chicano short stories, poems, a play. In graduate school, while working toward a Ph.D., I had to "argue" with one advisor after the other, semester after semester, before I was allowed to make Chicano literature an area of focus.

Even before I read books by Chicanos or Mexicans, it was the Mexican movies I saw at the drive-in—the Thursday night special of $1.00 a carload—that gave me a sense of belonging. "*Vámonos a las vistas*," my mother would call out and we'd all—grandmother, brothers, sister and cousins—squeeze into the car. We'd wolf down cheese and bologna white bread sandwiches while watching Pedro Infante in melodramatic tearjerkers like *Nosotros los pobres*, the first "real" Mexican movie (that was not an imitation of European movies). I remember seeing *Cuando los hijos se van* and surmising that all Mexican movies played up the love a mother has for her children and what ungrateful sons and daughters suffer when they are not devoted to their mothers. I remember the singing-type "westerns" of Jorge Negrete and Miguel Aceves Mejía. When watching Mexican movies, I felt a sense of homecoming as well as alienation. People who were to amount to something didn't go to Mexican movies, or *bailes* or tune their radios to *bolero*, *rancherita*, and *corrido* music.

The whole time I was growing up, there was *norteño* music sometimes called North Mexican border music, or Tex-Mex music, or Chicano music, or *cantina* (bar) music. I grew up listening to *conjuntos*, three- or four-piece bands made up of folk musicians playing guitar, *bajo sexto*, drums and button accordion, which Chicanos had borrowed from the German immigrants who had come to Central Texas and Mexico to farm and build breweries. In the Rio Grande Valley, Steve Jordan and Little Joe Hernández were popular, and Flaco Jiménez was the accordion king. The rhythms of Tex-Mex music are those of the polka, also adapted from the Germans, who in turn had borrowed the polka from the Czechs and Bohemians.

I remember the hot, sultry evenings when *corridos*—songs of love and death on the Texas-Mexican borderlands—reverberated out of cheap amplifiers from the local *cantinas* and wafted in through my bedroom window.

Corridos first became widely used along the South Texas/Mexican border during the early conflict between Chicanos and Anglos. The *corridos* are usually about Mexican heroes who do valiant deeds against the Anglo oppressors. Pancho Villa's song, "*La cucaracha*," is the most famous one. *Corridos* of John F. Kennedy and his death are still very popular in the Valley. Older Chicanos remember Lydia Mendoza, one of the great border *corrido* singers who was called *la Gloria de Tejas*. Her "*El tango negro*," sung during the Great Depression, made her a singer of the people. The everpresent *corridos* narrated one hundred years of border history, bringing news of events as well as entertaining. These folk musicians and folk songs are our chief cultural mythmakers, and they made our hard lives seem bearable.

I grew up feeling ambivalent about our music. Country-western and rock-and-roll had more status. In the 50s and 60s, for the slightly educated and *agringado* Chicanos, there existed a sense of shame at being caught listening to our music. Yet I couldn't stop my feet from thumping to the music, could not stop humming the words, nor hide from myself the exhilaration I felt when I heard it.

~

There are more subtle ways that we internalize identification, especially in the forms of images and emotions. For me food and certain smells are tied to my identity, to my homeland. Woodsmoke curling up to an immense blue sky; woodsmoke perfuming my grandmother's clothes, her skin. The stench of cow manure and the yellow patches on the ground; the crack of a .22 rifle and the reek of cordite. Homemade white cheese sizzling in a pan, melting inside a folded *tortilla*. My sister Hilda's hot, spicy *menudo, chile colorado* making it deep red, pieces of *panza* and hominy floating on top. My brother Carito barbecuing *fajitas* in the backyard. Even now and 3,000 miles away, I can see my mother spicing the ground beef, pork and venison with *chile*. My mouth salivates at the thought of the hot steaming *tamales* I would be eating if I were home.

Si le preguntas a mi mamá, "¿Qué eres?"

> "Identity is the essential core of who
> we are as individuals, the conscious
> experience of the self inside."
> —Kaufman[9]

Nosotros los Chicanos straddle the borderlands. On one side of us, we are constantly exposed to the Spanish of the Mexicans, on the other side we hear the Anglos' incessant clamoring so that we forget our language. Among ourselves we don't say *nosotros los americanos, o nosotros los españoles, o nosotros los hispanos.* We say *nosotros los mexicanos* (by *mexicanos* we do not mean citizens of Mexico; we do not mean a national identity, but a racial one). We distinguish between *mexicanos del otro lado* and *mexicanos de este lado*. Deep in our hearts we believe that being Mexican has nothing to do with which country one lives in. Being Mexican is a state of soul—not one of mind, not one of citizenship. Neither eagle nor serpent, but both. And like the ocean, neither animal respects borders.

> *Dime con quien andas y te diré quien eres.*
> (Tell me who your friends are and I'll tell you who
> you are.)
> —Mexican saying

Si le preguntas a mi mamá,"¿Qué eres?" te dirá,"Soy mexicana." My brothers and sister say the same. I sometimes will answer *"soy mexicana"* and at others will say *"soy Chicana" o "soy tejana."* But I identified as *"Raza"* before I ever identi-fied as *"mexicana"* or "Chicana."

As a culture, we call ourselves Spanish when referring to ourselves as a lin-guistic group and when copping out. It is then that we forget our predomi-nant Indian genes. We are 70 to 80% Indian.[10] We call ourselves Hispanic[11] or Spanish-American or Latin American or Latin when linking ourselves to other Spanish-speaking peoples of the Western hemisphere and when cop-ping out. We call ourselves Mexican-American[12] to signify we are neither Mexican nor American, but more the noun "American" than the adjective "Mexican" (and when copping out).

Chicanos and other people of color suffer economically for not acculturat-ing. This voluntary (yet forced) alienation makes for psychological conflict, a kind of dual identity—we don't identify with the Anglo-American cultural values and we don't totally identify with the Mexican cultural values. We are a synergy of two cultures with various degrees of Mexicanness or Angloness. I have so internalized the borderland conflict that sometimes I feel like one cancels out the other and we are zero, nothing, no one. *A veces no soy nada ni nadie. Pero hasta cuando no lo soy, lo soy.*

When not copping out, when we know we are more than nothing, we call ourselves Mexican, referring to race and ancestry; *mestizo* when affirming both our Indian and Spanish (but we hardly ever own our Black ancestry); Chicano when referring to a politically aware people born and/or raised in the U.S.; *Raza* when referring to Chicanos; *tejanos* when we are Chicanos from Texas.

Chicanos did not know we were a people until 1965 when Cesar Chavez and the farmworkers united and *I Am Joaquín* was published and *la Raza Unida* party was formed in Texas. With that recognition, we became a distinct people. Something momentous happened to the Chicano soul—we became aware of our reality and acquired a name and a language (Chicano Spanish) that reflected that reality. Now that we had a name, some of the fragmented pieces began to fall together—who we were, what we were, how we had evolved. We began to get glimpses of what we might eventually become.

Yet the struggle of identities continues, the struggle of borders is our reality still. One day the inner struggle will cease and a true integration take place. In the meantime, *tenémos que hacer la lucha. ¿Quién está protegiendo los ranchos de mi gente? ¿Quién está tratando de cerrar la fisura entre la india y el blanco en nues-tra sangre? El Chicano, si, el Chicano que anda como un ladrón en su propia casa.*

~

Los Chicanos, how patient we seem, how very patient. There is the quiet of the Indian about us.[13] We know how to survive. When other races have given up their tongue, we've kept ours. We know what it is to live under the hammer blow of the dominant *norteamericano* culture. But more than we count the blows, we count the days the weeks the years the centuries the eons until the white laws and commerce and customs will rot in the deserts they've created, lie bleached. *Humildes* yet proud, *quietos* yet wild, *nosotros los mexicanos-Chicanos* will walk by the crumbling ashes as we go about our business. Stubborn, persevering, impenetrable as stone, yet possessing a malleability that renders us unbreakable, we, the *mestizas* and *mestizos*, will remain.

Notes

1. Ray Gwyn Smith, *Moorland Is Cold Country*, unpublished book.

2. Irena Klepfisz, "*Di rayze aheym*/The Journey Home," in *The Tribe of Dina: A Jewish Women's Anthology*, Melanie Kaye/Kantrowitz and Irena Klepfisz, eds. (Montpelier, VT: Sinister Wisdom Books, 1986), 49.

3. R. C. Ortega, *Dialectología Del Barrio*, trans. Hortencia S. Alwan (Los Angeles, CA: R. C. Ortega Publisher & Bookseller, 1977), 132.

4. Eduardo Hernandéz-Chávez, Andrew D. Cohen, and Anthony F. Beltramo, *El Lenguaje de los Chicanos: Regional and Social Characteristics of Language Used by Mexican Americans* (Arlington. VA: Center for Applied Linguistics, 1975), 39.

5. Hernandéz-Chávez, xvii.

6. Irena Klepfisz, "Secular Jewish Identity: Yidishkayt in America," in *The Tribe of Dina*, Kaye/Kantrowitz and Klepfisz, eds., 43.

7. Melanie Kaye/Kantrowitz, "Sign," in *We Speak in Code: Poems and Other Writings* (Pittsburgh, PA: Motheroot Publications, Inc., 1980), 85.

8. Rodolfo Gonzales, *I Am Joaquín/Yo Soy Joaquín* (New York, NY: Bantam Books, 1972). It was first published in 1967.

9. Gershen Kaufman, *Shame: The Power of Caring* (Cambridge: Schenkman Books, Inc. 1980), 68.

10. John R. Chávez, *The Lost Land: The Chicano Images of the Southwest* (Albuquerque, NM: University of New Mexico Press, 1984), 88–90.

11. "Hispanic" is derived from *Hispanis* (*España*, a name given to the Iberian Peninsula in ancient times when it was a part of the Roman Empire) and is a term designated by the U.S. government to make it easier to handle us on paper.

12. The Treaty of Guadalupe Hidalgo created the Mexican-American in 1848.

13. Anglos, in order to alleviate their guilt for dispossessing the Chicano, stressed the Spanish part of us and perpetrated the myth of the Spanish Southwest. We have accepted the fiction that we are Hispanic, that is Spanish, in order to accommodate ourselves to the dominant culture and its abhorrence of Indians. Chávez, 88–91.

From *On Immunity: An Inoculation*

EULA BISS

Eula Biss is a non-fiction writer and poet whose works include Notes from No Man's Land: A Collection of American Essays *and* The Balloonists, *a book of narrative prose poems. The following excerpt is taken from Biss's 2014 work,* On Immunity: An Inoculation, *in which she addresses the timely and controversial subject of immunization. As a researcher and writer, Biss deftly navigates a wide variety of sources—from scientific literature to children's literature, Carson's* Silent Spring *to Stoker's* Dracula—*in her efforts to understand the complex issue of vaccination. Combining personal narrative, academic research, and cultural criticism,* On Immunity *offers a multifaceted study of the history, science, politics, economics, and social dynamics of immunization in the United States.*

The novel flu virus warnings issued by the CDC in my son's first year seemed to produce, more than anything else, a proliferation of antibacterial soap and hand sanitizer. Sanitizing wipes were stationed by the carts in grocery stores in addition to pumps of sanitizer at every checkout counter. Large pumps of sanitizer appeared at the entrance to security in the airport, in the post office, and at the circulation desk in my library. These sanitizers remained long after the threat of flu had abated.

I was reluctant to be routinely sanitized. My father, whose own hands were often cracked from repeated washing during his rounds in the hospital, had instilled in me a skepticism of anything that promised to kill germs. Not all germs should be put to death, he maintained. Killing germs, rather than washing them away, reminded him of the Crusades, when an abbot who was asked how to tell the faithful from the heretics replied, "Kill them all—God will know his own."

While hand sanitizers were killing indiscriminately, studies were finding the chemical triclosan in the urine of pregnant women, in the cord blood of newborn babies, and in the breast milk of nursing mothers. Triclosan, an antimicrobial agent used in toothpaste, mouthwash, deodorant, cleaning products, and laundry detergent, among other things, is also the active ingredient in nearly all antibacterial liquid soaps and many hand sanitizers.

What we know about triclosan is that at low concentrations it can prevent both "good" and "bad" microbes from reproducing, and at higher concentrations it can kill them. We know that it is in our wastewater, it is in our streams, and it is in our finished drinking water. It is in wild fish all over the world, it is in earthworms, and it is in the blood of bottlenose dolphins. What we do not know is exactly what this means for our ecosystem.

The upshot of quite a bit of research involving unfortunate mice, rats, and rabbits is that triclosan is probably not very toxic to humans. But the long-term effects of a lifetime of constant exposure are not yet known. Despite the protests of at least one large chemical company, the Food and Drug Administration nominated triclosan for further research at the National Toxicology Program in 2008. Scott Masten, the toxicologist I spoke with there, was rather dispassionate on the subject of triclosan. "I don't buy antibacterial soap," he allowed, when pressed, "not because I'm afraid of it, but because it doesn't have any benefit." A number of studies have found that washing with antibacterial soaps is actually no more effective at reducing bacteria than washing with regular soap and water. Triclosan is in soaps, Dr. Masten suggested, only because companies have found a market for antibacterial products that promise to kill rather than just clean.

I was interested, I explained to him, in thinking about how the risks posed by triclosan might compare to the risks posed by some of the components of vaccines. Our exposure to triclosan is nearly constant, and it can even be found in the urine of people who do not use any products that contain it. In comparison, our exposure to traces of other chemicals through vaccination is limited to a couple dozen instances. But I did not want to make the mistake of exaggerating the dangers associated with triclosan, I told Dr. Masten, in pursuit of this idea. "Relative risk problems are hard to communicate," he agreed. The health risks triclosan poses for humans are probably low, but any degree of risk, he reminded me, should be unacceptable in a product that does not do any good.

Fears of vaccines do not seem easily quieted by an abundance of expert risk-benefit analyses assuring us that the good they do is far greater than the harm. Serious side effects from vaccination are rare. But it is difficult to quantify exactly how rare, in part because many of the complications associated with vaccines are also caused by the natural infections those vaccines are designed to prevent. Natural infections of measles, mumps, chicken pox, and influenza can all cause encephalitis, a swelling of the brain. We do not know what the base rate of encephalitis would be in a population with no disease and no vaccination against disease. But we do know that 1 in about every 1,000 cases of measles leads to encephalitis, and that encephalitis has been reported after vaccination in about 1 out of every 3 million doses of the MMR (measles-mumps-rubella) vaccine. This incidence is so rare that researchers have been unable to definitely determine whether or not encephalitis is caused by the vaccine.

A comprehensive report on vaccine "adverse events" was released in 2011 by a committee of eighteen medical experts who reviewed 12,000 studies of vaccination for the Institute of Medicine. They found convincing evidence that the MMR vaccine can, very rarely, cause a condition called measles inclusion body encephalitis in people with compromised immune systems. The MMR can also cause fever-induced seizures that are usually mild and result in no long-term harm. The chicken pox vaccine can cause chicken pox, particularly in people with weakened immune systems. And six different vaccines can cause an anaphylactic allergic reaction in people with severe allergies. The injection of any type of vaccine can produce fainting and muscle pain caused not by the vaccine, but by the act of injection itself.

What vaccines do not cause, the report explained, is significantly harder to establish than what they do cause. While a substantial amount of evidence is acceptable as proof that an event does and can happen, there is never enough evidence to prove that an event cannot happen. Even so, the evidence reviewed by the committee "favors rejection" of the theory that the MMR vaccine causes autism. This report was released shortly after a national survey revealed that a quarter of the parents who responded believed that vaccines cause autism. And over half of the parents expressed concern about serious side effects from vaccines.

"Perceptions of risk—the intuitive judgments that people make about the hazards of their world," the historian Michael Willrich observes, "can be stubbornly resistant to the evidence of experts." We do not tend to be afraid of the things that are most likely to harm us. We drive around in cars, a lot. We drink alcohol, we ride bicycles, we sit too much. And we harbor anxiety about things that, statistically speaking, pose us little danger. We fear sharks, while mosquitoes are, in terms of sheer numbers of lives lost, probably the most dangerous creature on earth.

"Do people know which risks lead to many deaths and which risks lead to few?" the legal scholar Cass Sunstein asks. "They do not. In fact, they make huge blunders." Sunstein draws this observation from the work of Paul Slovic, author of *The Perception of Risk*. In a study that invited people to compare various causes of death, Slovic found that people tended to believe that accidents cause more deaths than disease and that homicide causes more deaths than suicide, when the opposite is true in both cases. In another study, people significantly overestimated the fatality rates of highly publicized or dramatic dangers like cancer or tornadoes.

One could interpret this, as Sunstein does, to mean that most people are just wrong about risk. But risk perception may not be about quantifiable risk so much as it is about immeasurable fear. Our fears are informed by history and economics, by social power and stigma, by myths and nightmares. And as with other strongly held beliefs, our fears are dear to us. When we encounter information that contradicts our beliefs, as Slovic found in one of his studies, we tend to doubt the information, not ourselves.

Bicycles, the *New York Times* reports, "are involved in more accidents than any other consumer product, but beds rank a close second." This does not alarm me, though I am a frequent user of both beds and bicycles. I carry my son on the back of my bicycle and allow him to sleep in my bed, despite public service posters of a baby sleeping with a butcher knife that warn me, "Your baby sleeping with you can be just as dangerous." The disregard for statistical risk that researchers observe in people like me may be at least partly due to an unwillingness to live lives dictated by danger. We sleep with our babies because the benefits, as we see them, outweigh the risks. The birth of my son, which posed a greater risk to my health than I anticipated when I became pregnant, gave me a new appreciation for the idea that there are some risks worth taking. "Having children," a friend with grown children reminds me, "is the greatest risk you can take."

"Perhaps what matters," Sunstein muses, "is not whether people are right on the facts, but whether they are frightened." And people do seem to be frightened. We are locking our doors and pulling our children out of public school and buying guns and ritually sanitizing our hands to allay a wide range of fears, most of which are essentially fears of other people. All the while we are also, in our way, reckless. We get *intoxicated*, from the Latin "to poison," for fun. This contradiction leads Sunstein to worry that regulatory laws based on the priorities of the general public may be prone to a pattern of "paranoia and neglect." Too much attention may be spent on minimal risks, while too little is paid to pressing threats.

Paranoia, the theorist Eve Sedgwick observes, tends to be contagious. She calls it a "strong theory," meaning a wide-ranging, reductive theory that displaces other ways of thinking. And paranoia very frequently passes for intelligence. As Sedgwick observes, "to theorize out of anything *but* a paranoid critical stance has come to seem naïve, pious, or complaisant." She does not believe that paranoid thinking is necessarily delusional or wrong, but only that there is value to approaches that are less rooted in suspicion. "Paranoia," Sedgwick writes, "knows some things well and others poorly."

Intuitive toxicology is the term that Slovic uses for the way most people assess the risk of chemicals. His research reveals that this approach is distinct from the methods used by toxicologists, and that it tends to produce different results. For toxicologists, "the dose makes the poison." Any substance can be toxic in excess. Water, for instance, is lethal to humans in very high doses, and overhydration killed a runner in the 2002 Boston Marathon. But most people prefer to think of substances as either safe or dangerous, regardless of the dose. And we extend this thinking to exposure, in that we regard any exposure to chemicals, no matter how brief or limited, as harmful.

In exploring this thinking, Slovic suggests that people who are not toxicologists may apply a "law of contagion" to toxicity. Just as brief exposure to a microscopic virus can result in lifelong disease, we assume that exposure to any amount of a harmful chemical will permanently contaminate our bodies. "Being contaminated," Slovic observes, "clearly has an all-or-none quality to it—like being alive or pregnant."

Fear of contamination rests on the belief, widespread in our culture as in others, that something can impart its essence to us on contact. We are forever polluted, as we see it, by contact with a pollutant. And the pollutants we have come to fear most are the products of our own hands. Though toxicologists tend to disagree with this, many people regard natural chemicals as inherently less harmful than man-made chemicals. We seem to believe, against all evidence, that nature is entirely benevolent.

One of the appeals of alternative medicine is that it offers not just an alternative philosophy or an alternative treatment but also an alternative language. If we feel polluted, we are offered a "cleanse." If we feel inadequate, lacking, we are offered a "supplement." If we fear toxins, we are offered "detoxification." If we fear that we are rusting with age, physically oxidizing, we are reassured with "antioxidants." These are metaphors that address our base anxieties. And what the language of alternative medicine understands is that when we feel bad we want something unambiguously good.

Most of the pharmaceuticals available to us are at least as bad as they are good. My father has the habit of saying, "There are very few perfect therapies in medicine." True as it may be, the idea that our medicine is as flawed as we are is not comforting. And when comfort is what we want, one of the most powerful tonics alternative medicine offers is the word *natural*. This word implies a medicine untroubled by human limitations, contrived wholly by nature or God or perhaps intelligent design. What *natural* has come to mean to us in the context of medicine is *pure* and *safe* and *benign*. But the use of *natural* as a synonym for *good* is almost certainly a product of our profound alienation from the natural world.

"Obviously," the naturalist Wendell Berry writes, "the more artificial a human environment becomes, the more the word 'natural' becomes a term of value." If, he argues, "we see the human and the natural economies as necessarily opposite or opposed, we subscribe to the very opposition that threatens to destroy them both. The wild and the domestic now often seem isolated values, estranged from one another. And yet these are not exclusive polarities like good and evil. There can be continuity between them, and there must be."

Allowing children to develop immunity to contagious diseases "naturally," without vaccination, is appealing to some of us. Much of that appeal depends on the belief that vaccines are inherently unnatural. But vaccines are of that liminal place between humans and nature—a mowed field, Berry might suggest, edged by woods. Vaccination is a kind of domestication of a wild thing, in that it involves our ability to harness a virus and break it like a horse, but its action depends on the natural response of the body to the effects of that once-wild thing.

The antibodies that generate immunity following vaccination are manufactured in the human body, not in factories. "In the pharmaceutical world," the writer Jane Smith observes, "the great division is between biologicals and chemicals-drugs that are made from living substances and drugs that are made from chemical compounds." Using ingredients sourced from organisms, once living or still alive, vaccines invite the immune system to produce its own protection. The live viruses in vaccines are weakened, sometimes by having been passed through the bodies of animals, so that they cannot infect a healthy person. The most unnatural aspect of vaccination is that it does not, when all goes well, introduce disease or produce illness.

Infectious disease is one of the primary mechanisms of natural immunity. Whether we are sick or healthy, disease is always passing through our bodies. "Probably we're diseased all the time," as one biologist puts it, "but we're hardly ever ill." It is only when disease manifests as illness that we see it as unnatural, in the "contrary to the ordinary course of nature" sense of the word. When a child's fingers blacken on his hand from Hib disease, when tetanus locks a child's jaw and stiffens her body, when a baby barks for breath from pertussis, when a child's legs are twisted and shrunken with polio—then disease does not seem natural.

Before Christopher Columbus landed in the Bahamas, the epidemic diseases of Europe and Asia did not exist in the Americas. There was no smallpox, no hepatitis, no measles, no influenza. The bacteria that cause diphtheria, tuberculosis, cholera, typhus, and scarlet fever were all unknown in this hemisphere. "The first recorded epidemic, perhaps due to swine flu, was in 1493," Charles Mann writes in his book *1493*. From that year onward, earthworms and honeybees imported by Europeans would forever change the ecology of the Americas, cattle and apple trees would transform its landscape, and novel diseases would decimate its people. Within the next two hundred years, three-quarters or more of the native population of the Americas would die of disease. Considering this course of events "natural" favors the perspective of the people who subsequently colonized the land, but it fails to satisfy the "not made or caused by humankind" definition of the term. While the ecosystem of the Americas can never be restored to its pre-Columbian state, our efforts to limit epidemic diseases through vaccination may be one small measure of habitat restoration.

"The history of the recent centuries has its black passages—the slaughter of the buffalo on the western plains, the massacre of the shorebirds by the market gunners, the near-extermination of the egrets for their plumage," Rachel Carson wrote in *Silent Spring*. She was writing in the late fifties, at a moment of acute atomic awareness, and the next of these black passages would be, she warned, a "new kind of fallout." The pesticides and herbicides of postwar industry, some of them originally developed for war, were being sprayed from airplanes over acres of fields and forests. One of these, DDT, was making its way into groundwater, accumulating in fish, and killing birds. Over fifty years later, DDT persists in the bodies of fish and birds all over the world, as well as in the milk of nursing mothers.

The publication of *Silent Spring* in 1962 led to the creation of the Environmental Protection Agency and a ban on the production of DDT in this country. The book popularized the idea that human health depends on the health of the ecosystem as a whole, but Carson did not use the word *ecosystem*. She preferred the metaphor of an "intricate web of life," in which a disturbance anywhere on the web sends tremors across the entire web. "*Silent Spring*," Carson's biographer Linda Lear writes, "proved that our bodies are not boundaries."

Our bodies are not boundaries, but DDT is not exactly what Carson feared it was. DDT, she warned, was a widespread cause of cancer. This hypothesis was not supported by the decades of research on DDT that followed the publication of *Silent Spring*. Numerous studies on factory and farm workers with high DDT exposure failed to find an association between DDT and cancer. And studies of specific cancers found no evidence that DDT increased the incidence of breast cancer, lung cancer, testicular cancer, liver cancer, or prostate cancer. I mention this to my father, an oncologist, and he recalls the DDT sprayed all over his town from trucks when he was young. He and his siblings were kept inside during the spraying, but they ran out to play as soon as the trucks had passed, when the leaves of trees were still dripping DDT and the smell of the chemical was in the air. It does not bother him that Carson may have overstated of the dangers of DDT, and that she got some things wrong, because, as he says, "she got the job done." She woke us up.

"Few books have done more to change the world," the journalist Tina Rosenberg acknowledges. "DDT killed bald eagles because of its persistence in the environment," she writes. "*Silent Spring* is now killing African children because of its persistence in the public mind." The blame for this may belong more to us, the inheritors of *Silent Spring*, than to the book, but either way malaria has resurged in some countries where DDT is no longer used against mosquitoes. One African child in twenty now dies from malaria, and more are left brain damaged by the disease. Ineffective treatments, toxic prophylactics, and environmentally damaging insecticides all remain in use because there is no viable vaccine against malaria.

For now, DDT is, unfortunately, one of the more effective means of controlling malaria in some places. Applied to the interior walls of homes once a year, DDT has nearly eliminated malaria in parts of South Africa. Compared to spraying DDT across millions of acres from airplanes, as was done in the United States, the environmental impact of this application is relatively small. But DDT remains an imperfect solution. Few chemical companies produce it, donors are unwilling to finance it, and many countries are reluctant to use a chemical that is banned elsewhere. "Probably the worst thing that ever happened to malaria in poor nations," Rosenberg writes, "was its eradication in rich ones."

Colonization and the slave trade brought malaria to the Americas, where it was once common as far north as Boston. Malaria never had quite as strong a hold in this country as it has in Africa, but it was difficult to eradicate here nonetheless. Beginning around the 1920s, thousands of miles of ditches were dug, swamps were drained, window screens were installed, and tons of an arsenic-based insecticide were spread. This was all to destroy breeding grounds and repel the mosquitoes that spread malaria. In a final push, DDT was applied to the walls of millions of homes, insecticides were sprayed from airplanes, and malaria was eliminated from the United States by 1949. Among other advantages, this contributed to the growth of our economy. Matthew Bonds, an economist at Harvard Medical School, compares the global effects of disease to widespread crime or government corruption. "Infectious diseases," he says, "systematically steal human resources."

"Such a catalog of illnesses!" Carson complained to a friend when an eye inflammation left her unable to read her own writing. Her work on *Silent Spring* had already been slowed by an ulcer, pneumonia, a staph infection, and two tumors. She kept this cancer, which would kill her shortly after the publication of *Silent Spring*, a secret. She did not want her work to appear to be driven by anything other than scientific evidence. And so her personal struggle with cancer was told only through dwindling numbers of bald eagles, through eggs that did not hatch, and through the robins that lay dead on the lawns of suburbia.

Even as Carson proposed that DDT could cause cancer, she recognized its utility for disease prevention. "No responsible person," she wrote, "contends that insect-borne disease should be ignored." Chemicals should be used in response to real threats, she suggested, rather than "mythical situations." She advocated for the informed, judicious use of chemicals, not the neglect of African children. But the enduring power of her book owes less to its nuances than to its capacity to induce horror.

Silent Spring begins with a "Fable for Tomorrow" in which Carson imagines an idyllic landscape of oaks, ferns, and wildflowers that is rapidly transformed into an apocalyptic wasteland where birds no longer sing. In the pages that follow, workers who have been picking oranges fall violently ill, a housewife who hates spiders develops leukemia, and a boy who runs to greet his father, just back from spraying the potato fields, dies that night from pesticide poisoning. It is a horror story in which man's creation, his monster, turns against him. Like Dracula, this monster moves through the air as mist and lies dormant in the soil. And like the plot of *Dracula*, the drama of *Silent Spring* depends on emblematic oppositions—good and evil, human and inhuman, natural and unnatural, ancient and modern. The monster in *Dracula* has ancient origins, but in *Silent Spring* evil takes the form of modern life.

Triclosan is destroying our environment and slowly poisoning us all, I determined shortly after I began reading about its toxicity. Or, triclosan is harmless to humans and not a serious threat to the environment. Uncertain how to interpret the data, I called the author of one of the studies I had read, an FDA researcher with a kindly voice. I explained my problem and he said that he would like to help me, but he was not supposed to talk to the press. It had not occurred to me that I was the press, though I was writing an article for *Harper's* magazine at the time.

Frustrated, I hung up the phone and fell asleep with my face on a pile of articles about herd immunity. I woke to find that a fragment of print had been transferred to my cheek. It spelled "munity," from the Latin *munis* for service or duty. "Munity is what you are really writing about," a colleague would say to me months later, "not immunity." This struck me as true, though I was writing about both.

As I rode my bicycle to my son's preschool after failing to determine how good or bad triclosan might be, it began to rain. I ran one block from the school to the public library through the rain, carrying my son, who was laughing. Inside, he darted through the stacks selecting picture books at random, while the question of whether or not I was the press continued to bother me. I understood it as a broader question of belonging. In my mind, I do not belong to the press even if my writing is published by the press. And if the opposite of the press is a poet, then I am both.

My son returned with a book about a baby alien who gets lost on Earth where nobody speaks her language, a book about a bat who lives with a family of birds who do not hang upside down like she does, and a book about a monkey who is teased for walking on two legs instead of four. The wordplay in *Gakky Two-Feet* was very funny to my son, but he did not understand the central conflict. Why, he wondered, does it bother the other monkeys when Gakky walks on two feet? "They feel threatened by his difference," I said. "What does *threatened* mean?" he asked.

It took me some time to define *threatened* because I was looking back through the books. Belonging and not belonging is a common theme of children's books, and maybe of childhood itself, but I was surprised that all these books were about the same thing. They were all about the problem of "us" and "them." The bat does not really belong with the birds even though she lives with the birds, and the alien is not at home on Earth. In the end, the bat is reunited with her bat mother and the alien is rescued by her alien parents, but some questions remain. "How can we be so different and feel so much alike?" one of the birds asks the bat. "And how can we feel so different and be so much alike?" another bird wonders.

Bats and birds may be of different biological classes, but they are both, as any child can see, flying things. *Stellaluna*, the book about the bat, allows for some confusion of categories, some disruption of boundaries. But "us" and "them" thinking insists on one belonging firmly to one category or another—it does not make room for ambiguous identities or outsider insiders. It does not allow for bat-bird alliances or resident aliens or monkeys who are in the process of evolving. And so the opposition between "us" and "them" becomes, as Wendell Berry warns, "the very opposition that threatens to destroy them both."

"I know you're on my side," an immunologist once remarked to me as we discussed the politics of vaccination. I did not agree with him, but only because I was uncomfortable with both sides, as I had seen them delineated. The debate over vaccination tends to be described with what the philosopher of science Donna Haraway would call "troubling dualisms." These dualisms pit science against nature, public against private, truth against imagination, self against other, thought against emotion, and man against woman.

The metaphor of a "war" between mothers and doctors is sometimes used for conflicts over vaccination. Depending on who is employing the metaphor, the warring parties may be characterized as ignorant mothers and educated doctors, or intuitive mothers and intellectual doctors, or caring mothers and heartless doctors, or irrational mothers and rational doctors—sexist stereotypes abound.

Rather than imagine a war in which we are ultimately fighting against ourselves, perhaps we can accept a world in which we are all irrational rationalists. We are bound, in this world, to both nature and technology. We are all "cyborgs, hybrids, mosaics, chimeras," as Haraway suggests in her feminist provocation "A Cyborg Manifesto." She envisions a cyborg world "in which people are not afraid of their joint kinship with animals and machines, not afraid of permanently partial identities and contradictory standpoints."

All of us who have been vaccinated are cyborgs, the cyborg scholar Chris Hables Gray suggests. Our bodies have been programmed to respond to disease, and modified by technologically altered viruses. As a cyborg and a nursing mother, I join my modified body to a breast pump, a modern mechanism, to provide my child with the most primitive food. On my bicycle, I am part human and part machine, a collaboration that exposes me to injury. Our technology both extends and endangers us. Good or bad, it is part of us, and this is no more unnatural than it is natural.

When a friend asked, years ago, if my son's birth was a "natural" birth, I was tempted to say that it was an animal birth. While his head was crowning, I was trying to use my own hands to pull apart my flesh and bring him out of my body. Or so I have been told, but I do not remember any intention to tear myself open—all I remember is the urgency of the moment. I was both human and animal then. Or I was neither, as I am now. "We have never been human," Haraway suggests. And perhaps we have never been modern, either.

Outcomes, Testing, Learning: What's at Stake?

PETER BROOKS

In this peer-reviewed article published in the academic journal Social Research *in 2012, Peter Brooks explores the current "crisis" in American higher education and how this has caused us to question the value of a college education and the purpose of assessing students' learning. Brooks explores the value of training in the humanities and ways the seemingly intangible value of reading and interpretation can be measured. Brooks is a widely published professor of comparative literature and also the Andrew W. Mellon Foundation Scholar at Princeton University.*

The American university, like American education in general, is in crisis. So we are told by countless books that have been rolling out since the 1980s, from *Profscam* (Skyes 1989) and *Tenured Radicals* (Kimball 1990, 1998) to *Academically Adrift* (Arum and Roska 2010) and *Higher Education? How Colleges are Wasting Our Money and Failing our Kids—and What We Can Do About It* (Hacker and Dreiftis 2010). Last fall, the *New York Review of Books* billed an article by my colleague Anthony Grafton "Our Flunking Universities." Perhaps more than anything else, it is the outrageous sticker price of a college education, and its steep upward climb in seeming defiance of the rest of the economy, that has fueled a demand to know why American families should sacrifice so much to a possibly dubious product. The frightening levels of debt incurred by students in the course of a college education have in fact become the stuff of political contention.

The very value of university education, for so many decades a central article of American faith, now has been put into doubt. The whole enterprise may be a waste of time, money, and national commitment. There is even a philanthropy, the Thiel Foundation, that offers prizes of $100,000 to induce smart kids to drop out of college and become entrepreneurs on their own, on the theory that college impedes rather than enhances the development of creative ideas.

Awash in such a tsunami of crisis rhetoric, there has been a natural reaction: to seek to evaluate what really goes on in the universities, to measure what students learn during their years of college. There are now more and more public calls for testing of the "value added" by college education—and more and more journalists and administrators listening to the calls. The notion that universities need to be held accountable for their use of resources and the outcomes they produce has become something of an article of faith, reiterated not only by the cultural right (*The Wall Street Journal*) but also the cultural center (*The New York Times*).

Pause for just a moment on the notion of "value added" that is supposed to be the testable achievement of a college education. It resonates with the "value added tax" long familiar to Europeans, a tax on costs accrued to a product on its way to market, and thus an incentive to cut production costs. The analogy fits well—perhaps too closely for comfort—with the demand on college education. It implies that a student entering college is something like a microchip waiting to be etched with a program. When you go back to the 2006 Spellings Commission report, which sounded the national call for assessment of college learning on the model of "No Child Left Behind" for the schools, you find the assertion that "we want to bring much-needed transparency and accountability to our colleges and universities," and that this will depend on collecting better data on student outcomes. The report stresses

> a lack of clear, reliable information about the cost and quality of postsec-ondary institutions, along with a remarkable absence of accountability mechanisms to ensure that colleges succeed in educating students. The result is that students, parents, and policymakers are often left scratch-ing their heads over the answers to basic questions, from the true cost of private colleges (where most students do not pay the official sticker price) to which institutions do a better job than others not only of graduating students but of teaching them what they need to learn (*A Test of Leader-ship* 2006, x).

The Spellings report (named for Secretary of Education Margaret Spellings) continues: "parents and students have no solid evidence, comparable across institutions, of how much students learn in colleges or whether they learn more at one college than another." This becomes the basis for a proposed requirement of national "outcomes" or "value added" testing:

> We believe that improved accountability is vital to ensuring the success of all the other reforms we propose. Colleges and universities must become

more transparent about cost, price, and student success outcomes, and must willingly share this information with students and families. Student achievement, which is inextricably connected to institutional success, must be measured by institutions on a "value-added" basis that takes into account students' academic baseline when assessing their results. This information should be made available to students, and reported publicly in aggregate form to provide consumers and policymakers an accessible, understandable way to measure the relative effectiveness of different colleges and universities.

I will come back to the "how much" language of the report: language that we all might reach for, but disturbing if it is taken to describe a college education—and entirely consonant with "value added." Spellings goes on to note that "policymakers" need such data to decide "whether the national investment in higher education is paying off" (13). And Spellings endorses, as probably the best metric available for getting the needed data, the Collegiate Learning Assessment (CLA), which "promotes a culture of evidence-based assessment in higher education" (22). This could then lead to what has been described by Frederick Hess, director of education policy at the American Enterprise Institute, as "coercive accountability" mechanisms to force universities to rethink what they are doing.

I don't pretend to be an expert on the Collegiate Learning Assessment, which is designed to test "core outcomes espoused by all of higher education—critical thinking, analytical reasoning, problem solving and writing" (Arum and Roska 2011, 21), but I have looked at some samples. One (touted in the much-reviewed *Academically Adrift*) asks the student to play the role of assistant to the president of DynaTech, a company that makes precision electronic instruments and navigational equipment. A member of the sales force has recommended that DynaTech purchase a small corporate plane, the SwiftAir 235, in order to reach customers more efficiently. But then a SwiftAir 235 crashes. The student is given a set of documents: newspaper articles about the crash, a federal accident report on in-flight breakups on single-engine planes, charts on SwiftAir's performance characteristics, an article from *Amateur Pilot* magazine comparing the 235 to competitive planes, and internal company emails on the proposed purchase. The student then must prepare a memo that assesses the information given and provides a recommendation as to whether or not DynaTech should purchase the plane.

This is fun. It resembles the real-world simulations that a student would work through if he or she took a job with McKinsey Consulting. In fact it is much like the case studies pioneered at Harvard Business School and now standard in business education. It does test the capacity to assess data, some of it conflicting, and to write a report that ought to lay out options, with their benefits and liabilities, and to show the process by which one reaches a conclusion on the basis of the available facts and interpretations. Nonetheless, there is much that it does not test—essentially, the whole of the humanities, where interpretation of data (texts, artworks, artifacts, often partial and incomprehensible without a deep understanding of historical, linguistic, stylistic, sociopolitical or other context) is very different, aimed not at an instrumental result—should DynaTech buy the plane or not—but at some understanding of a past culture or the worth of a present cultural innovation. It is simply and profoundly a different kind of learning and knowledge.

The CLA promotes an idea that has already made too many inroads in our culture, and in our universities: that knowledge is instrumental. Actually, I refuse to believe that what I teach—my field is comparative literature—is noninstrumental, but the way in which it may help my students in dealing with the world is hard to specify. It has to do with an ability to read the messages that daily claim our attention, or mostly our inattention, with a critical sense of how meaning is created—what Aristotle called "poetics." It's why when I teach French, for instance, I don't want students to think about language simply in instrumental terms—how do I order a croissant or buy a Hermès foulard—but also as a vehicle for cultural and literary expression that will tax them to step outside their cultural givens, to see those givens as almost frighteningly arbitrary, in need—if they are to be cultural and not just economic global citizens—of Copernican revision. I have not devised a test for the effectiveness of my teaching of what I want to teach. But if I could concoct such a test, I think it would have to be given to the student around the time of his or her twenty-fifth reunion. It is that kind of temporal arc that I think teaching in the humanities is about.

One further example of a CLA test, which I cite directly from the Council for Aid to Education website:

Pat Stone is running for reelection as mayor of Jefferson, a city in the state of Columbia. Mayor Stone's opponent in this contest is Dr. Jamie Eager. Dr. Eager is a member of the Jefferson City Council. You are a consultant to Mayor Stone.

Dr. Eager made the following three arguments during a recent TV interview: First, Mayor Stone's proposal for reducing crime by increasing the number of police officers is a bad idea. Dr. Eager said "it will only lead to more crime." Dr. Eager supported this argument with a chart that shows that counties with a relatively large number of police officers per resident tend to have more crime than those with fewer officers per resident.

Second, Dr. Eager said "we should take the money that would have gone to hiring more police officers and spend it on the STRIVE drug treatment program." Dr. Eager supported this argument by referring to a news release by the Washington Institute for Social Research that describes the effectiveness of the STRIVE drug treatment program. Dr. Eager also said there were other scientific studies that showed the STRIVE program was effective.

Third, Dr. Eager said that because of the strong correlation between drug use and crime in Jefferson, reducing the number of addicts would lower the city's crime rate (Council for Aid).

You are to prepare a memo to the mayor analyzing Dr. Eager's three points. You are given some seven documents—crime statistics, reviews of drug treatment effectiveness, newspaper articles—on which to base your assessments. Again, this is policy-oriented thinking—and in this case, the finding of arguments that will be politically persuasive—that surely has a place in testing critical thinking and argument, but a limited one. Is this all that college should be teaching? If we move to "outcomes assessments" and "value-added testing" I fear it may be, and that the outcomes of college learning will be those mandated by the test. We will repeat on the college level the sins of "No Child Left Behind," which pushed schools into teaching to the test to such an extent that a number of states sought exemption from it: a failed solution replicated.

I have been teaching a multiyear seminar under the rubric "The Ethics of Reading and the Cultures of Professionalism." It was inspired originally by reading the "torture memos" when they began to come to the light. These are the memos from the Justice Department's Office of Legal Counsel during the Bush administration justifying those "enhanced interrogation techniques" that I think by now we can agree to call torture. When I first read these ingeniously argued perversions of legal interpretation, I said to myself: no one trained in the analytic reading and interpretation of poetry could permit herself or himself to offer such twisted construals of what the texts (in this case, the Convention Against Torture and Cruel and Inhuman Treatment as incorporated in the US Criminal Code) really mean. There are rules for construing meaning, and though literary interpreters will gleefully disagree about meanings, they will mostly agree about how you should go about looking for them.

I am possibly overvaluing my own profession. But I thought it would at least be interesting to make the claim that we who teach the interpretive humanities have something to say to those whose professional practice should to a high degree depend on interpretative probity. I am convinced that the serious study of poetry and novel does inculcate an ethics of reading. I would go so far as to claim that there is no better way to understand the meaning and the importance of human rights than in the study of literature.

I can't really justify such an extravagant claim here. I want to make it clear, though, that I am not arguing that reading good books necessarily makes you a better person. It may—but we know people can study the humanities and join in mass murder. I don't subscribe to a feel-good version of culture. My argument takes place on the level of the practice of reading itself, which can be a rigorous discipline when the reader submits his or her work of interpretation to continuing testing. To make sure that your interpretation can be defended in the context of the text itself and its own contexts means that—unlike the authors of the "torture memos"—you must constantly submit what you want the writing to mean to the constraints of the lexicon, the historical horizon, and the text as a whole. In the classroom, teachers of literature (and history and philosophy) often have the strange experience of not speaking quite with or in their own voices—of letting other voices, from the past for instance, speak through them. As interpreters, they are mouthpieces of others; they are ventriloquists of the ideas and words of others. This submission to an otherness—in the largest sense, to culture as something beyond one's individuality—is in itself a discipline. It's a version of what T. S. Eliot meant when he claimed that all great art is impersonal.

This experience of otherness, something like what Keats called "negative capability"—the capacity to sink one's own personality into the imaginative realization of the personality of others, to see the world from inside other minds and hearts—seems to me characteristic of reading and interpretation in the humanities at their best. Such a submission to otherness leads to a kind of ethics: a self-dispossession in favor of the text, the other voice in the room. The attitude implied is ethical in that it allows the voice of the other to develop its full force, its full articulation, without censoring it, in a kind of dualism of feeling.

The discipline of close reading lies in this attempted fidelity to another voice, an evoked presence that must be treated with the utmost interpretive respect. When we talk of "sympathy" and "empathy" as central to the experience of studying the textual humanities, this need not suggest an easy sentimentalism, though often it does. In the practice of reading there is a test and trial of empathy. Historian Lynn Hunt has argued that human rights discourse originates in the eighteenth-century novel, which first led readers to a sympathetic identification with other fates and consciousnesses. I would agree with that claim, not on the level of the content of novels (or of any other works of art) but in the exercise of their reading. To espouse texts seriously, to bring them sustained and inquiring attention, does entail an engagement with central questions of what it means to be human, and to behave to other human beings in recognition of their kinship.

To circle back to my subject: how are we to test the value of training in the humanities? The American "system" of higher education has generally left the evaluation of student learning to those who teach the students—not the case in many other countries, which have systems of national exams, or else have students examined, typically at the end of their college years, by some group of faculty distinct from their course teachers. We are in fact somewhat peculiar in that the same people teach and certify student outcomes. I recall that in May 1968 France, the American system of course exams—rather than a make-or-break exam at the end of the cursus—became a reformist idea, what the French dubbed "contrôle continu" ongoing monitoring of student learning rather than a final hurdle to which all the student's work tended. And in many instances the French system indeed moved to a form of contrôle continu.

I offer that as a suggestion that there may be advantages to our way of doing things: it certainly offers teachers and students more opportunity for mid-course correction than systems that end-load their testing. And our system allows for the diversity—which is of course also the lack of quality control—that characterizes what we can only call a higher education "system" with lots of quotation marks. No doubt the universal institution of something like the CLA would provide more uniformity in that unsystematic system. Whether that is what we want, rather than some distinct effort to improve the lower echelons of the system, should give us pause. We all should be deeply concerned about the fate of public higher education, which is being savaged by the crisis of state finances, and through startling increases in tuition and fees failing on the American promise to provide higher education to those who qualify. There, I think, is the true crisis today.

I would go so far as to make the contrarian argument that those parents who are straining their budgets to send their children to the so-called elite colleges and those students who are negotiating the nightmare of acceptance to the elite colleges are not uninformed consumers who need to be told by the US Department of Education that they are wasting their money. On the contrary, I think their behavior is wholly rational. In the great American system of inequality—always with us, though much aggravated by tax and other policies—the rich universities have continued to get richer and to offer more. Not just more amenities—though the state-of-the-art fitness rooms and food courts can be excessive—but an education that has the luxury of resisting the instrumental and utilitarian, of preserving arcane subjects, such as Assyriology, pre-Socratic philosophy, Mycenaean archeology, that would not survive in a world dominated by CLA. Preserving also a faculty large enough that there can be small seminars and pampered enough that they go about their teaching (very often, in my experience) with a sense of dedication. If it weren't for our elite universities and the example they have set, I think American higher education would be far less good than it is. I want them to continue to have the freedom to flourish.

I want, too—and I repeat that this is our current crisis—for the affordable public sector to continue to be able to strive to rival the elite privates. There was a moment when the great state universities—UC Berkeley, Wisconsin, Michigan—offered as much as Harvard and Chicago. That's now in jeopardy, if only from the increasing disparity in faculty salaries, research funding, student support—even discounting the political onslaught on teachers at all levels of the system. I have tried to suggest that the calls for outcome assessments, measures of value added, voiced in the Spellings report don't seem to me to speak to our real problems. So why are they so loud, and so listened to? There is money to be made in assessment examinations, of course, and the movement has the backing of a number of conservative nonprofits and foundations. And there is ideology, a *ressentiment* directed to the academy that is not wholly rational, but part of a long history of American anti-intellectualism. I would suggest that ultimately the animus behind the Spellings report and its sequels is political. It is one legacy of the "culture wars" fought in the 1980s and '90s and never concluded by an armistice—a curious one, because the American right once seemed largely libertarian and even anarchic. That is no longer the case: cultural conformity is on the agenda. Intellectual deviance, experimentation, and the devotion to reading freed from pragmatic ends are under suspicion. I think those of us who believe in noninstrumental education, and in the ethical value of the humanities, need to resist.

References

Arum, Richard, and Josipa Roksa. 2011. *Academically Adrift: Limited Learning on College Campuses.* Chicago: University of Chicago Press.

Council for Aid to Education, n.d. *Architecture of the CLA Tasks.* <http://www.collegiatelearningassessment.org/files/Architecture_of_the_CLA_Tasks.pdf>.

Hacker, Andrew, and Claudia Dreifus. 2011. *Higher Education? How Colleges Are Wasting Our Money and Failing Our Kids—And What We Can Do About It.* New York: Times Books.

Grafton, Anthony. 2011. "Our Flunking Universities." *The New York Review of Books,* November 24. <http://www.nybooks.com/articles/archives/2011/nov/24/our-universities-why-are-they-failing/pagination=false>.

Hunt, Lynn. 2008. *Inventing Human Rights: A History.* New York: Norton.

Kimball, Roger. 1990. *Tenured Radicals: How Politics Has Corrupted Our Higher Education.* New York: HarperCollins.

Sykes, Charles J. 1989. *Profscam: Professors and the Demise of Higher Education.* New York: St. Martin's Press.

A Test of Leadership: Charting the Future of U.S. Higher Education. 2006. A Report of the Commission Appointed by Secretary of Education Margaret Spellings. <http://www2.ed.gov/about/bdscomm/list/hiedfuture/reports.html>. Accessed June 1, 2012.

All Can Be Lost: The Risk of Putting Our Knowledge in the Hands of Machines

NICHOLAS CARR

Nicholas Carr is an American writer who has published a number of widely read books and articles on technology and culture. In this essay—originally published in the Atlantic *and later chosen for inclusion in the 2014 edition of* The Best American Science and Nature Writing—*Carr calls attention to the ever-rising ubiquity of automation in the 21st century. Carr suggests that automation provides us with a great many conveniences, but they come at an ever-increasing cost to our human facility for deep learning, understanding, and developing advanced skill sets. He moves from anecdotal examples to historical evidence to recent case studies in his examination of the rise of automation, providing his audience with various opportunities to engage with the subject matter. Carr is especially careful to organize his essay in an effective manner, considering carefully the order in which he presents information.*

On the evening of February 12, 2009, a Continental Connection commuter flight made its way through blustery weather between Newark, New Jersey, and Buffalo, New York. As is typical of commercial flights today, the pilots didn't have all that much to do during the hour-long trip. The captain, Marvin Renslow, manned the controls briefly during takeoff, guiding the Bombardier Q400 turboprop into the air, then switched on the autopilot and let the software do the flying. He and his co-pilot, Rebecca Shaw, chatted—about their families, their careers, the personalities of air-traffic controllers—as the plane cruised uneventfully along its northwesterly route at 16,000 feet. The Q400 was well into its approach to the Buffalo airport, its landing gear down, its wing flaps out, when the pilot's control yoke began to shudder noisily, a signal that the plane was losing lift and risked going into an aerodynamic stall. The autopilot disconnected, and the captain took over the controls. He reacted quickly, but he did precisely the wrong thing: he jerked back on the yoke, lifting the plane's nose and reducing its airspeed, instead of pushing the yoke forward to gain velocity. Rather than preventing a stall, Renslow's action caused one. The plane spun out of control, then plummeted. "We're down," the captain said, just before the Q400 slammed into a house in a Buffalo suburb.

The crash, which killed all 49 people on board as well as one person on the ground, should never have happened. A National Transportation Safety Board investigation concluded that the cause of the accident was pilot error. The captain's response to the stall warning, the investigators reported, "should have been automatic, but his improper flight control inputs were inconsistent with his training" and instead revealed "startle and confusion." An executive from the company that operated the flight, the regional carrier Colgan Air, admitted that the pilots seemed to lack "situational awareness" as the emergency unfolded.

The Buffalo crash was not an isolated incident. An eerily similar disaster, with far more casualties, occurred a few months later. On the night of May 31, an Air France Airbus A330 took off from Rio de Janeiro, bound for Paris. The jumbo jet ran into a storm over the Atlantic about three hours after takeoff. Its air-speed sensors, coated with ice, began giving faulty readings, causing the autopilot to disengage. Bewildered, the pilot flying the plane, Pierre-Cedric Bonin, yanked back on the stick. The plane rose and a stall warning sounded, but he continued to pull back heedlessly. As the plane climbed sharply, it lost velocity. The airspeed sensors began working again, providing the crew with accurate numbers. Yet Bonin continued to slow the plane. The jet stalled and began to fall. If he had simply let go of the control, the A330 would likely have righted itself. But he didn't. The plane dropped 35,000 feet in three minutes before hitting the ocean. All 228 passengers and crew members died.

The first automatic pilot, dubbed a "metal airman" in a 1930 *Popular Science* article, consisted of two gyroscopes, one mounted horizontally, the other vertically, that were connected to a plane's controls and powered by a wind-driven generator behind the propeller. The horizontal gyroscope kept the wings level, while the vertical one did the steering. Modern autopilot systems bear little resemblance to that rudimentary device. Controlled by onboard computers running immensely complex software, they gather information from electronic sensors and continuously adjust a plane's attitude, speed, and bearings. Pilots today work inside what they call "glass cockpits." The old analog dials and gauges are mostly gone. They've been replaced by banks of digital displays. Automation has become so sophisticated that on a typical passenger flight, a human pilot holds the controls for a grand total of just three minutes. What pilots spend a lot of time doing is monitoring screens and keying in data. They've become, it's not much of an exaggeration to say, computer operators.

And that, many aviation and automation experts have concluded, is a problem. Overuse of automation erodes pilots' expertise and dulls their reflexes, leading to what Jan Noyes, an ergonomics expert at Britain's University of Bristol, terms "a de-skilling of the crew." No one doubts that autopilot has contributed to improvements in flight safety over the years. It reduces pilot fatigue and provides advance warnings of problems, and it can keep a plane airborne should the crew become disabled. But the steady overall decline in plane crashes masks the recent arrival of "a spectacularly new type of accident," says Raja Parasuraman, a psychology professor at George Mason University and a leading authority on automation. When an autopilot system fails, too many pilots, thrust abruptly into what has become a rare role, make mistakes. Rory Kay, a veteran United captain who has served as the top safety official of the Air Line Pilots Association, put the problem bluntly in a 2011 interview with the Associated Press: "We're forgetting how to fly." The Federal Aviation Administration has become so concerned that in January 2013 it issued a "safety alert" to airlines, urging them to get their pilots to do more manual flying. An overreliance on automation, the agency warned, could put planes and passengers at risk.

The experience of airlines should give us pause. It reveals that automation, for all its benefits, can take a toll on the performance and talents of those who rely on it. The implications go well beyond safety. Because automation alters how we act, how we learn, and what we know, it has an ethical dimension. The choices we make, or fail to make, about which tasks we hand off to machines shape our lives and the place we make for ourselves in the world. That has always been true, but in recent years, as the locus of labor-saving technology has shifted from machinery to software, automation has become ever more pervasive, even as its workings have become more hidden from us. Seeking convenience, speed, and efficiency, we rush to off-load work to computers without reflecting on what we might be sacrificing as a result.

Doctors use computers to make diagnoses and to perform surgery. Wall Street bankers use them to assemble and trade financial instruments. Architects use them to design buildings. Attorneys use them in document discovery. And it's not only professional work that's being computerized. Thanks to smartphones and other small, affordable computers, we depend on software to carry out many of our everyday routines. We launch apps to aid us in shopping, cooking, socializing, even raising our kids. We follow turn-by-turn GPS instructions. We seek advice from recommendation engines on what to watch, read, and listen to. We call on Google, or Siri, to answer our questions and solve our problems. More and more, at work and at leisure, we're living our lives inside glass cockpits.

~

A hundred years ago, the British mathematician and philosopher Alfred North Whitehead wrote, "Civilization advances by extending the number of important operations which we can perform without thinking about them." It's hard to imagine a more confident expression of faith in automation. Implicit in Whitehead's words is a belief in a hierarchy of human activities: Every time we off-load a job to a tool or a machine, we free ourselves to climb to a higher pursuit, one requiring greater dexterity, deeper intelligence, or a broader perspective. We may lose something with each upward step, but what we gain is, in the long run, far greater.

History provides plenty of evidence to support Whitehead. We humans have been handing off chores, both physical and mental, to tools since the invention of the lever, the wheel, and the counting bead. But Whitehead's observation should not be mistaken for a universal truth. He was writing when automation tended to be limited to distinct, well-defined, and repetitive tasks—weaving fabric with a steam loom, adding numbers with a mechanical calculator. Automation is different now. Computers can be programmed to perform complex activities in which a succession of tightly coordinated tasks is carried out through an evaluation of many variables. Many software programs take on intellectual work—observing and sensing, analyzing and judging, even making decisions—that until recently was considered the preserve of humans. That may leave the person operating the computer to play the role of a high-tech clerk—entering data, monitoring outputs, and watching for failures. Rather than opening new frontiers of thought and action, software ends up narrowing our focus. We trade subtle, specialized talents for more routine, less distinctive ones.

Most of us want to believe that automation frees us to spend our time on higher pursuits but doesn't otherwise alter the way we behave or think. That view is a fallacy—an expression of what scholars of automation call the "substitution myth." A labor-saving device doesn't just provide a substitute for some isolated component of a job or other activity. It alters the character of the entire task, including the roles, attitudes, and skills of the people taking part. As Parasuraman and a colleague explained in a 2010 journal article, "Automation does not simply supplant human activity but rather changes it, often in ways unintended and unanticipated by the designers of automation."

Psychologists have found that when we work with computers, we often fall victim to two cognitive ailments—complacency and bias—that can undercut our performance and lead to mistakes. Automation complacency occurs when a computer lulls us into a false sense of security. Confident that the machine will work flawlessly and handle any problem that crops up, we allow our attention to drift. We become disengaged from our work, and our awareness of what's going on around us fades. Automation bias occurs when we place too much faith in the accuracy of the information coming through our monitors. Our trust in the software becomes so strong that we ignore or discount other information sources, including our own eyes and ears. When a computer provides incorrect or insufficient data, we remain oblivious to the error.

Examples of complacency and bias have been well documented in high-risk situations—on flight decks and battlefields, in factory control rooms—but recent studies suggest that the problems can bedevil anyone working with a computer. Many radiologists today use analytical software to highlight suspicious areas on mammograms. Usually, the highlights aid in the discovery of disease. But they can also have the opposite effect. Biased by the software's suggestions, radiologists may give cursory attention to the areas of an image that haven't been highlighted, sometimes overlooking an early-stage tumor. Most of us have experienced complacency when at a computer. In using e-mail or word-processing software, we become less proficient proofreaders when we know that a spell-checker is at work.

The way computers can weaken awareness and attentiveness points to a deeper problem. Automation turns us from actors into observers. Instead of manipulating the yoke, we watch the screen. That shift may make our lives easier, but it can also inhibit the development of expertise. Since the late 1970s, psychologists have been documenting a phenomenon called the "generation effect." It was first observed in studies of vocabulary, which revealed that people remember words much better when they actively call them to mind—when they generate them—than when they simply read them. The effect, it has since become clear, influences learning in many different circumstances. When you engage actively in a task, you set off intricate mental processes that allow you to retain more knowledge. You learn more and remember more. When you repeat the same task over a long period, your brain constructs specialized neural circuits dedicated to the activity. It assembles a rich store of information and organizes that knowledge in a way that allows you to tap into it instantaneously. Whether it's Serena Williams on a tennis court or Magnus Carlsen at a chessboard, an expert can spot patterns, evaluate signals, and react to changing circumstances with speed and precision that can seem uncanny. What looks like instinct is hard-won skill, skill that requires exactly the kind of struggle that modern software seeks to alleviate.

~

In 2005, Christof van Nimwegen, a cognitive psychologist in the Netherlands, began an investigation into software's effects on the development of know-how. He recruited two sets of people to play a computer game based on a classic logic puzzle called Missionaries and Cannibals. To complete the puzzle, a player has to transport five missionaries and five cannibals (or, in van Nimwegen's version, five yellow balls and five blue ones) across a river, using a boat that can accommodate no more than three passengers at a time. The tricky part is that cannibals must never outnumber missionaries, either in the boat or on the riverbanks. One of van Nimwegen's groups worked on the puzzle using software that provided step-by-step guidance, highlighting which moves were permissible and which weren't. The other group used a rudimentary program that offered no assistance.

As you might expect, the people using the helpful software made quicker progress at the outset. They could simply follow the prompts rather than having to pause before each move to remember the rules and figure out how they applied to the new situation. But as the test proceeded, those using the rudimentary software gained the upper hand. They developed a clearer conceptual understanding of the task, plotted better strategies, and made fewer mistakes. Eight months later, van Nimwegen had the same people work through the puzzle again. Those who had earlier used the rudimentary software finished the game almost twice as quickly as their counterparts. Enjoying the benefits of the generation effect, they displayed better "imprinting of knowledge."

What van Nimwegen observed in his laboratory—that when we automate an activity, we hamper our ability to translate information into knowledge—is also being documented in the real world. In many businesses, managers and other professionals have come to depend on decision-support systems to analyze information and suggest courses of action. Accountants, for example, use the systems in corporate audits. The applications speed the work, but some signs suggest that as the software becomes more capable, the accountants become less so. One recent study, conducted by Australian researchers, examined the effects of systems used by three international accounting firms. Two of the firms employed highly advanced software that, based on an accountant's answers to basic questions about a client, recommended a set of relevant business risks to be included in the client's audit file. The third firm used simpler software that required an accountant to assess a list of possible risks and manually select the pertinent ones. The researchers gave accountants from each firm a test measuring their expertise. Those from the firm with the less helpful software displayed a significantly stronger understanding of different forms of risk than did those from the other two firms.

What's most astonishing, and unsettling, about computer automation is that it's still in its early stages. Experts used to assume that there were limits to the ability of programmers to automate complicated tasks, particularly those involving sensory perception, pattern recognition, and conceptual knowledge. They pointed to the example of driving a car, which requires not only the instantaneous interpretation of a welter of visual signals but also the ability to adapt seamlessly to unanticipated situations. "Executing a left turn across oncoming traffic," two prominent economists wrote in 2004, "involves so many factors that it is hard to imagine the set of rules that can replicate a driver's behavior." Just six years later, in October 2010, Google announced that it had built a fleet of seven "self-driving cars," which had already logged more than 140,000 miles on roads in California and Nevada.

Driverless cars provide a preview of how robots will be able to navigate and perform work in the physical world, taking over activities requiring environmental awareness, coordinated motion, and fluid decision making. Equally rapid progress is being made in automating cerebral tasks. Just a few years ago, the idea of a computer competing on a game show like Jeopardy would have seemed laughable, but in a celebrated match in 2011, the IBM supercomputer Watson trounced Jeopardy's all-time champion, Ken Jennings. Watson doesn't think the way people think; it has no understanding of what it's doing or saying. Its advantage lies in the extraordinary speed of modern computer processors.

In *Race Against the Machine*, a 2011 e-book on the economic implications of computerization, the MIT researchers Erik Brynjolfsson and Andrew McAfee argue that Google's driverless car and IBM's Watson are examples of a new wave of automation that, drawing on the "exponential growth" in computer power, will change the nature of work in virtually every job and profession. Today, they write, "computers improve so quickly that their capabilities pass from the realm of science fiction into the everyday world not over the course of a human lifetime, or even within the span of a professional's career, but instead in just a few years."

~

Who needs humans, anyway? That question, in one rhetorical form or another, comes up frequently in discussions of automation. If computers' abilities are expanding so quickly and if people, by comparison, seem slow, clumsy, and error-prone, why not build immaculately self-contained systems that perform flawlessly without any human oversight or intervention? Why not take the human factor out of the equation? The technology theorist Kevin Kelly, commenting on the link between automation and pilot error, argued that the obvious solution is to develop an entirely autonomous autopilot: "Human pilots should not be flying planes in the long run." The Silicon Valley venture capitalist Vinod Khosla recently suggested that health care will be much improved when medical software—which he has dubbed "Doctor Algorithm"—evolves from assisting primary-care physicians in making diagnoses to replacing the doctors entirely. The cure for imperfect automation is total automation.

That idea is seductive, but no machine is infallible. Sooner or later, even the most advanced technology will break down, misfire, or, in the case of a computerized system, encounter circumstances that its designers never anticipated. As automation technologies become more complex, relying on interdependencies among algorithms, databases, sensors, and mechanical parts, the potential sources of failure multiply. They also become harder to detect. All of the parts may work flawlessly, but a small error in system design can still cause a major accident. And even if a perfect system could be designed, it would still have to operate in an imperfect world.

In a classic 1983 article in the journal *Automatica*, Lisanne Bainbridge, an engineering psychologist at University College London, described a conundrum of computer automation. Because many system designers assume that human operators are "unreliable and inefficient," at least when compared with a computer, they strive to give the operators as small a role as possible. People end up functioning as mere monitors, passive watchers of screens. That's a job that humans, with our notoriously wandering minds, are especially bad at. Research on vigilance, dating back to studies of radar operators during World War II, shows that people have trouble maintaining their attention on a stable display of information for more than half an hour. "This means," Bainbridge observed, "that it is humanly impossible to carry out the basic function of monitoring for unlikely abnormalities." And because a person's skills "deteriorate when they are not used," even an experienced operator will eventually begin to act like an inexperienced one if restricted to just watching. The lack of awareness and the degradation of know-how raise the odds that when something goes wrong, the operator will react ineptly. The assumption that the human will be the weakest link in the system becomes self-fulfilling.

Psychologists have discovered some simple ways to temper automation's ill effects. You can program software to shift control back to human operators at frequent but irregular intervals; knowing that they may need to take command at any moment keeps people engaged, promoting situational awareness and learning. You can put limits on the scope of automation, making sure that people working with computers perform challenging tasks rather than merely observing. Giving people more to do helps sustain the generation effect. You can incorporate educational routines into software, requiring users to repeat difficult manual and mental tasks that encourage memory formation and skill building.

Some software writers take such suggestions to heart. In schools, the best instructional programs help students master a subject by encouraging attentiveness, demanding hard work, and reinforcing learned skills through repetition. Their design reflects the latest discoveries about how our brains store memories and weave them into conceptual knowledge and practical know-how. But most software applications don't foster learning and engagement. In fact, they have the opposite effect. That's because taking the steps necessary to promote the development and maintenance of expertise almost always entails a sacrifice of speed and productivity. Learning requires inefficiency. Businesses, which seek to maximize productivity and profit, would rarely accept such a trade-off. Individuals, too, almost always seek efficiency and convenience. We pick the program that lightens our load, not the one that makes us work harder and longer. Abstract concerns about the fate of human talent can't compete with the allure of saving time and money.

~

The small island of Igloolik, off the coast of the Melville Peninsula in the Nunavut territory of northern Canada, is a bewildering place in the winter. The average temperature hovers at about 20 degrees below zero, thick sheets of sea ice cover the surrounding waters, and the sun is rarely seen. Despite the brutal conditions, Inuit hunters have for some 4,000 years ventured out from their homes on the island and traveled across miles of ice and tundra to search for game. The hunters' ability to navigate vast stretches of the barren Arctic terrain, where landmarks are few, snow formations are in constant flux, and trails disappear overnight, has amazed explorers and scientists for centuries. The Inuit's extraordinary way-finding skills are born not of technological prowess—they long eschewed maps and compasses—but of a profound understanding of winds, snowdrift patterns, animal behavior, stars, and tides.

Inuit culture is changing now. The Igloolik hunters have begun to rely on computer-generated maps to get around. Adoption of GPS technology has been particularly strong among younger Inuit, and it's not hard to understand why. The ease and convenience of automated navigation makes the traditional Inuit techniques seem archaic and cumbersome.

But as GPS devices have proliferated on Igloolik, reports of serious accidents during hunts have spread. A hunter who hasn't developed way-finding skills can easily become lost, particularly if his GPS receiver fails. The routes so meticulously plotted on satellite maps can also give hunters tunnel vision, leading them onto thin ice or into other hazards a skilled navigator would avoid. The anthropologist Claudio Aporta, of Carleton University in Ottawa, has been studying Inuit hunters for more than 15 years. He notes that while satellite navigation offers practical advantages, its adoption has already brought a deterioration in way-finding abilities and, more generally, a weakened feel for the land. An Inuit on a GPS-equipped snowmobile is not so different from a suburban commuter in a GPS-equipped SUV: as he devotes his attention to the instructions coming from the computer, he loses sight of his surroundings. He travels "blindfolded," as Aporta puts it. A unique talent that has distinguished a people for centuries may evaporate in a generation.

Whether it's a pilot on a flight deck, a doctor in an examination room, or an Inuit hunter on an ice floe, knowing demands doing. One of the most remarkable things about us is also one of the easiest to overlook: each time we collide with the real, we deepen our understanding of the world and become more fully a part of it. While we're wrestling with a difficult task, we may be motivated by an anticipation of the ends of our labor, but it's the work itself—the means—that makes us who we are. Computer automation severs the ends from the means. It makes getting what we want easier, but it distances us from the work of knowing. As we transform ourselves into creatures of the screen, we face an existential question: Does our essence still lie in what we know, or are we now content to be defined by what we want? If we don't grapple with that question ourselves, our gadgets will be happy to answer it for us.

Vanishing Languages
DAVID CRYSTAL

David Crystal, the Wales-based author of The Cambridge Encyclopedia of Language, *has written about language for academic audiences as well as the general public. In "Vanishing Languages," which appeared in the magazine* Civilization *in 1997, Crystal draws on his expert knowledge of linguistics and his personal experiences with Welsh to introduce an educated public audience to the issue of language extinction. By using examples of endangered languages around the world, Crystal shows how language connects to culture, identity, and power.*

There's a Welsh proverb I've known for as long as I can remember: *"Cenedl heb iaith, cenedl heb galon."* It means, "A nation without a language [is] a nation without a heart," and it's become more poignant over the years as more and more families who live around me in North Wales speak in English instead of Welsh across the dinner table.

Welsh, the direct descendant of the Celtic language that was spoken throughout most of Britain when the Anglo-Saxons invaded, has long been under threat from English. England's economic and technological dominance has made English the language of choice, causing a decline in the number of Welsh speakers. And although the decline has steadied in the last 15 years, less than 20 percent of the population of Wales today can speak Welsh in addition to English.

The Welsh language is clearly in trouble. Someday, it may even join the rapidly growing list of extinct languages, which includes Gothic and Hittite, Manx and Cornish, Powhatan and Piscataway. If present trends continue, four of the world's languages will die between the publication of this issue of *Civilization* and the next. Eighteen more will be gone by the end of 1997. A century from now, one-half of the world's 6,000 or more languages may be extinct.

The decline is evident the world over. Consider the case of Sene: In 1978 there were fewer than 10 elderly speakers remaining in the Morobe province of Papua New Guinea. Or Ngarla: In 1981 there were just two speakers of the Aboriginal language still alive in northwest Western Australia. And in 1982 there were 10 surviving speakers of Achumawi out of a tribal population of 800 in northwestern California. Does it matter? When the last representatives of these people die, they take with them their oral history and culture, though their passing is rarely noticed. Sometimes, years later, we find hints of a culture's existence, in the form of inscriptions or fragments of text, but many of these—the Linear A inscriptions from ancient Crete, for example—remain undeciphered to this day.

There is some controversy over exactly how to count the number of languages in the world. A great deal depends on whether the speech patterns of different communities are viewed as dialects of a single language or as separate languages. The eight main varieties of spoken Chinese, for example, are as mutually unintelligible as, say, French and Spanish—which suggests that they are different languages. On the other hand, they share a writing system, and so perhaps are best described as dialects of the same language. If you opt for the first solution, you will add eight to your tally of the world's languages. If you opt for the second, you will add just one.

Taking a conservative estimate of 6,000 languages worldwide, one fact becomes immediately clear: Languages reveal enormous differences in populations. At one extreme, there is English, spoken by more people globally than any other language in history, probably by a third of the world's population as a first, second or foreign language. At the other extreme is Ngarla (and most of the other languages of the native peoples of Australia, Canada and the United States), whose total population of speakers may amount to just one or two. And then there are closely related groups of languages like the Maric family in Queensland, Australia, which consists of 12 languages. When it was surveyed in 1981, only one of these, Bidyara, had as many as 20 speakers. Most had fewer than five. Five of them had only one speaker each.

The loss of languages may have accelerated recently, but it is hardly a new problem. In the 19th century, there were more than 1,000 Indian languages in Brazil, many spoken in small, isolated villages in the rain forest; today there are a mere 200, most of which have never been written down or recorded. In North America, the 300 or more indigenous languages spoken in the past have been halved.

People sometimes talk of "the beauty of Italian" or of "German's authority," as if such characteristics might make a language more or less influential. But there is no internal mechanism in a language that settles its fate. Languages are not, in themselves, more or less powerful. People don't adopt them because they are more precise. They gain ascendancy when their speakers gain power, and they die out when people die out or disperse. It's as simple as that.

A dramatic illustration of how a language disappears took place in Venezuela in the 1960s. As part of the drive to tap the vast resources of the Amazonian rain forests, a group of Western explorers passed through a small village on the banks of the Coluene River. Unfortunately, they brought with them the influenza virus, and the villagers, who lacked any immunity, were immediately susceptible to the disease. Fewer than 10 people survived. A human tragedy, it was a linguistic tragedy too, for this village contained the only speakers of the Trumai language. And with so few people left to pass it on, the language was doomed.

Other languages—such as Welsh and Scottish Gaelic—have been threatened when indigenous populations have moved or been split up. Brighter economic prospects tempt young members of the community away from the villages. And even if they choose to stay, it doesn't take much exposure to a dominant culture to motivate ambitious young people to replace their mother tongue with a language that gives them better access to education, jobs and new technology.

A language's fortunes are tied to its culture's. Just as one language holds sway over others when its speakers gain power—politically, economically or technologically—it diminishes, and may even die, when they lose that prominence. Latin, now used almost exclusively in its written form, had its day as a world language because of the power of Rome. English, once promoted by the British Empire, is thriving today chiefly because of the prominence of the U.S.A., but it was once an endangered language, threatened by the Norman invaders of Britain in the 11th century, who brought with them a multitude of French words. In South America, Spanish and Portuguese, the language of colonists, have replaced many of the indigenous Indian tongues.

The death of languages is most noticeable in parts of the world where large numbers of languages are concentrated in a few small geographical regions. Travel to the tropical forests of the Morobe province in Papua New Guinea and you'll find five isolated villages in a mountain valley where fewer than 1,000 people speak the Kapin language. They support themselves by agriculture and have little contact with outsiders. Other tiny communities, speaking completely different languages, live in neighboring valleys. Linguists estimate that in the country as a whole there is approximately one language for every 200 people. Indeed, three countries, which together amount to less than 2 percent of the earth's land area, support 1,700—or a quarter—of the world's living languages: Papua New Guinea has 862; Indonesia, 701; and Malaysia, 140. These countries' isolation and physical geography account in large part for the existence of such concentrations, and it is hardly surprising to find that, as remote areas of the globe have opened up for trade and tourism, there has been a dramatic increase in the rate of language death. Valuable reserves of gold, silver, and timber in Papua New Guinea, for example, are bringing speculators to the islands—and with them their languages.

There has been little research into exactly what happens when a language begins to die. The process depends on how long there has been contact between the users of the minority language and their more powerful neighbors. If the contact has been minimal, as in the case of the Trumai in the Amazon, the minority language might remain almost unchanged until the last of the speakers dies. But if two languages have been in contact for generations, the dominant language will slowly erode the pronunciation, vocabulary and grammar of the minority language. Take the Celtic languages of northwest Europe. Following the death of the last mother-tongue speakers of Cornish (spoken in Cornwall until the 19th century) and Manx (spoken in the Isle of Man until the 1940s), the only remaining Celtic languages are Breton (in northwest France), Irish and Scottish Gaelic, and Welsh. All have been in steady decline during the 20th century. Equally, all have been the focus of strenuous efforts to revive their fortunes (or, in the case of Cornish and Manx, to resurrect a new first-language base). But the effects of four centuries of domination by English are evident everywhere.

Walk into the stores of the strongly Welsh-speaking areas of North Wales, as I regularly do, and you will hear the Welsh language widely used—and apparently in good health. But there is also a great deal of recognizable English vocabulary scattered throughout the speech. Of course, all languages have what linguists refer to as "loan words"—words taken from other languages to supplement the vocabulary. English itself has tens of thousands of words borrowed from French, Spanish, Latin and other languages. But there is an important difference between traditional vocabulary borrowing and what takes place in an endangered language. When arsenic, lettuce and attorney came into English in the Middle Ages, it was because these items did not already exist in the English- speaking community: The nouns were introduced to describe new objects, and so to supplement the existing vocabulary. But in the case of an endangered language, the loan words tend to replace words that already exist. And as the decline continues, even quite basic words in the language are replaced.

I meet this phenomenon every day on the Welsh island of Anglesey, where I live. It's become quite unusual to hear locals referring to large sums of money in anything other than English. In a Holyhead butcher's shop recently, I overheard someone say *"Mae'n twelve fifty"* (It's twelve fifty), where the first part of the sentence is colloquial Welsh and the second part is colloquial English. As I waited for a train at the station the same day, I heard a porter calling out to disgruntled passengers *"Mae'n late"* (It's late). And I later heard a group of people using the English word *injection* as they stood in a street describing in Welsh someone's visit to a doctor's clinic. In all these cases, perfectly good Welsh words already exist, but the speakers did not use them. Why they chose not to is not at all clear. Maybe they did not know the Welsh words, or maybe it is a sign of status or education to use the English equivalents. But when something as basic as its number system is affected, a language is clearly in danger.

Mixed languages are an inevitable result of language contact, and they exist all over the world, often given a dismissive label by more educated speakers: Wenglish, Franglais, Spanglish. Such mixed varieties often become complex systems of communication in their own right—and may even result in brand new languages, or pidgins such as Tok Pisin, which is now spoken by more than 1 million people in Papua New Guinea. But when one of the languages in question has no independent existence elsewhere in the world, as in the case of Welsh, mixed languages are a symptom of linguistic decline.

In the West, when a population fears that its language is threatened, speakers often react defensively, establishing a committee or board to oversee and coordinate political policy and to plan dictionaries, grammars and local broadcasting. The best-known example is France, home of the Académie Française, where there is now a law banning the use of English words—such as *le week-end* and *le computeur*—in official publications if a native French term already exists (in these cases, *la fin de semaine* and *l'ordinatuer*). Often two levels of language ability emerge as a consequence. There is an educated standard, used as a norm in education and the media. And there is a colloquial standard, used by the majority of the population (including many educated users, who thereby become bilingual—more technically, bidialectal—in their own language). It is the usage of the elite minority that is called by the majority the "proper" or "correct" language, even though it often represents a far more artificial style of speech than the language of the streets.

The plight of the indigenous languages of America was made vivid by James Fenimore Cooper as long ago as 1826, when the Indian chief Tamenund lamented that "before the night has come, have I lived to see the last warrior of the wise race of the Mohicans." There are 200 North American Indian languages, but only about 50 have more than 1,000 speakers, and only a handful have more than 50,000. Just over a year ago, Red Thunder Cloud, the last known fluent speaker of the Siouan language Catawba, died. The only surviving fluent speaker of Quileute is 80-year old Lillian Pullen, of La Push, Washington. But at least the decline of the American Indian languages has begun to attract widespread attention from politicians and the media—sources of support that are unlikely to help such equally threatened but less well known cases as Usku in Irian Jaya or Pipil in El Salvador.

In Europe, public attention is regularly focused on language rights by the European Bureau for Lesser Used Languages, head-quartered in Brussels. A recent book, A Week in Europe, edited by the Welsh magazine editor Dylan Iorwerth, offers a glimpse of Western European life by journalists writing in minority languages. Some of these are minority uses of major languages, such as German in Denmark, Swedish in Finland, and Croatian in Italy; but in most cases the entire language-using community is found in a single region, such as Scottish Gaelic, Galacian, Alsatian, Welsh, Catalan, Asturian, Breton, Friulian, Basque, Sorbian, Occitan, Provençal, Frisian and Irish. Political concern over the status of minority languages is regularly voiced by the European Parliament, and occasionally words are backed up with financial commitment—to local newspapers and broadcasting, literary festivals and teaching programs.

When an endangered language (such as Gaelic) is spoken in a culture whose historical significance is widely appreciated—perhaps because it is associated with prowess in arts and crafts, or because it is known for its literary achievements—it may provoke widespread concern. And sometimes endangered languages that have suffered as a result of colonial expansion win support from speakers of the dominant language, who wish to distance themselves from the aggression of their ancestors. But in most cases, anxiety, like charity, begins at home. In the 1970s, Gwynfor Evans held a hunger strike as part of his (successful) campaign for a Welsh-language TV channel. And in 1952 in Madras, India, Potti Sriramulu died following a hunger strike in support of the Telugu language. Language, as that Welsh proverb reminds us, is truly at the heart of a culture. It is a matter of identity, of nationhood.

With enough personal effort, time and money, and a sympathetic political climate, it is possible to reverse the fortunes of an endangered language. Catalan, spoken in northeast Spain, was allocated the status of an official language, and it now has more native speakers than it did 30 years ago. And the Hoçak, or Winnebago tribe in Wisconsin is hoping to develop a full Hoçak-speaking school system. In an effort funded entirely by profits from the tribe's casinos, schoolchildren use interactive multimedia computer programs to gain familiarity with a language that was traditionally passed down orally from parent to child. Such advances generally depend upon collaboration between minority groups, such as those who united to form the European Bureau for Lesser Used Languages. Together they have a realistic chance of influencing international policies, without overlooking the vast differences between the political and cultural situations of minority languages: Welsh, Gaelic, Maori, Quechua and Navajo demand very different solutions.

Welsh, strongly supported by Welsh-language broadcasting and Welsh-medium schools, is alone among the Celtic languages in stopping its decline. The census figures for the last 20 years show a leveling out, and even some increase in usage among certain age groups, especially young children. A similar vigorous concern seems to be simulating Navajo and several other American languages, as well as some minority languages in continental Europe. But it is quite clear that most of the endangered languages of the world are beyond practical help, in the face of economic colonialism, the growth of urbanization and the development of global communication systems. And, given the difficulty there has been in achieving language rights for such well known communities as the Navajo or the Welsh, the likelihood of attracting world interest in the hundreds of languages of Papua New Guinea, each of which has only a few speakers left, is remote. Clearly, with some 3,000 languages at risk, the cost of supporting them on a worldwide scale would be immense. Can, or should, anything be done?

On an intellectual level, the implications are clear enough: To lose a language is to lose a unique insight into the human condition. Each language presents a view of the world that is shared by no other. Each has its own figures of speech, its own narrative style, its own proverbs, its own oral or written literature. Preserving a language may also be instructive; we can learn from the way in which different languages structure reality, as has been demonstrated countless times in the study of comparative literature. And there is no reason to believe that the different accounts of the human condition presented by the peoples of say, Irian Java will be any less insightful than those presented by writers in French, English, Russian and Sanskrit. Moreover, the loss of a language means a loss of inherited knowledge that extends over hundreds or thousands of years. As human beings have spread around the globe, adapting to different environments, the distilled experience of generations have been retained chiefly through the medium of language. At least when a dying language has been written down, as in the case of Latin or Classical Greek, we can usually still read its messages. But when a language without a writing system disappears, its speakers experience its loss forever. The Bithynian, Cappadocian and Cataonian cultures are known today only from passing references in Greek literature. Language loss is knowledge loss, and it is irretrievable.

Such intellectual arguments may persuade the dispassionate observer, but most arguments in favor of language preservation are quite the opposite: They are particular, political and extremely passionate. Language is more than a shared code of symbols for communication. People do not fight and die, as they have done in India, to preserve a set of symbols. They do so because they feel that their identity is at stake—that language preservation is a question of human rights, community status and nationhood. This profoundly emotional reaction is often expressed in metaphors. Language nationalists see their language as a treasure house, as a repository of memories, as a gift to their children, as a birthright. And it is this conviction that has generated manifestoes and marches in Montreal on behalf of French; civil disobedience in India and Pakistan, in Belgium and in Spain.

Such demonstrations stand in stark contrast to places where cultural and linguistic pluralism works successfully, as in Switzerland and Sweden, where the dominant culture respects the identities and rights of its linguistic minorities, and provides educational opportunities for speakers. Successful multilingual communities such as Sweden's serve as examples for the United Nations, UNESCO, the Council of Europe, and the European Parliament as they act to preserve minority language use.

Conversely, several countries have actively repressed minority languages, such as Basque by the Spanish fascists, or Sorbian (a Slavic language spoken in southern Germany) by the Nazis. And laws forbidding the use of minority languages have been commonplace; children have been punished for using a minority language in school; street signs in a minority language have been outlawed; the publication of books in the language have been banned; people's names have been forcibly changed to their equivalents in the language of the dominant power. Whole communities, such as several in the Basque-speaking parts of northern Spain, have had their linguistic identity deliberately eliminated.

Political arguments for and against preservation have been expressed with such vehemence that they tend to dominate any discussion of minority languages. Does the loss of linguistic diversity present civilization with a problem analogous to the loss of a species in biology? Not entirely. A world containing only one species is impossible. But a world containing only one language is by no means impossible, and may not be so very far away. Indeed, some argue strongly in favor of it. The possibility of creating a unilingual world has motivated artificial-language movements (such as Esperanto) since the 16th century, and there are many who currently see the remarkable progress of English as a promising step towards global communication. They argue that mutual intelligibility is desirable and should be encouraged: Misunderstandings will decrease; individuals and countries will negotiate more easily; and the world will be more peaceful.

This kind of idealism wins little sympathy from language nationalists, who point out that the use of a single language by a community is no guarantee of civil peace—as is currently evident in the states of the former Yugoslavia or in Northern Ireland. But language nationalists are faced with major practical concerns: How can one possibly evaluate the competing claims of thousands of endangered languages? Is it sensible to try and preserve a language (or culture) when its recent history suggests that it is heading for extinction? In the next few years, international organizations may have to decide, on chiefly economic grounds, which languages should be kept alive and which allowed to die.

The publication in the early 1990s of major surveys of the world's languages has brought some of these issues before the public. UNESCO's Endangered Languages (established in the U.K. in 1995) and the Linguistic Society of America's Committee on Endangered Languages and their preservation are fostering research into the status of minority languages. Information is gradually becoming available on the Internet—such as through the World Wide Web site of the Summer Institute of Linguistics. And a clearinghouse for the world's endangered languages was established in 1995, by request of UNESCO, at the University of Tokyo.

But after the fact-finding, the really hard work consists of tape-recording and transcribing the endangered languages before they die. The fieldwork procedures are well established among a small number of dedicated linguists, who assess the urgency of the need, document what is already known about the languages, extend that knowledge as much as possible, and thus help preserve languages, if only in archive form.

The concept of a language as a "national treasure" still takes many people by surprise—and even English has no international conservation archive. It is hard to imagine the long hours and energy needed to document something as complex as a language—and it's often a race against time. Thirty years ago, when anthropologist J.V. Powell began working with the Quileute Indians in Washington state, 70 members of the tribe were fluent speakers. Around that time the tribal elders decided to try to revitalize the language, writing dictionaries and grammars, and imagining a day when their children would sit around chanting in Quileute. "But," says Powell, "their prayers haven't been answered." Now they've scaled back to a more modest goal: basic familiarity rather than fluency. Powell recognizes that they will not save Quileute, but it will be preserved in recordings for future scholars—and will serve as a symbol of the tribe's group identity. That may seem like a small success, but it's a far better fate than the one facing most endangered languages.

Mail

ANNE FADIMAN

"Mail" is one of the many essays Anne Fadiman wrote during her tenure as the editor of The American Scholar, *a quarterly magazine published by the Phi Beta Kappa Society. Fadiman, an award-winning essayist and reporter, uses memories of her father's love of receiving, sorting, and answering mail as a starting point for examining the history of the British postal service as well as her own use of email. First published in 2000 and later reprinted in* At Large and at Small, *this essay combines meticulous research with personal reflection to suggest timeless questions about how technology shapes our reading and writing practices.*

Some years ago, my parents lived at the top of a steep hill. In his study, my father kept a pair of binoculars with which, like a pirate captain hoisting his spyglass to scan the horizon for treasure ships, he periodically inspected the mailbox to check the position of the flag. When the mail finally arrived, he trudged down the driveway and opened the extra-large black metal box, purchased by my mother in the same accommodating spirit with which some wives buy their husbands extra-large trousers. The day's load—a mountain of letters and about twenty pounds of review books packed in Jiffy bags, a few of which had been pierced by their angular contents and were leaking what my father called "mouse dirt"—was always tightly wedged. But he was a persistent man, and after a brief show of resistance the mail would surrender, to be carried up the hill in a tight clinch and dumped onto a gigantic desk. Until that moment, my father's day had not truly begun.

His desk was made of steel, weighed more than a refrigerator, and bristled with bookshelves and secret drawers and sliding panels and a niche for a cedar-lined humidor. (He believed that cigar-smoking and mail-reading were natural partners, like oysters and Muscadet.) Several books were written on that desk, but its finest hours were devoted to sorting the mail. My father hated Sundays and holidays because there was nothing new to spread on it. Vacations were taxing, the equivalent of forced relocations to places without food. His homecomings were always followed by daylong orgies of mail-opening—feast after famine—at the end of which all the letters were answered; all the bills were paid; the outgoing envelopes were affixed with stamps from a brass dispenser heavy enough to break your toe; the books and manuscripts were neatly stacked; and the empty Jiffy bags were stuffed into an enormous copper wastebasket, cheering confirmation that the process of postal digestion was complete.

"One of my unfailing minor pleasures may seem dull to more energetic souls: opening the mail," he once wrote.

> Living in an advanced industrial civilization is a kind of near-conquest over the unexpected.... Such efficiency is of course admirable. It does not, however, by its very nature afford scope to that perverse human trait, still not quite eliminated, which is pleased by the accidental. Thus to many tame citizens like me the morning mail functions as the voice of the unpredictable and keeps alive for a few minutes a day the keen sense of the unplanned and the unplannable.

What unplanned and unplannable windfalls might the day's yield contain? My brother asked him, when he was in his nineties, what kinds of mail he liked best. "In my youth," he replied, "a love letter. In middle age, a job offer. Today, a check." (That was false cynicism, I think. His favorite letters were from his friends.) Whatever it was, it never came soon enough. Why were deliveries so few and so late (he frequently grumbled), when, had he lived in central London in the late seventeenth century, he could have received his mail ten or twelve times a day?

~

We get what we need. In 1680, London had mail service nearly every hour because there were no telephones. If you wished to invite someone to tea in the afternoon, you could send him a letter in the morning and receive his reply before he showed up at your doorstep. Postage was one penny.

If you wished to send a letter to another town, however, delivery was less reliable and postage was gauged on a scale of staggering complexity. By the mid-1830s,

> the postage on a single letter delivered within eight miles of the office where it was posted was...twopence, the lowest rate beyond that limit being fourpence. Beyond fifteen miles it became fivepence; after which it rose a penny at a time, but by irregular augmentation, to one shilling, the charge for three hundred miles.... There was as a general rule an additional charge of a half-penny on a letter crossing the Scotch border; while letters to or from Ireland had to bear, in addition, packet rates, and rates for crossing the bridges over the Conway and the Menai.

So wrote Rowland Hill, the greatest postal reformer in history, who in 1837 devised a scheme to reduce and standardize postal rates and to shift the burden of payment from the addressee to the sender.

Until a few years ago, I had no idea that if you sent a letter out of town—and if you weren't a nobleman, a member of Parliament, or some other VIP who had been granted the privilege of free postal franking—the postage was paid by the recipient. This dawned on me when I was reading a biography of Charles Lamb, whose employer, the East India House, allowed clerks to receive letters gratis until 1817: a substantial perk, sort of like being able to receive your friends' calls on your office's 800 number. (Lamb, who practiced stringent economies, also wrote much of his personal correspondence on company stationery. His most famous letter to Wordsworth—the one in which he refers to Coleridge as "an Archangel a little damaged"—is inscribed on a page whose heading reads "Please to state the Weights and Amounts of the following Lots.")

Sir Walter Scott liked to tell the story of how he had once had to pay "five pounds odd" in order to receive a package from a young New York lady he had never met. It contained an atrocious play called *The Cherokee Lovers*, accompanied by a request to read it, correct it, write a prologue, and secure a producer. Two weeks later, another large package arrived for which he was charged a similar amount. "Conceive my horror," he told his friend Lord Melville, "when out jumped the same identical tragedy of *The Cherokee Lovers*, with a second epistle from the authoress, stating that, as the winds had been boisterous, she feared the vessel entrusted with her former communication might have foundered, and therefore judged it prudent to forward a duplicate." Lord Melville doubtless found this tale hilarious, but Rowland Hill would have been appalled. He had grown up poor, and, as Christopher Browne notes in *Getting the Message*, his splendid history of the British postal system, "Hill had never forgotten his mother's anxiety when a letter with a high postal duty was delivered, nor the time when she sent him out to sell a bag of clothes to raise 3s for a batch of letters."

Hill was a born Utilitarian who, at the age of twelve, had been so frustrated by the irregularity of the bell at the school where his father was principal that he had instituted a precisely timed campanological schedule. Thirty years later, he published a report called "Post Office Reform: Its Importance and Practicability." Why, he argued, should legions of accountants be employed to figure out the byzantine postal charges? Why should Britain's extortionate postal rates persist when France's revenues had risen, thanks to higher mail volume, after its rates were lowered? Why should postmen waste precious time waiting for absent addressees to come home and pay up? A national Penny Post was the answer, with postage paid by the senders, "using a bit of paper...covered at the back with a glutinous wash, which the bringer might, by the application of a little moisture, attach to the back of the letter."

After much debate, Parliament passed a postal reform act in 1839. On January 10, 1840, Hill wrote in his diary, "Penny Postage extended to the whole kingdom this day!...I guess that the number despatched to-night will not be less than 100,000, or more than three times what it was this day twelve-months. If less I shall be disappointed." On January 11, he wrote, "The number of letters despatched exceeded all expectation. It was 112,000, of which all but 13,000 or 14,000 were prepaid." On May 6, the Post Office introduced the Penny Black, a gummed rectangle, printed with lampblack in linseed oil, that bore the profile of Queen Victoria: the first postage stamp. (Some historians—a small, blasphemous minority—confer that honor on a prepaid paper wrapper, inscribed with the date of transit, introduced in 1653 by Jean-Jacques Renouard de Villayer, the proprietor of a private postal service in Paris. But his wrapper wasn't sticky and it wasn't canceled, and thus, in my opinion, it bears the same relation to a stamp as a mud pie to a Sacher torte. In any case, Villayer's plan failed because practical jokers put mice in his postboxes and the mail got chewed.) The British press, pondering the process of cancellation, fretted about the "untoward disfiguration of the royal person," but Victoria became an enthusiastic philatelist who waived the royal franking privilege for the pleasure of walking to the local post office from Bal-moral Castle to stock up on stamps and gossip with the postmaster. When Rowland Hill—by that time, *Sir* Rowland Hill—retired as Post Office Secretary in 1864, a Punch cartoon was captioned, "Should ROWLAND HILL have a statue? Certainly, if OLIVER CROMWELL should. For one is celebrated for cutting off the head of a bad King, and the other for sticking on the head of a good Queen."

The Penny Post, wrote Harriet Martineau, "will do more for the circulation of ideas, for the fostering of domestic affections, for the humanizing of the mass generally, than any other single measure that our national wit can devise." It was incontrovertible proof, in an age that embraced progress on all fronts ("every mechanical art, every manufacture, everything that promotes the convenience of life," as Macaulay put it in a typical gush of national pride), that the British were the most civilized people on earth. Ancient Syrian runners, Chinese carrier pigeons, Persian post riders, Egyptian papyrus bearers, Greek *hemerodromes*, Hebrew dromedary riders, Roman equestrian relays, medieval monk-messengers, Catalan *troters*, international couriers of the House of Thurn and Taxis, American mail wagons—what could these all have been leading up to, like an ever-ascending staircase, but the Victorian postal system?

And yet (to raise a subversive question), might it be possible that, whatever the benefit in efficiency, there may have been a literary cost associated with the conversion from payment by addressee to payment by sender? If you knew that your recipient would have to bear the cost of your letter, wouldn't courtesy motivate you to write an extra good one? On the other hand, if you paid for it yourself, wouldn't you be more likely to feel you could get away with "Having a great time, wish you were here"?

~

I used to think my father's attachment to the mail was strange. I now feel exactly the way he did. I live in a five-story loft building and, with or without binoculars, I cannot see my mailbox, one of thirteen dinky aluminum cells bolted to the lobby wall. The mail usually comes around four in the afternoon (proving that the postal staircase that reached its highest point with Rowland Hill has been descending ever since), which means that at around three, *just in case*, I'm likely to visit the lobby for the first of several reconnaissance trips. There's no flag, but over the years my fingers have become so postally sensitive that I can tell if the box is full by giving it the slightest of pats. If there's a hint of convexity—it's very subtle, nothing as obvious, let us say, as the bulge of a tuna-fish can that might harbor botulism—I whip out my key with the same eagerness with which my father set forth down his driveway.

There the resemblance ends. The excitement of the treasure hunt is followed all too quickly by the glum realization that the box contains only four kinds of mail: 1) junk; 2) bills; 3) work; and 4) letters that I will read with enjoyment, place in a folder labeled "To Answer," and leave there for a geologic interval. The longer they languish, the more I despair of my ability to live up to the escalating challenge of their response. It is a truism of epistolary psychology that a Christmas thank-you note written on December 26 can say any old thing, but if you wait until February, you are convinced that nothing less than *Middlemarch* will do.

In the fall of 1998 I finally gave in and signed up for e-mail. I had resisted for a long time. My husband and I were proud of our retrograde status. Not only did we lack a modem, but we didn't own a car, a microwave, a Cuisinart, an electric can opener, a CD player, or a cell phone. It's hard to give up that sort of backward image. I worried that our friends wouldn't have enough to make fun of. I also worried that learning how to use e-mail would be like learning how to program our VCR, an unsuccessful project that had confirmed what excellent judgment we had shown in not purchasing a car, etc.

As millions of people had discovered before me, e-mail was fast. Sixteenth-century correspondents used to write "Haste, haste, haste, for lyfe, for lyfe, haste!" on their most urgent letters; my "server," a word that conjured up a luxurious sycophancy, treated *every* message as if someone's life depended on it. It got there instantly, caromed in a series of digital cyberpackets through the nodes of the Internet and restored to its original form by its recipient's 56,000-bit-per-second modem. (I do not understand a word of what I just wrote, but that is immaterial. Could the average Victorian have diagrammed the mail-coach route from Swansea to Tunbridge Wells?) More important, I *answered* e-mail fast—sometimes within seconds of its arrival. No more guilt! I used to think I didn't like writing letters. I now realize that what I didn't like was folding the paper, sealing the envelope, looking up the address, licking the stamp, getting in the elevator, crossing the street, and dropping the letter in the postbox.

At first I made plenty of mistakes. I clicked on the wrong icons, my attachments didn't stick, and, not yet having learned how to file addresses, I sent an X-rated message to my husband (I thought) at gcolt@aol.com instead of georgecolt@aol.com. I hope Gerald or Gertrude found it flattering. But the learning curve was as steep as my parents' driveway, and pretty soon I was batting out fifteen or twenty e-mails in the time it had once taken me to avoid answering a single letter. My box was nearly always full—no waiting, no binoculars, no convexity checks, no tugging. I began to look forward every morning to the perky green arrow with which AT&T Worldnet beckoned me into my father's realm of the unplanned and the unplannable. What fresh servings of spam awaited me? Would I be invited to superboost my manhood, regrow my thinning hair, cleanse my intestines with blue-green algae, bulletproof my tires, say no to pain, work at home in my underwear, share the fortune of a highly placed Nigerian petroleum official, obtain a diploma based on my life experience from a prestigious nonaccredited university, or win a Pentium III 500 MHz computer (presumably in order to receive such messages even faster)? Or would I find a satisfying little clutch of friendly notes whose responses could occupy me until I awoke sufficiently to tackle something that required intelligence? As Hemingway wrote to Fitzgerald, describing the act of letter-writing: "Such a swell way to keep from working and yet feel you've done something."

My computer, without visible distension, managed to store a flood tide of mail that in nonvirtual form would have silted up my office to the ceiling. This was admirable. And when I wished to commune with my friend Charlie, who lives in Taipei, not only could I disregard the thirteen-hour time difference, but I was billed the same amount as if I had dialed his old telephone number on East Twenty-second Street. The German critic Bernhard Siegert has observed that the breakthrough concept behind Rowland Hill's Penny Post was "to think of all Great Britain as a single city, that is, no longer to give a moment's thought to what had been dear to Western discourse on the nature of the letter from the beginning: the idea of distance." E-mail is a modern Penny Post: the world is a single city with a single postal rate.

Alas, our Penny Post, like Hill's, comes at a price. If the transfer of postal charges from sender to recipient was the first great demotivator in the art of letter-writing, e-mail was the second. "It now seems a good bet," Adam Gopnik has written, "that in two hundred years people will be reading someone's collected e-mail the way we read Edmund Wilson's diaries or Pepys's letters." That may be true—but will what they read be any good? E-mails are brief. (One doesn't blather; an overlong message might induce carpal tunnel syndrome in the recipient from excessive pressure on the DOWN arrow.) They are also—at least the ones I receive—frequently devoid of capitalization, minimally punctuated, and creatively spelled. E-mail's greatest strength—speed—is also its Achilles' heel. In effect, it's always December 26. You are not expected to write *Middlemarch*, and therefore you don't.

In a letter to his friend William Unwin, written on August 6, 1780, William Cowper noted that "a Letter may be written upon any thing or Nothing." This observation is supported by the index of *The Faber Book of Letters, 1578–1939*. Let us examine the first few entries from the *d* section:

damnation, 87
dances and entertainments, 33, 48, 59, 97, 111, 275
death, letters written before, 9, 76, 84, 95, 122, 132, 135, 146, 175, 195, 199, 213, 218, 219, 235, 237, 238, 259, 279
death, of children, 31, 41, 100, 153
dentistry, 220
depressive illness, 81, 87
Dictionary of the English Language, Johnson's, 61
Diggers, 22
dolphins, methods of cooking, 37

I have never received an e-mail on any of these topics. Instead, I am informed that Your browser is not Y2K-compliant. Your son left his Pokémon turtle under our sofa. Your essay is 23 lines too long.

Important pieces of news, but, as Lytton Strachey (one of the all-time great letter writers) pointed out, "No good letter was ever written to convey information, or to please its recipient: it may achieve both these results incidentally; but its fundamental purpose is to express the personality of its writer." *But wait!* you pipe up. *Someone just e-mailed me a joke!* So she did, but wasn't the personality of the sender slightly muffled by the fact that she forwarded it from an e-mail she received and sent it to thirty-seven additional addressees?

I also take a dim, or perhaps a buffaloed, view of electronic slang. Perhaps I should view it as a linguistic milestone, as historic as the evolution of Cockney rhyming slang in the 1840s. But will the future generations who pry open our hard drives be stirred by the eloquence of the e-acronyms recommended by a Web site on "netiquette"?

BTDT	been there done that
FC	fingers crossed
IITYWTMWYBMAD	if I tell you what this means will you buy me a drink?
MTE	my thoughts exactly
ROTFL	rolling on the floor laughing
RTFM	read the fucking manual
TANSTAAFL	there ain't no such thing as a free lunch
TAH	take a hint
TTFN	ta ta for now

Or by the "emoticons," otherwise known as "smileys"—punctional images, read sideways—that "help readers interpret the e-mail writer's attitude and tone"?

:-)	ha ha
:-(	boo hoo
(-:	I am left-handed
:-&	I am tongue-tied
%-)	I have been staring at this screen for 15 hours straight
{:-)	I wear a toupee
:-[	I am a vampire
:-F	I am a bucktoothed vampire with one tooth missing
=|:-)=	I am Abraham Lincoln
*:o)	I am Bozo the Clown

"We are of a different race from the Greeks, to whom beauty was everything," boasted a character in an 1855 novel by Elizabeth Gaskell. "Our glory and our beauty arise out of our inward strength, which makes us victorious over material resistance." We have achieved a similar victory of efficiency over beauty. The posthorn, a handsome brass instrument that once announced the arrival of mail coaches and made a cameo appearance in the sixth movement of Mozart's *Posthorn Serenade*, has been supplanted by an irritating voice that chirps, "You've got mail!" I wouldn't give up e-mail if you paid me, but I'd feel a pang of regret if the epistolary novels of the future were to revolve around such messages as

Subject: R U Kidding?

From: Clarissa Harlowe <claha@virtue.com>

To: Robert Lovelace <lovelaceandlovegirlz@vice.com>

hi bob, TAH. if u think im gonna run off w/ u, :-F. do u really think im that kind of girl?? if your looking 4 a trollop, CLICK HERE NOW: http://www hotpix com. TTFN.

~

I own a letter written by Robert Falcon Scott, the polar explorer, to G. T. Temple, Esq., who helped procure the footgear for Scott's first Antarctic expedition. The date is February 26, 1901. The envelope and octavo stationery have black borders because Queen Victoria had died the previous month. The paper is yellowed, the handwriting is messy, and the stamp bears the Queen's profile—and the denomination ONE PENNY. I bought the letter many years ago because, unlike a Cuisinart, which would have cost about the same, it was something I believed I could not live without. I could never feel that way about an e-mail.

I also own my father's old copper wastebasket, which now holds my own empty Jiffy bags. Several times a day I use his heavy brass stamp dispenser; it is tarnished and dinged, but still capable of unspooling its contents with a singular smoothness. And my file cabinets hold hundreds of his letters, the earliest written in his sixties in small, crabbed handwriting, the last in his nineties, after he lost much of his sight, penned with a Magic Marker in huge capital letters. I hope my children will find them someday, as Hart Crane once found his grandmother's love letters in the attic,

> *pressed so long*
> *Into a corner of the roof*
> *That they are brown and soft,*
> *And liable to melt as snow.*

I Can't Afford to Get Sick

LESLIE FEINBERG

In this speech delivered to a national transgender health conference, Leslie Feinberg shows us the limitations of the American health care system for those in poverty and for those who do not fit into rigid gender stereotypes. Feinberg, a self-identified American transgender, butch, lesbian activist, uses hir own experience with the health care system to demonstrate how biological determinism is used as a means of oppression and to call for an understanding of gender that does not limit people to the gender they were assigned at birth. As an activist, Feinberg has written several books including Stone Butch Blues *(1993). "I Can't Afford to Get Sick" is from Feinberg's collection* Transliberation *(1998), which includes speeches and texts that argue for the rights of all trans people.*

Ironically, the morning I arrived at the Boston Convention Center to speak to the 2nd Transgender Health Conference, I felt sick as a dog. As I climbed the steps to the stage, I wasn't sure I'd be able to stand and speak. From the podium, I could see about 350 people, filling the auditorium. I knew some worked at AIDS service centers; others were health care providers. Some were gay, lesbian, and bi; others were heterosexual; a few were trans. Some were assigned by their agencies to attend; others came on their own accord.

I felt so ill the room seemed to spin. Yet if I stepped down from this podium, where would I go to seek health care? I decided to attempt to speak, and if I couldn't continue, I'd ask for help from the audience.

I'm very lucky to be alive today and able to speak to you about the health care crisis for trans people. I hovered near death all last year—unable to secure a diagnosis, tests, or a cure. Two obstacles blocked my path like boulders: bigotry and poverty. Both are deadly roadblocks in an economic system that organizes health care as a profit-driven industry.

When my fever first spiked, I did not have a doctor to call. As a transgender adult, I had only sought treatment in life-and-death situations. Moments when I was weakened and scared because of illness were times I least relished a stranger examining my body; I felt vulnerable to potential hostility.

I remembered the resident who, while examining me for strep throat, suddenly shoved his hand down my pants shouting, "You're a freak!"

I remembered the doctor who told me in a quiet voice that the devil—not Jesus—had encouraged me to choose the path I've walked in life.

I remembered every moment of humiliation I'd ever experienced at the hands of health care providers. That's why I always made up a phony nom de guerre and gave bogus ID to emergency room staff. Get out with a quick medical evaluation, a prescription and my dignity—that was always my aim.

Of course that meant I'd never had any continuity of care from a primary physician who I could trust to treat my body with caring and respect. Instead I'd had to grapple with the fear that the malice or contempt of the doctor or nurse would result in poor or malicious mistreatment.

Unfortunately, this is not an individual crisis. Throughout the United States, masculine females and, feminine males, cross-dressers, transsexuals and intersexuals are home alone dealing with pain, fevers, the trauma of gang rape and beatings, and other emergencies, hoping the symptoms will go away so they don't have to reveal themselves to a venomously hostile doctor or nurse.

In 1995 my symptoms did not go away. I was incubating a deadly bacterial heart infection, and as a result, I developed acute cytomegalovirus and other diseases.

Like tens of millions of documented workers in this country, and uncounted millions of undocumented workers, I had no health insurance. Paying the rent and buying food has always been a struggle for me. As a visibly transgendered person I have always had low-wage jobs, if any. I had no savings or pension fund to dip into. And in fact, no working person can afford a catastrophic illness, even if they save a small nest egg.

So with a raging fever I made my way on the subway, through a sleet storm, to a clinic that has a sliding payment scale. The waiting area was standing room only. Young mothers held a crying infant in one arm and clutched a restless toddler's hand with another. Elderly people sat alone; they leaned their heads back against the wall, or they doubled over coughing.

The staff was sometimes rude to us. But they were just as abrupt with each other. Five hours later, as I still sat waiting to be seen, I had a better sense of how overworked they were.

In fact, the staff was so overburdened that the clinic was nearly dysfunctional. The results of my blood test were misplaced. Had they not been lost, I could have been cured after eight weeks of intravenous treatment. This was just the first of the tragedy of errors and hurdles to health care that resulted in a year of grave illness, needless intravenous medications, discrimination, abuse, powerlessness, and rage.

You see, I could be like a transgender Scheherazade. I could tell you horror stories about how I and other trans people have been treated by the health care system from now to my last breath and there'd still be more outrages to relate.

You might feel such seething rage at health care workers that you would stand up with us as trans people *against* them. But that's not my goal. I want you to be angry about the abuses we have suffered. I want you to help us create zero tolerance for gender-phobia and trans-phobia in the health care industry. But I believe that pitting patients against health care staff only exacerbates the problem. The only way we can begin to create change in the care of trans people is to open up a dialogue with health care workers.

But there are obstacles that prevent such a discussion from taking place. Bigotry is pandemic in this society, so the education of health care workers has to be part of our larger struggle to build alliances between everyone who suffers from discrimination and prejudice.

The owners and CEOs of the lucrative health care industry try to block a large-scale dialogue from developing between staff and patients, as well. For example, I can't name the doctor who told me my fever was a result of my being "a very troubled person." I can't name the hospital in which I awoke at night to find staff gawking at me, laughing and referring to me as "it." I can't name the staff who referred to me as a Martian.

If I did, the hospital administrators, on behalf of the owners, could sue me. Is this litigation threat meant to protect hospital workers? No, the threats of libel suits are designed to protect the hospital corporations from financial damages.

We as trans people have no interest in hurting health care workers. We have a stake in building camaraderie between us. We can offer important feedback on how the administration of health care is structured in ways that create a schism between trans patients and health care workers. For example, the hospital into which I was admitted mandated that patients be placed in wards based on birth biology. That meant that I was placed on a female ward, where my masculinity created an immediate furor. This same hospital places male-to-female transsexual women who have completed sex-reassignment surgery on male wards. In which ward will intersexual people fit?

Some might argue that this is a division based on nature. I heard similar arguments used to defend racial segregation in health care services when I was a child. Racial segregation wasn't decreed by nature; it was rooted in racism. Trans oppression is not identical to racial oppression. But prejudice and hatred nearly killed me because I didn't fit into the rigid female or male ward system.

Wouldn't it make sense to create wards based on the type of injury or disease and the degree of care required? Many hospitals place females and males in separate rooms within mixed wards without dire consequence. In such a situation, the patient's gender expression or sex creates much less of a stir.

And we have a right to demand that health care institutions provide mandatory sensitivity classes in which representatives from diverse trans communities can have an opportunity to speak to the staff.

Some nurses and physicians' assistants and doctors will hear us and quickly understand that trans people deserve to be treated with respect. But I say to those who hold opinions about transgender and intersexuality and transsexuality that they're not willing to let go of: If you feel you can't treat us compassionately then do us both a favor—remove yourself from the situation. Let us work with someone on the staff who is sensitive to our humanity.

Even well-intentioned health care providers can be hampered in their approach to trans patients based on what they've been taught is natural. A very caring nurse recently told me she wished trans people would inform her of that fact right away. If she finds out later, she feels duped. And she believes it's important for their care that she knows what their birth biology is.

To be blunt, it's really not her business. Each trans patient must have the fundamental right to privacy. The question of patient self-revelation can't be seen solely through a clinical lens. There are larger social issues. Maybe you feel you would treat this patient the same way once they came out to you. But when you put it in their chart, or mention it to the next staff member, the trans patient may be mistreated.

Underlying the anger or embarrassment of health care workers who feel "tricked" by a trans patient is the feeling that "I thought you were one sex, but you're *really* another." You're really another. What does that mean? That trans people are pretending to be something that they're not?

This view is based on biological determinism—a weapon used for centuries to justify the oppression of women. Biological determinism only regards the sex we are assigned at birth as authentic.

All of our lives and our identities are valid and real. But if we don't come out to health care personnel, it's not because we are duplicitous. It's because we are oppressed.

Winning more sensitive care for trans people is not enough to save our lives. Not if we can't afford to see a doctor or go to a hospital. The fight against bigotry must go hand in hand with the battle to make health care affordable.

And in this fight, trans people do not stand alone.

Today we are witnessing the final stages of the transfer of health care to an industry run solely to make profits. The changes in health care parallel those now occurring in all large businesses and financial institutions. Smaller hospitals and health care facilities are consolidating into large-scale corporations. Hospitals are closing their doors in communities that desperately need them because the facilities are deemed unprofitable. Public health centers are being privatized. Profits are being maximized by downsizing the number of workers and speeding up those still employed.

Patients' lives are held hostage to the weed of the pharmaceutical giants that patent drugs used to treat life-threatening diseases. When I contracted acute cytomegalovirus during a catastrophic illness last year, the cost for one month's medication v as out of reach for me: $13,000. With government deregulation, private insurance companies pick and choose those they feel are healthy, and reject disabled, ill, and elderly people.

Medical science can achieve microsurgical organ transplants, gene manipulation and splicing. In this epoch of rapidly expanding medical knowledge, why is a treatable disease like tuberculosis again on the rise amongst the poor in this country? Why are more and more people being shunted into HMOs where treatment cost is the bottom line? Why are Medicaid and Medicare being whittled away instead of expanded?

Because the productive growth under capitalism isn't designed to meet human needs. Each hospital, each insurance carrier, is only concerned with its own bottom line.

How can we wage a political battle to expand access to affordable, adequate, and sensitive health care? By fusing the power of the poorest and most oppressed communities, people with AIDS and their service providers, elders, the lesbian, gay, bi, and trans movements, civil rights organizations, the women's movement, and labor—employed and unemployed.

Together we can demand that the government channel the necessary funds to meet public health emergencies like AIDS and breast cancer. And that welfare, Medicaid, and Medicare assistance be restored and expanded to all who need it. We can demand that every patient be treated with respect, and that every vestige of prejudice must be eradicated from health care.

We can demand that every form of health care be free—from emergency to preventive care, from open-heart surgery to prenatal care, from eyeglasses to dentures, from lab work to drugs. Open the doors of medical schools to all who want an education and eliminate the staggering costs of tuition. We deserve free health care because it is a right, not a privilege.

Do you think that's a lot to ask for? That it sounds utopian? Well, my partner Minnie Bruce just returned from three weeks of working and living with families in Cuba—a tiny island of 11 million people burdened by the legacy of colonialism and being economically strangled by an illegal U.S. blockade. One of the many achievements of the Revolution that most impressed her was that every single person in Cuba receives free health care—from the womb to the tomb. And preventive care—not just emergency attention. Glasses, braces, surgery, prescriptions—all are free to everyone. Medical schools—all education—is free too, because education, like health care and a job, is considered the birthright of every human being.

The United States is the richest country in the world, we are often told.

So show us the money!

In fact, the greatest polarization of wealth and poverty in the world exists here in the United States. That's why it will take a *collective* fight to win the health care we deserve. Remember how Medicaid and Medicare were won in the first place? By people who got fed up waiting for the next election. They took to the streets to vote with their feet in picket lines and marches and sit-ins and rallies.

It will take just such a mighty movement to provide every human being with sensitive, respectful, and free health care.

Each of us deserves nothing less.

From "Vignettes: Locations of Writing"

The following two essays appeared in the academic journal College Composition and Communication. *This special edition of the journal, "Vignettes: Locations of Writing," asks questions about how location influences writing and writers as they make sense of the worlds in which they find themselves.*

In her vignette "Splintered Literacies," Amanda Hayes explores the "splintered worlds" of writing and literacy in Appalachia, reflecting on the separation between home and school and what that separation means for the way people connect to their cultural histories. Hayes is a scholar of Composition and Rhetoric at Ohio University.

In the vignette "Writing in Sacred Spaces," Brian McNely reflects on his experience observing parishioners writing while in a Catholic Adoration chapel, specifically focusing on how the very act of writing can help some parishioners come to terms with their ineffable and intangible experiences of spirituality. McNely is a professor of writing and rhetoric at University of Kentucky.

Splintered Literacies

AMANDA HAYES

Writing and literacy are splintered worlds in Appalachia.

My family resides on a ridge of woods and farmland that's been passed through the generations for 150 years. I grew up related to my closest neighbors, learning from them stories that got told from ear to ear and often from generation to generation. (I could, for example, quote words spoken by my grandfather's grandfather, who fought for the Union in the Civil War. The former Private Thomas Gallagher thought it important that his own children hear his stories, and not mistake war for glory. He said to them often, "I run a mile to join the army. After I was in it, I'd a-run ten miles to get out and been grateful just to go home." It's an old story by now, yes, but one that unfortunately still has resonance.)

Reading and writing were parts of the stories, too, in particular ways. The weakness of oral cultures is that they can die in a generation, and my mother recognized this. I can remember her using a typewriter (exciting, when I was a child) as she wrote out some of the family stories and put each story in a box frame with its corresponding heirlooms, such as a great-great-grandmother's pin framed with the story of her travels to these hills from the east, to marry and become a local midwife. And often when she read to us, my mother chose books she could relate to our family stories. My favorite was Laura Ingalls Wilder's *Little House in the Big Woods*, which Momma read to us more than once. "This may be what life was like for Pap's grandparents," she would say, keeping us well acquainted with those ancestors who built the first tiny house in our big woods, a house that still stood in ruins twenty feet from our front porch. Stories were important this way, because they meant holding on to life, even for those long dead. More and more as I've grown I've seen that there is something deeply rhetorical in these multigenerational tales, something I'm only beginning to grasp about making meaning of the place I live. Writing records and preserves what is valuable, but my mother's work of writing these stories and reading similar ones also created that value for me, a child who would grow up fascinated by the very acts of literacy.

In my school literacy, on the other hand, writing was not constructed as playing the preserving role it did in my early life. I can't recall once writing a school essay about my family or our land—the two things I learned earliest were worth writing about—until college. And I certainly learned not to write in the way I talked at home. I remember, for example, a middle school English teacher who became so frustrated by our "bad" English that she threw chalk at us and lamented our inability to learn "finer sensibilities." Even those teachers who weren't outright insulting about our Appalachian dialects and home lives seemed to take for granted that these subjects were not acceptably "academic" enough for school writing. A hillbilly background was a thing to be overcome, not embraced; therefore we didn't, and couldn't, write Appalachia in school. The more I study and teach about writing and culture, the more troubled I become by this conceptual separation. Formal schools have almost entirely taken over the educational roles once played by families in the region, and students can easily see when their home literacies are not valued. It's what we lose when we stop valuing those literacies that scares me.

My mother's example made certain I valued my home literacy, but not all children are so fortunate. A local newspaper article recently lamented the prevalence of hunger in our county, with need by far outstripping the ability of food pantries to supply. My grandparents, who as octogenarians still gardened and stocked a basement pantry with home-preserved foodstuffs at the end of each summer, read stories like this with deep distress. They, children of poverty by any standard, didn't grow up hungry. That so few people, in a region with both rich land and a traditional pride in self-sufficiency, can now grow food or preserve it is an absurdity. And while food science and writing might seem unrelated, I would argue that they are not, especially not here. Those starving people in our rural county almost certainly had grandparents who knew how to garden. Why was this not bothered to be taught or learned? There's a vicious conceptual cycle at play here, the root of which is what literacy means, what writing means, and how we continue to define and value what we need to know to live well. The stories that get told, or not told, and where we're allowed to tell them, can shape the knowledge we value. And that value, or its lack, can hurt us.

Writing in Sacred Spaces: Tangible Practices for Understanding Intangible Spirituality

BRIAN J. McNELY

Sometimes meaningful self-sponsored literacy practices take place in unexpected locations.

In early 2011, after almost one year of preparation, I began fieldwork for a multi-sited visual ethnography of Eucharistic adoration practices. For Roman Catholics, the Eucharist is the true body, blood, soul, and divinity of Christ; in Eucharistic adoration, participants meditate with and reflect upon what they believe is the real presence of the ineffable. In Adoration chapels, parishioners spend time—from a few minutes to a few hours—in Christ's Eucharistic presence, ensconced in a tabernacle (see Figure 1). In more formal services of Exposition and Benediction, the Eucharist is displayed in a monstrance on the altar (see Figure 2), exposed and glorified in the sanctuary. Several participants in my study engage in daily or weekly adoration practices; my research aim was formulating a better understanding of their extradiscursive rhetorics in these contemplative and sacred locations—the material assemblages of participant practice, sensory rhetorics (olfactory, haptic, aural), the roles of visuality and (in)visibility, and embodied meaning making. Though my semistructured interviews contain two general questions about alphabetic literacies, I had not expected to observe so many instances of writing and reading *in situ*—before the Eucharist—or to hear participants describe how location-specific writing was central to their experiential knowing and being with Christ.

Field notes from one of my initial observations of Eucharistic Exposition—a Thursday evening service popular with college-age parishioners—detail how some participants in the sanctuary were reading and intensively *writing*:

> The young woman who sits crisscross applesauce [in line for confession] remains seated that way, and she now has a journal in which she's writing…. I wonder why she writes in the presence of the Eucharist, what she

Figure 1. Adoration chapel and tabernacle.

Figure 2. Participating in Eucharistic Exposition: the Eucharist in a monstrance on the altar.

writes, how she uses this time as a literate moment.... [Ten minutes later] The young woman continues to write in her journal. She started on a left-hand page and is now more than halfway down the following page. She readjusts her sitting posture, looks up for a moment, then returns, intently, to her writing. She stops a moment, places the tip of the cap of her ballpoint pen to her lips, returns it to the journal. Raises the pen to her mouth again, appears to think some more, then returns to writing.... She's reading what she's written now. Runs a hand through her long blonde hair. Returns to writing.

[Thirty minutes later, observing a different parishioner] The young woman lying down [prone, very near the altar] writes a LOT in a small script on what appears to be a blank yellow piece of paper. [Twelve minutes later] The young woman who was lying down has moved and now sits with her back to the wall, legs and feet out in front of her, still writing furiously. I'm dying to know what it is she's writing. The predominant sounds in the sanctuary right now are the flowing water [of the baptismal font] and the crackles of paper as this woman's hand moves across the pages sitting on the uneven surface of her thighs. She's writing furiously fast, filling up pages.

These examples were not anomalous; I observed parishioners, young and old, male and female, reading and writing consistently in adoration chapels and in sanctuaries during Eucharistic exposition. But in my attempts to discuss these kinds of writing events with participants during semistructured interviews, I often met with trepidation. Such writing, I learned, was intensely personal and situationally meaningful.

Jason, a twenty-six-year-old college missionary, explained his own daily writing practices during adoration (which occurred in the small chapel pictured in Figure 1). During interviews with Jason, I came to better understand why locations of writing matter for the deeply personal and spiritual literacy practices I observed. Jason spends one hour each morning in the adoration chapel; without fail, he brings along his Bible, a spiritual book of some kind, and his journal. During adoration, there is an interplay between scripture (reading), his physical orientation to the tabernacle (sensory interactions and movements), and his journal (writing). Jason explains this interplay:

> If I'm meditating upon a particular [scripture] passage, through prayer [I'm] having a conversation with the Lord about it—writing down my thoughts and my feelings and what I am experiencing and, just allowing that meditation to also be prayer that can be conversation that I can record, because I don't maybe want to forget it, or want to go back to it in a time of desolation or dryness in prayer and say "Oh yeah, I remember this, Lord.... This was a great time of prayer for me." And so it's there and it's tangible.

Jason is one of the few participants to have shared his journals with me. They contain frank and personal reflections on his spirituality, composed in the adoration chapel. In one instance, he showed me a passage that he described as "an outpouring of my experience—what I was sort of struggling with, just questions that were going through my mind [and] certain responses that I was having—just writing that down and thinking about it, praying with it."

The significance of writing and rhetorics in these locations is palpable, for they embody, as Jason notes, *tangible* practices for understanding *intangible* spirituality. In these sacred spaces, therefore, writing is a material way of knowing and being with God. The adoration chapel—and much more importantly, the presence of Christ in the Eucharist—frames specific forms of writing rich with implications for spiritual identification and ontologies. As Christ is embodied in the Eucharist for parishioners, so too is spiritual understanding and practice embodied in the situated materiality of writing.

What's the Language of the Future?

HENRY HITCHINGS

In "What's the Language of the Future," Henry Hitchings uses research to re-examine an everyday phenomenon (language) as historical, political, and cultural. Balancing competing perspectives, he steps into wider academic as well as more public conversations about the reasons for and critiques of the spread of English around the globe. The following essay is an excerpt from The Language Wars: A History of Proper English *(2011) and was also published in* Salon. *In addition to* Language Wars, *Hitchings has written four books on the history, culture, and politics of English language and literature.*

No language has spread as widely as English, and it continues to spread. Internationally the desire to learn it is insatiable. In the twenty-first century the world is becoming more urban and more middle class, and the adoption of English is a symptom of this, for increasingly English serves as the lingua franca of business and popular culture. It is dominant or at least very prominent in other areas such as shipping, diplomacy, computing, medicine and education. A recent study has suggested that among students in the United Arab Emirates "Arabic is associated with tradition, home, religion, culture, school, arts and social sciences," whereas English "is symbolic of modernity, work, higher education, commerce, economics and science and technology." In Arabic-speaking countries, science subjects are often taught in English because excellent textbooks and other educational resources are readily available in English. This is not something that has come about in an unpurposed fashion; the propagation of English is an industry, not a happy accident.

English has spread because of British colonialism, the technological advances of the Industrial Revolution, American economic and political ascendancy, and further (mostly American) technological developments in the second half of the twentieth century. Its rise has been assisted by the massive exportation of English as a second language, as well as by the growth of an English-language mass media. The preaching of Christianity, supported by the distribution of English-language Bibles, has at many times and in many places sustained the illusion, created by Wyclif and Tyndale and Cranmer, that English is the language of God.

The history of English's global diffusion is littered with important dates: the planting of the Jamestown colony in 1607; Robert Clive's victory at the Battle of Plassey in 1757, which ushered in the dominion of the British East India Company; the creation of the first penal colony in Australia in 1788; the British settlement at Singapore in 1819 and establishment of a Crown Colony in Hong Kong in 1842; the formal beginning of British administration in Nigeria in 1861; the foundation of the BBC in 1922 and the United Nations in 1945; the launch by AT&T of the first commercial communications satellite in 1962. This list is condensed. It takes no account, for instance, of the various waves of Anglomania that swept much of Europe in the eighteenth century. But it will be apparent that the diffusion of English has had a lot to do with material reward, the media, and its use as a language of instruction. A fuller list might intensify the impression of a whiff of bloodshed.

Wherever English has been used, it has lasted. Cultural might outlives military rule. In the colonial period, the languages of settlers dominated the languages of the peoples whose land they seized. They marginalized them and in some cases eventually drove them to extinction. All the while they absorbed from them whatever local terms seemed useful. The colonists' languages practised a sort of cannibalism, and its legacy is still sharply felt. English is treated with suspicion in many places where it was once the language of the imperial overlords. It is far from being a force for unity, and its endurance is stressful. In India, while English is much used in the media, administration, education and business, there are calls to curb its influence. Yet even where English has been denigrated as an instrument of colonialism, it has held on— and in most cases grown, increasing its numbers of speakers and functions.

In the early decades of the twentieth century, H.G. Wells imagined what would become known as World English in his prophetic novel, "The World Set Free." That term for the concept of English as an international language, a global second language, an intellectual and commercial lubricant, even an instrument of foreign policy on the part of the major English-speaking nations, grew common only in the 1960s. It has circulated since the 1920s, though, and the idea was touched upon earlier, not just by Wells, but also by Alexander Melville Bell, who had in 1888 presented World-English, a scheme of revised spellings intended to help learners acquire the language that, as he saw it, exceeded all others "in general fitness to become the tongue of the World." Robert Nares, writing in 1784, presented with no little relish a vision of English extending prodigiously around the globe. Even before that, John

Adams had prophesied that it would become the most widely spoken and read language—and "the most respectable."

The term World English is still in use, but is contested by critics who believe it strikes too strong a note of dominance. Today World English is known by several names, perhaps the most catchy of which is Globish (though personally I think this sounds silly), a term popularized by Jean-Paul Nerrière in his book *Don't Speak English, Parlez Globish*. Globish, as conceived by Nerrière, is a pragmatic form of English consisting of 1,500 words, intended to make it possible for everyone in the world to understand everyone else.

Nerrière's Globish is not alone. Madhukar Gogate, a retired Indian engineer, has independently come up with an idea for something he too calls Globish. It would use phonetic spellings to create what he considers a neater form of English. This could become a global language enabling links between people from different cultures. Meanwhile Joachim Grzega, a German linguist, is promoting Basic Global English, which has a mere twenty grammatical rules and a vocabulary comprising 750 words that learners are expected to supplement with an additional 250 words relevant to their individual needs.

Although these schemes may be intended in a different spirit, promoting a neutral form of English rather than one freighted with "Anglo" values, they are part of a larger, often invisible project: to establish a community, without territorial boundaries, of people who use English; to make its use seem not just normal, but also prestigious; and to market it as a language of riches, opportunity, scholarship, democracy and moral right. This is supported economically, politically, in education and the media, and sometimes also by military force. Much of the endorsement happens covertly. And as English continues to spread, it seems like a steamroller, squashing whatever gets in its way. True, it is often used alongside local languages and does not instantly replace them. Yet its presence shifts the cultural emphases in the lives of those who adopt it, altering their aspirations and expectations. English seems, increasingly, to be a second first language. It is possible to imagine it merely coexisting with other languages, but easy to see that coexistence turning into transcendence. As English impinges on the spaces occupied by other languages, so linguists are increasingly finding that they need to behave like environmentalists: instead of being scholars they have to become activists.

There have been attempts to create an artificial language for use by all the world. In the second half of the nineteenth century and then especially in the early years of the twentieth, schemes to construct new languages were numerous. Most of these are now forgotten: who remembers Cosmoglossa,

Spokil, Mundolingue, Veltparl, Interlingua, Romanizat, Adjuvilo or Molog? Some of the innovators sound like remarkably odd people. Joseph Schipfer, developer of Communicationssprache, was also known for promoting means of preventing people from being buried alive. Etienne-Paulin Gagne, who devised Monopanglosse, proposed that in time of famine Algerians help their families and friends by exchanging their lives or at least some of their limbs for food, and was willing if necessary to give up his own body to the needy.

Only two schemes enjoyed success. In 1879 a Bavarian pastor, Johann Martin Schleyer, devised Volapük. It was briefly very popular: within ten years of its invention, there were 283 societies to promote it, and guides to Volapük were available in twenty-five other languages. As Arika Okrent observes in her book *In the Land of Invented Languages*, Volapük is a gift to people with a puerile sense of humour: 'to speak' is *pükön*, and 'to succeed' is *plöpön*. More famous and less daft-sounding were the efforts of Ludwik Zamenhof, a Polish ophthalmologist of Lithuanian Jewish descent, who in the 1870s began work on creating Esperanto, a language without irregularities. He published his first book on the subject in 1887, summing up the language's grammar in sixteen rules and providing a basic vocabulary. Zamenhof's motives were clear; he had grown up in the ghettos of Bialystok and Warsaw, and, struck by the divisiveness of national languages, he dreamt of uniting humanity. Esperanto is certainly the most successful of modern invented languages, but although it still has enthusiastic supporters there is no prospect of its catching on as Zamenhof once hoped.

You are more likely to have heard Klingon, which was originated by Marc Okrand for the "Star Trek" films, and the Elvish languages—notably Quenya and Sindarin, modelled on Finnish and Welsh respectively—devised by J.R.R. Tolkien and faithfully used in Peter Jackson's films of "The Lord of the Rings." A more recent example of a new artificial language is the one conceived by Paul Frommer that is spoken by the blue-skinned Na'vi in James Cameron's 2009 film "Avatar." Where once they embodied political hopefulness in the real world, invented languages have become accessories of art and entertainment.

Today it is English, rather than any created alternative, that is the world's auxiliary tongue. There are more people who use English as a second language than there are native speakers. Estimates of the numbers vary, but even the most guarded view is that English has 500 million second-language speakers. Far more of the world's citizens are eagerly jumping on board than trying to resist its progress. In some cases the devotion appears religious and can involve what to outsiders looks a lot like self-mortification. According to

Mark Abley, some rich Koreans pay for their children to have an operation that lengthens the tongue because it helps them speak English convincingly. The suggestion is that it enables them to produce *r* and *l* sounds, although the evidence of the many proficient English-speakers among Korean immigrants in America and Britain makes one wonder whether the procedure is either necessary or useful. Still, it is a powerful example of the lengths people will go to in order to learn English, seduced by the belief that linguistic capital equals economic capital.

In places where English is used as a second language, its users often perceive it as free from the limitations of their native languages. They associate it with power and social status, and see it as a supple and sensuous medium for self-expression. It symbolizes choice and liberty. But while many of those who do not have a grasp of the language aspire to learn it, there are many others who perceive it as an instrument of oppression, associated not only with imperialism but also with the predations of capitalism and Christianity. (It is mainly thanks to Lenin's 1917 pamphlet about imperialism and capitalism that the two words have come to be pretty much synonymous.) The Australian scholar Alastair Pennycook neatly sums up English's paradoxical status as "a language of threat, desire, destruction and opportunity." Its spread can be seen as a homogenizing (some would say, Americanizing) force, eroding the integrity of other cultures. Yet it is striking that the language is appropriated locally in quite distinct ways. Sometimes it is used against the very powers and ideologies it is alleged to represent. Listening to Somali or Indonesian rappers, for instance, it seems sloppy to say that the use of English in their lyrics is a craven homage to the commercial and cultural might of America.

In his book *Globish* (2010), Robert McCrum diagnoses English's "subversive capacity to run with the hare and hunt with the hounds, to articulate the ideas of both government and opposition, to be the language of ordinary people as well as the language of power and authority, rock 'n' roll *and* royal decree." He considers it "contagious, adaptable, populist," and identifies the fall of the Berlin Wall in 1989 as the symbolic moment that signalled the beginning of "a new dynamic in the flow of information." McCrum sees English as performing a central role in what Thomas L. Friedman has catchily called "the flattening of the world," the new "single global network."

There are challenges to the position of English as the dominant world language in the twenty-first century. The main ones seem likely to come from Spanish and Mandarin Chinese. Both have more first-language users than English. But at present neither is much used as a lingua franca. The majority of speakers of Mandarin Chinese live in one country, and, excepting Spain, most Spanish-speakers are in the Americas. There is an argument that the revitalization of minority languages is good for English because it weakens English's large rivals and thus removes obstacles to the language's spread. So, for instance, the resurgence of Catalan, Basque and Galician weakens Castilian Spanish, making it a less powerful rival to English. Apologists for English invert this argument, claiming that the advance of English is good for minority languages. The inversion is spurious.

Nicholas Ostler, a linguist whose insights are often brilliantly surprising, observes that "If we compare English to the other languages that have achieved world status, the most similar—as languages—are Chinese and Malay." All three have subject-verb-object word order, and their nouns and verbs display few inflections. Moreover, "the peculiarly conservative, and hence increasingly anti-phonetic, system is another facet of English that bears a resemblance to Chinese," and "as has happened with Chinese...the life of English as it is spoken has become only loosely attached to the written traditions of the language." It's an intriguing link, but hardly a guide to what will happen next.

The main challenges to English may come from within. There is a long history of people using the language for anti-English ends—of creative artists and political figures asserting in English their distance from Englishness or Britishness or American-ness. For instance, many writers whose first language has not been English have infused their English writing with foreign flavours; this has enabled them to parade their heritage while working in a medium that has made it possible for them to reach a wide audience.

Two challenges stand out. I have mentioned India already; English is important to its global ambitions. The language's roots there are colonial, but English connects Indians less to the past than to the future. Already the language is used by more people in India than in any other country, the United States included. Meanwhile in China the number of students learning the language is increasing rapidly. The entrepreneur Li Yang has developed Crazy English, an unorthodox teaching method. It involves a lot of shouting. This, Li explains, is the way fo Chinese to activate their "international muscles." His agenda is patriotic. Kingsley Bolton, head of the English department at the City University of Hong Kong, calls this "huckster nationalism." It certainly has a flamboyant quality; one of Li's slogans is "Conquer English to Make China Strong." A few dissenting voices suggest that he is encouraging racism, but the enthusiasm for his populist approach is in no doubt, and it is a symptom of China's English Fever: the ardent conviction that learning English is the essential skill for surviving in the modern world.

The embrace of English in the world's two most populous countries means that the language is changing. Some of the changes are likely to prove disconcerting for its native speakers. The "Englishness" of English is being diluted. So, more surprisingly, is its American flavour. English's centre of gravity is moving; in fact, in the twenty-first century the language has many centres. As this continues, native English-speakers may find themselves at a disadvantage. Native speakers freight their use of the language with all manner of cultural baggage. An obvious example is the way we use sporting metaphors. If I say to a Slovakian associate, "you hit that for six," she probably won't have a clue what I am on about. Nor will an American. An Indian very likely will (the image is from cricket), but really I should choose my words with greater care. The trouble is, often I and many others like me do not exercise much care at all. To non-native speakers, quirks and elaborations of this kind are confusing. Non-native speakers of English often comment that they find conversing with one another easier than sharing talk with native speakers. Already many people who learn English do so with little or no intention of conversing with its native users. If I join their conversations, my involvement may prove unwelcome.

At the same time, native speakers of English tend to assume that their ability in this potent language makes it unimportant to learn other languages. The reality is different. British companies often miss out on export opportunities because of a lack of relevant language skills. Moreover, there is a chance that a command of English will within twenty or thirty years be regarded as a basic skill for business, and native speakers of the language will no longer enjoy any competitive advantage. When polled in 2005, more than 80 percent of people in the Netherlands, Denmark and Sweden claimed to be able to speak English. The figure was around 60 percent in Finland, 50 percent in Germany, 30 percent in France and Italy, and 20 percent in Spain and Turkey. These figures can safely be assumed to have increased. They come from a study published in 2006 by the British Council, an organization set up in 1934 and today operating as an "international cultural relations body" in more than a hundred countries. In 1989 its Director General, Sir Richard Francis, stated that "Britain's real black gold is not North Sea oil, but the English language." That view is often played down, but the role of the British Council in promoting British English ties in with British corporate interests. Large companies such as British Petroleum (now BP Amoco) have worked with the British Council, funding educational schemes to encourage foreign nationals to learn English. This is not exactly an act of altruism. As Robert Phillipson punchily says, "English for business is business for English." But while English is being pushed, it is also being pulled; it is the language, more than any other, that people want to learn.

The consequences are complex. Some, it would seem, are not as intended. Even as vast amounts are spent on spreading British English, the reality is that English is taking on more and more local colour in the different places where it is used. Accordingly, while the number of languages in the world is diminishing, the number of Englishes is increasing.

A Place Where the Soul Can Rest

bell hooks

In an essay from Belonging: A Culture of Place *(2009), cultural critic bell hooks reflects on her past and present to explore what it means to belong to a particular place. "A Place Where the Soul Can Rest" focuses on a particular and familiar place for many: the porch. hooks asks us to see the porches of her childhood and adult homes through her contexts as an African-American woman from the American South. Through an exploration of the porch as a gendered and racialized place, she opens up our ways of seeing and understanding the implications of how we interact with our own places. hooks is a feminist scholar, activist, and prolific writer who has published 40 books primarily on race, gender, and sexuality in education and other social contexts.*

Street corners have always been space that has belonged to men—patriarchal territory. The feminist movement did not change that. Just as it was not powerful enough to take back the night and make the dark a safe place for women to lurk, roam, and meander at will, it was not able to change the ethos of the street corner—gender equality in the workplace, yes, but the street corner turns every woman who dares lurk into a body selling herself, a body looking for drugs, a body going down. A female lurking, lingering, lounging on a street corner is seen by everyone, looked at, observed. Whether she wants to be or not she is prey for the predator, for the Man, be he pimp, police, or just passerby. In cities women have no outdoor territory to occupy. They must be endlessly moving or enclosed. They must have a destination. They cannot loiter or linger.

Verandas and porches were made for females to have outdoor space to occupy. They are a common feature of southern living. Before air conditioning cooled every hot space the porch was the summertime place, the place everyone flocked to in the early mornings and in the late nights. In our Kentucky world of poor southern black neighborhoods of shotgun houses and clapboard houses, a porch was a sign of living a life without shame. To come out on the porch was to see and be seen, to have nothing to hide. It signaled a willingness to be known. Oftentimes the shacks of the destitute were places where inhabitants walked outside straight into dust and dirt—there was neither time nor money to make a porch.

The porches of my upbringing were places of fellowship—outside space women occupied while men were away, working or on street corners. To sit on one's porch meant chores were done—the house was cleaned, food prepared. Or if you were rich enough and the proud possessor of a veranda, it was the place of your repose while the house-keeper or maid finished your cleaning. As children we needed permission to sit on the porch, to reside if only for a time, in that place of leisure and rest. The first house we lived in had no porch. A cinder-block dwelling made for working men to live in while they searched the earth for oil outside city limits, it was designed to be a waiting place, a place for folks determined to move up and on—a place in the wilderness. In the wilderness there were no neighbors to wave at or chat with or simply to holler at and know their presence by the slamming of doors as one journeyed in and out. A home without neighbors surely did not require a porch, just narrow steps to carry inhabitants in and out.

When we moved away from the wilderness, when we moved up, our journey of improved circumstance took us to a wood-frame house with upstairs and downstairs. Our new beginning was grand: we moved to a place with not one but three porches—a front porch, a side porch, and a back porch. The side porch was a place where folks could sleep when the heat of the day had cooled off. Taking one's dreams outside made the dark feel safe. And in that safeness, a woman, a child—girl or boy—could linger. Side porches were places for secret meetings, places where intimate callers could come and go without being seen, spend time without anyone knowing how long they stayed. After a year of living with a side porch and six teenaged girls, Daddy sheetrocked, made walls, blocked up the door so that it became our brother's room, an enclosed space with no window to the outside.

We sat on the back porch and did chores like picking walnuts, shucking corn, and cleaning fish, when Baba, Mama's mama, and the rest had a good fishing day, when black farmers brought the fruit of their labor into the city. Our back porch was tiny. It could not hold all of us. And so it was a limited place of fellowship. As a child I felt more comfortable there, unobserved, able to have my child's musings, my day-dreams, without the interruptions of folks passing by and saying a word or two, without folks coming up to sit a spell. At Mr. Porter's house (he was the old man who lived and died there before we moved in) there was feeling of eternity, of timelessness. He had imprinted on the soul of this house his flavor, the taste and scent of a long lived life. We honored that by calling his name when talking about the house on First Street.

To our patriarchal dad, Mr. V, the porch was a danger zone—as in his sexist mindset all feminine space was designated dangerous, a threat. A strange man walking on Mr.V's porch was setting himself up to be a possible target: walking onto the porch, into an inner feminine sanctum, was in the eyes of any patriarch just the same as raping another man's woman. And we were all of us—mother, daughters—owned by our father. Like any patriarch would, he reminded us from time to time whose house we lived in—a house where women had no rights but could indeed claim the porch—colonize it and turn it into a place where men could look but not touch—a place that did not interest our father, a place where he did not sit. Indeed, our daddy always acted as though he hated the porch. Often when he came home from work he entered through the back door, making his territory, taking us unaware.

We learned that it was best not to be seen on the porch often when he walked up the sidewalk after a long day's work. We knew our place: it was inside, making the world comfortable for the patriarch, preparing ourselves to bow and serve—not literally to bow, but to subordinate our beings. And we did. No wonder then that we loved the porch, longed to move outside the protected patriarchal space of that house that was in its own way a prison.

Like so much else ruined by patriarchal rage, so much other female space damaged, our father the patriarch took the porch from us one intensely hot summer night. Returning home from work in a jealous rage, he started ranting the moment he hit the sidewalk leading up to the steps, using threatening, ugly words. We were all females there on that porch, parting our bodies like waves in the sea so that Mama could be pushed by hurting hands, pushed through the front door, pushed into the house, where his threats to kill and kill again would not be heard by the neighbors. This trauma of male violence took my teenage years and smothered them in the arms of a deep and abiding grief—took away the female fellowship, the freedom of days and nights sitting on the porch.

Trapped in the interstices of patriarchal gender warfare, we stayed off the porch, for fear that just any innocent male approaching would be seen by our father and set off crazy rage. Coming in from the outside I would see at a distance the forlorn look of a decimated space, its life energy gone and its heart left lonely. Mama and Daddy mended the wounded places severed by rage, maintaining their intimate bond. They moved away from Mr. Porter's house into a small new wood frame structure, a house without a porch, and even when a small one was added it was not a porch for sitting, just a place for standing. Maybe this space relieved Dad's anxiety about the dangerous feminine, about female power.

Surely our father, like all good patriarchs, sensed that the porch as female gathering place represented in some vital way a threat to the male dominator's hold on the household. The porch as liminal space, standing between the house and the world of sidewalks and streets, was symbolically a threshold. Crossing it opened up the possibility of change. Women and children on the porch could begin to interpret the outside world on terms different from the received knowledge gleaned in the patriarchal household. The porch had no master; even our father could not conquer it. Porches could be abandoned but they could not be taken over, occupied by any one group to the exclusion of others.

A democratic meeting place, capable of containing folks from various walks of life, with diverse perspectives, the porch was free-floating space, anchored only by the porch swing, and even that was a symbol of potential pleasure. The swing hinted at the underlying desire to move freely, to be transported. A symbol of play, it captured the continued longing for childhood, holding us back in time, entrancing us, hypnotizing us with its back-and-forth motion. The porch swing was a place where intimacies could be forged, desire arising in the moment of closeness swings made possible.

In the days of my girlhood, when everyone sat on their porches, usually on their swings, it was the way we all became acquainted with one another, the way we created community. In M. Scott Peck's work on community-making and peace, *The Different Drum*, he explains that true community is always integrated and that "genuine community is always characterized by integrity." The integrity that emerged in our segregated communities as I was growing up was based on the cultivation of civility, of respect for others and acknowledgement of their presence. Walking by someone's house, seeing them on their porch, and failing to speak was to go against the tenets of the community. Now and then, I or my siblings would be bold enough to assume we could ignore the practice of civility, which included learning respect for one's elders, and strut by folks' houses and not speak. By the time we reached home, Mama would have received a call about our failure to show courtesy and respect. She would make us take our walk again and perform the necessary ritual of speaking to our neighbors who were sitting on their porches.

In *A World Waiting to Be Born: The Search for Civility*, M. Scott Peck extends his conversation on making community to include the practice of civility. Growing up in the segregated South, I was raised to believe in the importance of being civil. This was more than just a recognition of the need to be polite, of having good manners; it was a demand that I and my siblings remain constantly aware of our interconnectedness and interdependency on all the folk around us. The lessons learned by seeing one's neighbors on their porches and stopping to chat with them, or just to speak courteously, was a valuable way to honor our connectedness. Peck shares the insight that civility is consciously motivated and essentially an ethical practice. By practicing civility we remind ourselves, he writes, that "each and every human being—you, every friend, every stranger, every foreigner is precious." The etiquette of civility then is far more than the performance of manners: it includes an understanding of the deeper psychoanalytic relationship to recognition as that which makes us subjects to one another rather than objects.

African Americans have a long history of struggling to stand as subjects in a place where the dehumanizing impact of racism works continually to make us objects. In our small-town segregated world, we lived in communities of resistance, where even the small everyday gesture of porch sitting was linked to humanization. Racist white folks often felt extreme ire when observing a group of black folks gathered on a porch. They used derogatory phrases like "porch monkey" both to express contempt and to once again conjure up the racist iconography linking blackness to nature, to animals in the wild. As a revolutionary threshold between home and street, the porch as liminal space could also then be a place of antiracist resistance. While white folk could interpret at will the actions of a black person on the street, the black person or persons gathered on a porch defied such interpretation. The racist eye could only watch, yet never truly know, what was taking place on porches among black folk.

I was a little girl in a segregated world when I first learned that there were white people who saw black people as less than animals. Sitting on the porch, my siblings and I would watch white folks bring home their servants, the maids and cooks who toiled to make their lives comfortable. These black servants were always relegated to the back seat. Next to the white drivers in the front would be the dog and in the back seat the black worker. Just seeing this taught me much about the interconnectedness of race and class. I often wondered how the black worker felt when it came time to come home and the dog would be placed in front, where racism and white supremacy had decreed no black person could ride. Although just a child, witnessing this act of domination, I understood that the workers must have felt shamed, because they never looked out the window; they never acknowledged a world beyond that moving car.

It was as though they were riding home in a trance—closing everything out was a way to block out the shaming feelings. Silent shadows slouched in the back seats of fancy cars, lone grown-up workers never turned their gaze toward the porch where "liberated" black folks could be seen hanging together. I was the girl they did not see, sitting in the swing, who felt their pain and wanted to make it better. And I would sit there and swing, going back and forth to the dreaming rhythm of a life where black folks would live free from fear.

Leaving racialized fear behind, I left the rhythm of porch swings, of hot nights filled with caring bodies and laughter lighting the dark like june bugs. To the West Coast I went to educate myself, away from the lazy apartheid of a jim crow that had been legislated away but was still nowhere near gone, to the North where I could become the intellectual the South back then had told me I could not be. But like the black folks anthropologist Carol Stack writes about, who flee the North and go South again, yearning for a life they fear is passing them by, I too returned home. To any southerner who has ever loved the South, it is always and eternally home. From birth onward we breathed in its seductive heady scent, and it is the air that truly comforts. From birth onward as southerners we were seduced and imprinted by glimpses of a civic life expressed in communion not found elsewhere. That life was embodied for me in the world of the porch.

Looking for a home in the new South, that is, the place where jim crow finds its accepted expression in crude acting out, I entered a real-estate culture where material profit was stronger than the urge to keep neighborhoods and races pure. Seeking to live near water, where I could walk places, surrounded by an abundant natural tropical landscape, where I can visit Kentucky friends and sit on their porches, I found myself choosing a neighborhood populated mainly by old-school white folks. Searching for my southern home, I looked for a place with a porch. Refurbishing a 1920s bungalow, similar to ones the old Sears and Roebuck catalogue carried for less than seven hundred dollars with or without bathroom, I relished working on the porch. Speaking to neighbors who did not speak back, or one who let me know that they came to this side of town to be rid of lazy blacks, I was reminded how the black families who first bought homes in "white" neighborhoods during the civil rights era suffered—that their suffering along with the pain of their allies in struggle who worked for justice makes it possible for me to choose where I live. By comparison, what I and other black folk experience as we bring diversity into what has previously been a whites-only space is mere discomfort.

In their honor and in their memory, I speak a word of homage and praise for the valiant ones, who struggled and suffered so that I could and do live where I please, and I have made my porch a small everyday place of antiracist resistance, a place where I practice the etiquette of civility. I and my two sisters, who live nearby, sit on the porch. We wave at all the passersby, mostly white, mostly folks who do not acknowledge our presence. Southern white women are the least willing to be civil, whether old or young. Here in the new South there are many white women who long for the old days when they could count on being waited on by a black female at some point in their life, using the strength of their color to weigh her down. A black woman homeowner disrupts this racialized sexist fantasy. No matter how many white women turn their gaze away, we look, and by looking we claim our subjectivity. We speak, offering the southern hospitality, the civility, taught by our parents so that we would be responsible citizens. We speak to everyone.

Humorously, we call these small interventions yet another "Martin Luther King moment." Simply by being civil, by greeting, by "conversating," we are doing the antiracist work of nonviolent integration. That includes speaking to and dialoguing with the few black folk we see from the porch who enter our neighborhood mainly as poorly paid, poorly treated workers. We offer them our solidarity in struggle. In King's famous essay "Loving Your Enemies," he reminded us that this reaching out in love is the only gesture of civility that can begin to lay the groundwork for true community. He offers the insight, "Love is the only force that can turn an enemy into a friend. We never get rid of an enemy by meeting hate with hate; we get rid of an enemy by getting rid of enmity. By its very nature, hate destroys and tears down; by its very nature, love creates and builds up. Love transforms with redemptive power." Inside my southern home, I can forge a world outside of the racist enmity. When I come out on my porch I become aware of race, of the hostile racist white gaze, and I can contrast it with the warm gaze of welcome and recognition from those individual white folks who also understand the etiquette of civility, of community building and peace making.

The "starlight bungalow"—my southern home for now, given the name assigned it in the blueprint of the Sears and Roebuck 1920s catalogue (as a modern nomad I do not stay in place)—has an expansive porch. Stucco over wood, the house has been reshaped to give it a Mediterranean flavor. Architecturally it is not a porch that invites a swing, a rocking chair, or even a bench. Covered with warm sand-colored Mexican tiles, it is a porch that is not made for true repose. Expansive, with rounded arches and columns, it does invite the soul to open wide, to enter the heart of the home, crossing a peaceful threshold.

Returning to the South, I longed for a porch for fellowship and late-night gatherings. However, just as I am true to my inner callings, I accept what I feel to be the architectural will of the porch and let it stand as it is, without added seats, with only one tin star as ornament. It is a porch for short sittings, a wide standing porch, for looking out and gazing down, a place for making contact—a place where one can be seen. In the old Sears and Roebuck catalogue, houses were given names and the reader was told what type of life might be imagined in this dwelling. My "starlight bungalow" was described as "a place for distinct and unique living." When I first sat on the porch welcoming folk, before entering a dwelling full of light, I proclaimed, in old South vernacular, "My soul is rested." A perfect porch is a place where the soul can rest.

In Kentucky my house on the hill has a long wide porch facing the lake that is our water source. This is not a porch for meeting and greeting. Perched high on a hill, the house and the porch has no passersby. Like the "starlight bungalow" this is a porch for "quiet and repose." It invites one to be still—to hear divine voices speak.

occupation of space,

The IRL Fetish

NATHAN JURGENSON

In an essay published in the online magazine The New Inquiry, Nathan Jurgenson, a sociologist who focuses on social media, offers a nuanced analysis of the ways we understand our online interactions as distinct from our IRL— "in real life"—experiences. Critiquing the tendency to value time spent offline or unplugged as more authentic, meaningful, or "real," Jurgenson argues that the online-offline distinction fails to acknowledge the ways social media shapes how we think and act long after we've signed off.

The deep infiltration of digital information into our lives has created a fervor around the supposed corresponding loss of logged-off *real life*. Each moment is oversaturated with digital potential: Texts, status updates, photos, check-ins, tweets, and emails are just a few taps away or pushed directly to your buzzing and chirping pocket computer—anachronistically still called a "phone." Count the folks using their devices on the train or bus or walking down the sidewalk or, worse, crossing the street oblivious to drivers who themselves are bouncing back and forth between the road and their digital distractor. Hanging out with friends and family increasingly means also hanging out with their technology. While eating, defecating, or resting in our beds, we are rubbing on our glowing rectangles, seemingly lost within the infostream.

If the hardware has spread virally within physical space, the software is even more insidious. Thoughts, ideas, locations, photos, identities, friendships, memories, politics, and almost everything else are finding their way to social media. The power of "social" is not just a matter of the time we're spending checking apps, nor is it the data that for-profit media companies are gathering; it's also that the *logic* of the sites has burrowed far into our consciousness. Smartphones and their symbiotic social media give us a surfeit of options to tell the truth about who we are and what we are doing, and an audience for it all, reshaping norms around mass exhibitionism and voyeurism. Twitter lips and Instagram eyes: Social media is part of ourselves; the Facebook source code becomes our own code.

Predictably, this intrusion has created a backlash. Critics complain that people, especially young people, have logged on and checked out. Given the addictive appeal of the infostream, the masses have traded *real* connection for the virtual. They have traded human friends for Facebook friends. Instead of being present at the dinner table, they are lost in their phones. Writer after writer laments the loss of a sense of disconnection, of boredom (now redeemed as a respite from anxious info-cravings), of sensory peace in this age of always-on information, omnipresent illuminated screens, and near-constant self-documentation. Most famously, there is Sherry Turkle, who is amassing fame for decrying the loss of real, offline connection. In the *New York Times*, Turkle writes that "in our rush to connect, we flee from solitude...we seem almost willing to dispense with people altogether." She goes on:

> I spend the summers at a cottage on Cape Cod, and for decades I walked the same dunes that Thoreau once walked. Not too long ago, people walked with their heads up, looking at the water, the sky, the sand and at one another, talking. Now they often walk with their heads down, typing. Even when they are with friends, partners, children, everyone is on their own devices. So I say, look up, look at one another.

While the Cape Cod example is Kerry/Romney-level unrelatable, we can grasp her point: Without a device, we are heads up, eyes to the sky, left to ponder and appreciate. Turkle leads the chorus that insists that taking time out is becoming dangerously difficult and that we need to follow their lead and log off.

This refrain is repeated just about any time someone is forced to detether from a digital appendage. Forgetting one's phone causes a sort of existential crisis. Having to navigate without a maps app, eating a delicious lunch and not being able to post a photograph, having a witty thought without being able to tweet forces reflection on how different our modern lives really are. To spend a moment of boredom without a glowing screen, perhaps while waiting in line at the grocery store, can propel people into a *This American Life*–worthy self-exploration about how profound the experience was.

Fueled by such insights into our lost "reality," we've been told to resist technological intrusions and aspire to consume less information: turn off your phones, log off social media, and learn to reconnect offline. Books like Turkle's *Alone Together*, William Powers's *Hamlet's Blackberry*, and the whole Digital Sabbath movement[1] plead with us to close the Facebook tab so we can focus on one task undistracted. We should go out into the "real" world, lift our chins, and breathe deep the wonders of the offline (which, presumably, smells of Cape Cod).

But as the proliferation of such essays and books suggests, we are far from forgetting about the offline; rather we have become obsessed with being offline more than ever before. We have never appreciated a solitary stroll, a camping trip, a face-to-face chat with friends, or even our boredom better than we do now. Nothing has contributed more to our collective appreciation for being logged off and technologically disconnected than the very technologies of connection. The ease of digital distraction has made us appreciate solitude with a new intensity. We savor being face-to-face with a small group of friends or family in one place and one time far more thanks to the digital sociality that so fluidly rearranges the rules of time and space. In short, we've never cherished being alone, valued introspection, and treasured information disconnection more than we do now. Never has being disconnected—even if for just a moment—felt so profound.

The current obsession with the analog, the vintage, and the retro has everything to do with this fetishization of the offline. The rise of the mp3 has been coupled with a resurgence in vinyl. Vintage cameras and typewriters dot the apartments of Millennials. Digital photos are cast with the soft glow, paper borders, and scratches of Instagram's faux-vintage filters. The ease and speed of the digital photo resists itself, creating a new appreciation for slow film photography. "Decay porn"[2] has become a thing.

[Note: At Occupy Wall Street, there was a bunch of old-time-y cameras.[3]]

~

Many of us, indeed, have always been quite happy to occasionally log off and appreciate stretches of boredom or ponder printed books—even though books themselves were regarded as a deleterious distraction as they became more prevalent. But our immense self-satisfaction in disconnection is new. How proud of ourselves we are for fighting against the long reach of mobile and social technologies! One of our new hobbies is patting ourselves on the back by demonstrating how much we *don't* go on Facebook. People boast about not having a profile. We have started to congratulate ourselves for keeping our phones in our pockets and fetishizing the offline as something more real to be nostalgic for. While the offline is said to be increasingly difficult to access, it is simultaneously easily obtained—if, of course, you are the "right" type of person.

Every other time I go out to eat with a group, be it family, friends, or acquaintances of whatever age, conversation routinely plunges into a discussion of when it is appropriate to pull out a phone. People boast about their self-control over not checking their device, and the table usually reaches a self-congratulatory consensus that we should all just keep it in our pants. The pinnacle of such abstinence-only smartphone education is a game that is popular to talk about (though I've never actually seen it played) wherein the first person at the dinner table to pull out their device has to pay the tab. Everyone usually agrees this is awesome.

What a ridiculous state of affairs this is. To obsess over the offline and deny all the ways we routinely remain disconnected is to fetishize this disconnection. Author after author pretends to be a lone voice, taking a courageous stand in support of the offline in precisely the moment it has proliferated and become over-valorized. For many, maintaining the fiction of the collective loss of the offline *for everyone else* is merely an attempt to construct their own personal time-outs as more special, as allowing them to rise above those social forces of distraction that have ensnared the masses. "I am real. I am the thoughtful human. You are the automaton." I am reminded of a line from a recent essay by Sarah Nicole Prickett:[4] that we are "so obsessed with the real that it's unrealistic, atavistic, and just silly." How have we come to make the error of collectively mourning the loss of that which is proliferating?

In great part, the reason is that we have been taught to mistakenly view *online* as meaning *not offline*. The notion of the offline as real and authentic is a recent invention, corresponding with the rise of the online. If we can fix this false separation and view the digital and physical as enmeshed, we will understand that what we do while connected is inseparable from what we do when disconnected. That is, disconnection from the smartphone and social media isn't really disconnection at all: The logic of social media follows us long after we log out. There was and is no offline; it is a lusted-after fetish object that some claim special ability to attain, and it has always been a phantom.

Digital information has long been portrayed as an elsewhere, a new and different cyberspace,[5] a tendency I have coined the term "digital dualism"[6] to describe: the habit of viewing the online and offline as largely distinct. The common (mis)understanding is experience is zero-sum: time spent online means less spent offline. We are either jacked into the Matrix or not; we are either looking at our devices or not. When camping, I have service or not, and when out to eat, my friend is either texting or not. The smartphone has come to be "the perfect symbol"[7] of leaving the here and now for something digital, some other, *cyber*, space.

[Note: To be clear, the digital and physical *are not the same*, but we should aim to better understand the relationship of different combinations of information, be they analog or digital, whether using the technologies of stones, transistors, or flesh and blood. Also, technically, bits are atoms, but the language can still be conceptually useful.]

But this idea that we are trading the offline for the online, though it dominates how we think of the digital and the physical, is myopic. It fails to capture the plain fact that our lived reality is the result of the constant interpenetration of the online and offline. That is, we live in an augmented reality that exists at the intersection of materiality and information, physicality and digitality, bodies and technology, atoms and bits, the off and the online. It is wrong to say "IRL" to mean offline: *Facebook is real life*.

Facebook doesn't curtail the offline but depends on it. What is most crucial to our time spent logged on is what happened when logged off; it is the fuel that runs the engine of social media. The photos posted, the opinions expressed, the check-ins that fill our streams are often anchored by what happens when disconnected and logged-off. The Web has everything to do with reality; it comprises real people with real bodies, histories, and politics.[8] It is the fetish objects of the offline and the disconnected that are not real.

Those who mourn the loss of the offline are blind to its prominence online. When Turkle was walking Cape Cod, she breathed in the air, felt the breeze, and watched the waves with Facebook in mind. The appreciation of this moment of so-called disconnection was, in part, a product of online connection. The stroll ultimately was understood as and came to be fodder for her op-ed, just as our own time spent not looking at Facebook becomes the status updates and photos we will post later.

[Note: Turkle takes for granted not only her Cape Cod cottage but also her access to high-profile op-ed space, blinding her to others' similar need for media to declare how meaningful our lives are.]

The clear distinction between the on and offline, between human and technology, is queered beyond tenability. It's not real unless it's on Google; pics or it didn't happen. We aren't friends until we are Facebook friends. We have come to understand more and more of our lives through the logic of digital connection. Social media is more than something we log into; it is something we carry within us. We can't log off.

Solving this digital dualism also solves the contradiction: We may never fully log off, but this in no way implies the loss of the face-to-face, the slow, the analog, the deep introspection, the long walks, or the subtle appreciation of life sans screen. We enjoy all of this more than ever before. Let's not pretend we are in some special, elite group with access to the pure offline, turning the real into a fetish and regarding everyone else as a little less real and a little less human.

See hyperlinks embedded in this online article:

1. http://www.sabbathmanifesto.org/unplug

2. http://thesocietypages.org/cyborgology/tag/decay-porn/

3. http://thesocietypages.org/cyborgology/2011/11/02/retro-tech-ows-complicated-relationship-with-technology/

4. http://thenewinquiry.com/essays/speaking-in-tongues/

5. http://thenewinquiry.com/essays/the-myth-of-cyberspace/

6. http://thesocietypages.org/cyborgology/2011/02/24/digital-dualism-versus-augmented-reality/

7. http://www.theatlantic.com/technology/archive/2012/02/the-myth-of-the-disconnected-life/252672/

8. http://thesocietypages.org/cyborgology/2011/09/13/digital-dualism-and-the-fallacy-of-web-objectivity/

No Man's Land

TOMÁS M. KALMAR

In this excerpt from the first chapter of his book Illegal Alphabets and Adult Biliteracy: Latino Migrants Crossing the Linguistic Border, *Tomás Mario Kalmar describes how migrant workers in Illinois dealt with violence against their community through communication. This chapter provides a lens through which we can see different ways languages interact, as the communities acquired functional English literacies by translating English phrases into the Spanish alphabet* líricamente, *constructing new phrases that they could pronounce and that could also be understood by English speakers. Kalmar, a doctor of education and independent scholar, participated in this community for four years as an ethnographer to write this book.*

Quasi captivos sensus in suam linguam victoris iure transposuit.
—JEROME

I

Líricamente

On Monday, July 7, 1980, the temperature in Cobden, Illinois rose, as it had for the past week, to 110° in the shade. No one could remember it ever being this hot before. Many blamed it on atmospheric changes caused by the eruption of Mt. St. Helens in Washington state.

The two thousand people who picked the apples in the orchards around Cobden on that Monday did not, of course, work in the shade. When the day's work was done, some of the Mexicans gathered on the porch of Su Casa Grocery Store, as usual, to chat with one another and with their new Anglo friends. The Anglos were locals from Union and Jackson counties who came to Su Casa Grocery Store on weekday evenings in the hope of picking up a little Spanish in return for teaching a little English. That, at least, was how they first explained their reason for coming, when these gatherings had first begun about six weeks earlier. Week by week, the character of the meetings had gone through changes. People began gathering every weeknight (except

Friday). Some, on each "side" of the language barrier, came only once or twice. Others came often, and brought their friends. Sometimes there were only half-a-dozen of us, sometimes thirty or forty. Gradually, shyly, people who could not speak each other's language exchanged bits and pieces of ordinary speech, the common coin of each other's social customs. Gradually, face-to-face encounters between Anglos and Mexicans, between legal citizens and illegal migrant laborers, became less embarrassing. Under the guise of lowering the language barrier, in the "neutral territory" of the Mexican grocery store, people were, as the Mexicans put it, *ganando confianza*: building trust across the social (and legal) gulf that divided locals and migrants. Very quietly, almost invisibly, Cobden was beginning to desegregate itself.

On that Monday, July 7, 1980, people felt too hot, and too numerous, to crowd into the store. A few strolled down to the little park down the street, and others joined them. By around 7 p.m. I counted about eighty people in the park, locals and migrants, half and half. Little kids were on the swings, teenagers on the basketball court, and more mature adults on the bench or in the shade of the tree. This was more people than I had seen in the park before. The park, in fact, was usually empty.

On the basketball court two teams had formed. It was not Mexicans *versus* Anglos. Each team was mixed. But the game was pure basketball. Mexicans tend to regard basketball as quintessentially Mexican. It was played in pre-Columbian Mexico. North Americans tend to regard it as quintessentially yankee. Despite the language barrier, the rules of the game were common knowledge. Players and spectators kept up a supportive banter of phrases in English and Spanish. From time to time, to comment on a good or bad shot, players or spectators tried out some rather mild cusswords in each other's language. Much laughter.

While Mexican and Anglo body rhythms playfully contested possession of the ball on the court according to the well-known rules of the game, a group of us older, or at least less energetic, men shared the rhythms of Mexican and North American music, country-western and ranchera, bluegrass and corridos, sitting or standing in the shade of a tree that had lost a couple of branches to the recent tornado. We shared soft drinks and Kentucky Fried Chicken. Jim had brought his banjo; I had brought my guitar. Constantino, Pancho, Antonio, and some of the other men, were from los Altos de Jalisco and sang the old corridos—*La carcel de Cananea, Valentín de la Sierra, El veinticuatro de junio, Rosita Alvirez*[1]—in the old traditional style which demands that two men sing in such close harmony and with such complete recall of the entire text that you cannot tell who is leading and who is following, which is *la primera voz*, which *la segunda voz*—which is the first voice, which the second. To maintain concentration, you gaze into each other's eyes throughout all the verses, keeping your voices always a third apart (never, as in bluegrass harmony, an open fourth or fifth.) These corridos are invariably learned *líricamente*—"lyrically," that is to say by heart, by "word of mouth," orally, not from written texts.

Jim tried to accompany the corridos on his banjo, without much luck. His banjo licks fit in much better with the polka rhythms of the norteño style, especially this song, as sung by Pancho and Antonio on that day:

1] Porque somos los mojados
siempre nos busca la ley
porque andamos ilegales
y no sabemos inglés
la migra terca a sacarnos
y nosotros a volver.

Si unos sacan por Laredo
por Mexicali entran diez
por Ciudad Juárez, Tijuana,
y por Nogales también
¿quién puede sacar la cuenta
cuantos entramos al mes?

1]*Because we are "wetbacks"*
the law is always after us
because we go round illegal
and don't speak English
the INS is bent on throwing us out
and we're bent on coming back

For each one thrown out at Laredo
ten get in through Mexicali,
Ciudad Juárez, Tijuana,
and Nogales as well.
Who can keep score
how many of us come per month?

(<u>Chorus</u>:)
El problema de nosotros
fácil se puede arreglar
que nos den una gringuita
para poder emigrar
en cuanto nos den la mica
la mandamos a volar

2] ¿Si se acabara el mojado
de quién podrán depender?
¿Quién piscara el jitomate,
lechuga, y el betabel?
El limón, uva, y toronja—
todo se echara a perder.

Y los salones de baile
todos tendrán que cerrar
porque si se va el mojado
¿quienes van a ir a bailar?
y las que viven de welfare
¿quién las irá a consolar?[2]

(*Chorus:*)
Our problem
can easily be solved
let them give us a little gringa
so that we can emigrate
as soon as they give us our green card
we'll tell her to split

2] If there were no wetbacks
on whom could they depend?
Who'd pick the tomatoes,
the lettuce, the beet?
The lemons, grapes, grapefruit—
it would all go to waste.

And all the dance halls
will have to close down
because if the wetback leaves
who's going to go dancing?
And the women on welfare—
who's going to console them?

Then Jim and his friend Simon sang *Cold Cold Heart* and other old Hank Williams songs, in close country harmony, often in parallel thirds, which sounded, in this context, somewhat Mexican in flavor. When Jim sang *If you've got the money, I've got the time*, Alfredo and Raúl joined in. They were two of the most highly respected men in the Tarascan community. Alfredo was in his early fifties, Raúl—who had distinguished himself on the basketball court—in his late forties. Both men had traveled from Chéran to various regions of the United States and back again many times.

Later, Raúl and Alfredo decided to write down *toda la letra*—the whole text, the complete lyrics—of *You picked a fine time to leave me Lucille*, which had been sung more than once that night. They already knew it *líricamente*—they sang along with everyone else every time it got sung. They wanted to write it down so they could remember it on their own. Jim and Simon could remember the opening lines, the rest they "faked." Two lines satisfied Raúl. Alfredo wanted the whole thing. He went around collecting bits of it here and there, from one person, and another until finally he had the whole thing down pat. He looked at his score and sang it just like on the record.

Raúl	Alfredo	(Spanish version)
YO PICTI FAY TAIYO	LLU PICT FANY TAM	ME ABANDONASTE
TU LIVE MI LUCI	TO LIMI LUSIO	MUY PRONTO MUJER
FORR JANDRI CHOUREN	FOR JAGRE CHILDON	CON LA COSECHA,
HENE CROOF ENDÍ FIIL	EN COROP IN FIL	LOS HIJOS Y YO
	AYFRD SAN BE TAMS	
	LIBT TRU SAN SE TAMS	
	BAT DIS TAM	
	DU JORTN GUANT JIOL	
	LLU PICT FANY TAM	
	TO LIMI LUSIO	

Working together, Raúl and Alfredo and Jim and Santiago and me came up with a Spanish version. We had to keep counting syllables in each language to make sure it fit the tune. It took about fifteen minutes to translate just two lines. But these two lines sounded almost like a corrido:

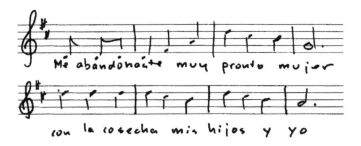

While his elders were making field transcriptions of local oral texts, Panchito was learning his first words in English. Panchito, about fifteen years old, was probably the youngest Tarascan man in the area. He had been in the United States less than a week and this was his first social encounter with friendly locals. He had been active in the basketball game and was now hanging out with Cipriano and Alfonso, two older teenagers from los Altos de Jalisco (i.e., not Tarascans). Cipriano and Alfonso had formed a friendship with Renée, a fourteen-year-old white picker who often came to the meetings with her mother. Tonight Renée had brought her friend Stephanie, a young woman her own age. Panchito kept looking at Stephanie. Finally he came over to where we were singing. In the softest possible voice, he asked "¿Como se dice en inglés ¿dónde vives??" How do you say *dónde vives* in English.

Panchito listened closely to Jim, Simon, and some of the other men saying *where d'you live?* He mimicked them until he got it off by heart, *líricamente*.

He borrowed a ball-point pen and a scrap of paper from Alfredo. He wrote
JUELLULIB.

He kept looking at his piece of paper and trying it out. "La lengua tiene que
doblarse donde uno la maneja," said Alfredo—your tongue has to fold the
way you tell it to. To my ears Panchito was wrapping his tongue around the
southern twang just fine. He echoed, I thought, Jim's local intonation and
rhythm perfectly. "Tiene la musiquita de la voz," said Raúl—he's caught the
melody of the voice. Panchito even pronounced the final *v* in *live* (represented
by the final B in his JUELLULIB.) Monolingual Spanish speakers have trouble
hearing this sound at the end of a word or phrase—and therefore have trouble
saying it—because the rhythms of spoken Spanish don't end that way. Panchito, Alfredo, and Raúl, however, were not monolingual. They were bilingual
in Tarascan and Spanish. And they were musicians.

Panchito looked across at Stephanie. Doubt flickered on his face, I urged him
to practice on Martha, who was standing nearby. A long silence, during which
he gazed at Martha, gazed pensively at his piece of paper. Finally something
overcame his shyness. He stepped up to Martha and touched her elbow.
When she turned to him he said, softly, "JUELLULIB?" "Carbondale," said
Martha. The smile that flowered on his lips as he crossed the language border
was the first smile I had seen on his face since the day he arrived from Cherán.

From that day on, he smiled more and more often, and by the end of the summer he had become something of a leader among his compañeros, some of
whom were a good deal older than he was.

I copied JUELLULIB into my own notebook and it made me smile in turn.
Panchito had a lot to learn. But so did I. JUELLULIB struck me, at the time, as
funny, and it took a number of subsequent experiences to convert my amuse-
ment into respect unmixed with condescension.

July death called accident

Body finally identified as migrant worker

THU NOV 6 1980

By H. B. Koplowitz
Of The Southern Illinoisan

The body of a man found dead July 12 on U.S. 51 south of Cobden has at last been positively identified.

According to Union County State's Attorney William Ballard, the Mexican Department of Defense identified the man last week as Leonardo Valdez, 21, of Michoacan Province, Mexico. The identification was made from fingerprint samples sent to Mexico by the state's attorney's office. X *murder list*

Valdez died July 12, apparently as the result of a late night hit-and-run accident. According to Union County deputy Jim Ray, three and perhaps four vehicles hit Valdez. Two cars stopped at the scene, but lab tests of paint chips found on the body indicated that those cars probably hit Valdez after he was already dead and lying along the highway.

There had been rumors of foul play concerning the incident, rumors partially fueled by a lack of information. Because the body was not positively identified immediately, an obituary was never printed. And, because the incident is still an open case, the Union County sheriff's department did not report it.

According to information compiled through the sheriff's department, the state's attorney's office and the Illinois Migrant Council, on the night of Valdez's death, he had been drinking at the Country Cafe in Cobden. There had been a disturbance at the bar and a Cobden policeman took Valdez to a migrant camp north of Cobden.

One of the mysteries about the incident is how Valdez got from the migrant camp north of Cobden to south of Cobden where his body was found.

Ballard said Valdez was probably standing when he was fatally injured because bones in his chest were broken. After that, his head was run over by a second car. The head was severely injured, which gave rise to reports of decapitation, Ballard said.

Valdez was apparently an illegal alien because no papers were found on him, Ballard said. Other migrants were able to identify Valdez, but it took several months to get an official identification from fingerprints.

The migrant community held a Mass for Valdez several months ago. He was buried in the Anna Cemetery.

Some people have suggested that Union County officials did not pursue their investigation of the incident as vigorously as they might have if Valdez had not been a migrant, a charge that Ballard pointedly denies.

"We didn't ignore the incident," said Ballard. "That's not our attitude down here at all."

Deputy Ray said the sheriff's department has followed up on about a dozen leads in the past four months, including two leads two weeks ago. But there still are no suspects in the case, which is still open.

138

II

The Death of Leonardo

At the end of that week, on Friday, July 11, the Chief of Police convened a meeting in Cobden. Present at the meeting were Gustavo, a bilingual South American law student who was working as an intern for the Illinois Migrant Legal Assistance Program based in Chicago; Rafael, a Puerto Rican, María, an upper-class Mexican, and Maximo, a bilingual middle-class Mexican student at Southern Illinois University, who together made up the Anti-Alcoholism Project; and me wearing my "hat" as the Illinois Migrant Council's regional Education Director.

The Police Chief began by explaining that he had called the meeting because people were saying that the Mexicans were taking over the town. "You gotta keep your boys in line," he told us.

He was referring to the *de facto* desegregation of the little village park which had been under way for a week. Where I saw people simply strolling over to the park because it was too hot and crowded in the store basement, he saw Mexicans crossing an invisible line that had never been crossed before. If what had impressed me was the way Raúl, Alfredo, and little Panchito used the alphabet to notate what they had already learned *líricamente*, what had impressed the Police Chief was the way they played basketball every night. He explained that as nephew of the largest grower in the region, he felt some responsibility for keeping things under control and making sure they didn't get out of hand.

My notes for the meeting record that the Police Chief went on to say that he himself was grateful to these hard-working Mexicans as long as they made no trouble; that during the heatwave one of the Mexicans had passed out on the street, been jailed, and, on being released, had passed out again; and that this was the *only* case in which he, the Chief of Police, had taken the steps necessary to have a Mexican deported. "What was he charged with?" asked Gustavo, the legal intern. "Improper use of the highway," explained the Chief of Police.

The meeting ended with Gustavo asking "What, precisely, is your policy towards the Mexicans in this area?" and the Chief of Police answering "Our policy is very simple: we are here to enforce the law."

~

That night, around midnight, the bartender at the Country Cafe took a baseball club and attacked three of his Mexican customers: Enrique, 17, Leonardo, a man in his 40's, and Calixto, also 17. There are two versions of what happened next. The unofficial version is that the police arrived and took Enrique and Leonardo home to their respective camps, leaving Calixto, who was relatively unscathed, to get home by himself. Enrique they left bleeding on his camp-bed, with his scalp split open and his right eye injured; Leonardo they left, no one knows how badly injured, at a different camp north of Cobden. The next day Enrique's uncle, Miguel, brought Enrique to my house in Carbondale. Enrique was in critical medical condition. (He was looked after by my house-mate, Dr. Jennifer FauntLeRoy, and was not well enough to return to work until two weeks later.) Leonardo's body, meanwhile, had been found at 4 a.m. (Saturday, July 12) lying on the main highway, US51, south of Cobden. His head had been severed from his body. The unofficial version was silent on the question of how Leonardo's body had got from his camp north of Cobden to the highway south of Cobden.

The official version was eventually published in the *Southern Illinoisan* on Thursday, November 6, 1980—almost four months later. (See above, p. 138.) Officially, Leonardo was the victim of a hit-and-run accident. The Illinois Bureau of Investigation analyzed flecks of paint found on the body and concluded that three "or maybe four" cars had run over Leonardo—hence the decapitation. Scientific evidence showed that Leonardo was already dead when at least two of the cars hit him. When the first car hit him, he was officially still alive: he "was probably standing when he was fatally injured because bones in his chest were broken." The unofficial Mexican version suggests that Leonardo may have been already dead before the first car hit him; the official version does not allow for this possibility.

As far as I could tell, the law was not enforced. The bartender at the Country Cafe was never charged with any crime, not even selling liquor to minors. (He eventually offered Enrique some money to make up for the two weeks' earnings Enrique had missed.) None of the Mexican witnesses were interviewed. Nor were the drivers of the three or four cars in the "hit-and-run" business ever publicly identified.

Since no documents of any sort had been found in Leonardo's empty pockets, he was "apparently an illegal alien," and no identification of the deceased was officially possible—until the Mexican army finally identified his fingerprints, months later.

Leonardo was, as far as I know, the only Tarascan in the area who was not from Cherán: he was said to be from Azajo. This was his first summer in Cobden. Unlike the Tarascans from Cherán (such as Calixto and Enrique), Leonardo seems to have had no friends or family in the United States.

Following Leonardo's death, Cobden was quiet for three weeks. Mexicans aimed for invisibility. The basketball court stood empty. Anglos stopped coming to Su Casa Grocery Store. Meanwhile Leonardo's body was not buried.

On Wednesday, July 30, a small group gathered again in the basement of Su Casa Grocery Store. This was (as far as I know) the first such "public" meeting since the death of Leonardo Valdez. I wasn't there, but I heard about it from Evaristo. As a "legal" Mexican-American (from Texas), Evaristo had been hired by the Illinois Migrant Council, on Department of Labor money, to manage the Su Casa Grocery Store. He often knew the latest word-of-mouth news. He told me people were planning to meet again a week later, on August 6. I decided to join them.

III

DOLÓ DASNT PROTECT AS

Breaking the Ground: Burying Leonardo

On Wednesday, August 6, 1980, when I arrived at Su Casa Grocery Store at around 6:30 p.m., there was no one there.

Some minutes later, Evaristo drove up, with María. María and I had not seen each other since the July 11 meeting with the Chief of Police. Evaristo and María explained that "everyone" was going to Anna.

Going to Anna was very unusual. People said the last black man in Anna had been lynched in 1948.

María, who had aristocratic Catholic connections, had persuaded the Catholic priest in Anna to say *a misa para el difunto*—a Mass for the deceased Leonardo. There was a Catholic church right in Cobden, but for some reason a mass in Cobden was out of the question. After the mass in Anna, Leonardo was, at long last, going to be buried. In the lily-white Anna cemetery.

María invited me to come too. I decided to stay and pass the word on to anyone who hadn't yet heard. A few minutes later, the Román family drove by, Calixto at the wheel. They hadn't heard about the funeral. They decided to go. Then Rob Tate showed up. He had been coming over from Carterville ever since the very first "language exchange" meetings and he was the only anglo who, after Leonardo's death, continued to come. He expressed no interest in attending a Catholic mass, and the two of us sat around waiting to see if anyone else would show.

The funeral in Anna was attended by 60 Mexicans, certainly the largest public gathering of illegal aliens ever seen in the region. María was firmly in control and delivered a homily in Spanish on the perils of drink. Leonardo was buried in an unmarked grave.

After the funeral, about a dozen men drove back from Anna to the grocery store in Cobden, mainly men who had come to many previous meetings, old-timers like the Jalisco clan, Alfonso, Cipriano and Constantino, but also a couple of men who had never come before, Juan known as El Peligroso, and Esequiel. No Tarascans. Neither Renée nor her friend Stephanie showed up. Nor did Martha. Perhaps they didn't know the meeting was taking place. By 8 p.m., no *gringuitas* had come. It looked as if maybe everyone might just call it a day and go home.

Breaking the Taboo: Covering the Topic

Then a car pulled up and two women stepped out. Two new *gringuitas* who had never come before. Bridget and Danon, freelance reporters working for the *Illinois Times* on an article about migrant workers in Illinois. Their arrival cast me in the role of interpreter, at least initially. I introduced them formally to each of the men in turn. Danon asked me if it would be all right to take photos. I translated her question into Spanish and translated the positive response back into English.

Whenever local anglos talked face-to-face with local *mojados* for the first time, there was an inevitable sense, on the side of the anglos, of a taboo being broken. If I was present at such initial encounters, my mediation as an interpreter lent a modicum of legitimacy to the ritual drama of breaking the taboo. By and large the *mojados* themselves welcomed the witness of any local anglos who crossed the no-man's-land between "legal" and "illegal," documented and undocumented, discourse and silence. On this night, having buried Leonardo, they especially welcomed the witness of these two female reporters from Springfield, the state capital.

Previously, before July 12, anglos who arrived at the grocery store around 8 p.m. walked in on a lively scene and could join in conversations that were already going on. Bridget and Danon did not know, of course, that people tonight were much more somber than usual. About Leonardo's burial in Anna they knew nothing. They seemed surprised that the *mojados* trusted them immediately. Everyone looked at each other in thoughtful silence and then Constantino suggested that we go down into the basement after all.

Three months later (on November 7, 1980), Bridget's incisive article and Danon's photos appeared in the *Illinois Times*. The informal encounter between these two freelance reporters and a group of *mojados* illuminates the paradoxical process of documenting the undocumentable. Many middle-class citizens in southern Illinois, especially intellectuals affiliated with Southern Illinois University, Carbondale, assumed they were doing the *mojados* a favor by letting silence cover the topic of their existence, their presence in the area, the economic importance of their work. All the same, there has long been a national public discourse on the topic of "illegal aliens." From time to time the local media "covered" this topic. In the summer and fall of 1979, the local radio station, WSIU, and the local daily, the *Southern Ilinoisan*, had reported, in detail, on the epidemic of Giardia Lamblia, a tropical disease that spread through the migrant camps and was at first blamed on the unsanitary toilet practices of the Mexicans but was ultimately traced to the contaminated water in nearby Alto Pass. In the fall of 1980, the *St. Louis Globe Democrat* carried an excellent article by Jim Orso under the headline "One grower says they're the best in the business." (The grower is quoted as saying "It would take 60 people to do what these [three dozen] boys are doing.") And in October 1980, *North Pass News*, a type-written six-page newspaper published and distributed in Makanda, the hometown of then congressman Paul Simon, devoted an issue to "The Tarascan People: Their Present and Future."

No-Man's Land

The newspaper articles also exemplify the difficulty of categorizing the meetings that took place in the basement of the grocery store. Jim Orso called them "dialogue sessions." Bridget and Danon seem to have imagined that what they witnessed on August 6 was a legitimate "class," authorized by the Illinois Migrant Council.

It was not a class in the ordinary sense of the word, and it was not sponsored by the Illinois Migrant Council or any other legitimate institution. These meetings were not constrained to play by the rules of the game which govern legitimate classroom activities, and the implications of this fact are worth spelling out in detail for the light they throw on what actually happened in the basement on August 6.

In that basement, that night as on other nights, there was no time-table, no agenda, no curriculum, no textbook. Gatherings began and ended at no fixed time, and were never the same twice. There was no gate-keeping mechanism. No one was paid to perform the role of teacher. No one claimed the gate-keeper's authority to admit some people and deny entry to others. No one kept public records of who was present and who was absent. No one knew in advance what direction any given gathering might take. No one played the role of student in return for thirty dollars a week. In short, no one was officially in control. I certainly wasn't. Which is surely why the meetings were perceived by the Police Chief as a threat to the status quo and why he instructed me to keep "my" boys in line. If it had been a "normal" class, under the auspices of the Illinois Migrant Council, it would have posed no such threat.

For the past ten years, the Illinois Migrant Council had been conducting Adult Basic Education classes (including English as a Second Language, GED, and Pre-Vocational Education) throughout the state of Illinois. None of these classes were perceived as posing a threat to existing power structures. Their stated goal was to help seasonal and migrant farmworkers settle out into the mainstream of the U.S. economy. The classes were funded (at more than $2,000,000 per year) by the U.S. Department of Labor. "Illegal aliens" were therefore *not* eligible to attend. These legitimate classes followed the rhythms of "government time" and reproduced the normal Discourse of public education. The federal funds were used to rent classrooms, buy texts and educational materials, pay a salary to the teachers, and above all to pay a CETA stipend to the students. Teachers were paid to teach. Students were paid to learn—or, at least, to attend. Teachers were responsible for handing out the weekly CETA checks to the students. The size of the check depended on the student's documented attendance. Roles were clear. Gate-keeping was firm. Record-keeping was adequate and, in principle, public.

If 1980 had been like previous years, the Illinois Migrant Council would, as usual, have run one such class in Cobden from mid-June to mid-September, with a total budget of about $10,000. This covered the costs of a small part-time ABE class for ten adults, meeting from 6 p.m. to 9 p.m., Monday through Wednesday, for fifteen weeks. In previous years, these summer classes had served as a gate through which the ten eligible migrants (and their local wives) could get on the escalator leading from English as a Second Language to Adult Basic Education to a GED to Vocational Education to legitimate job placement. Migrant workers who were not "illegal" and were still showing up in class at the height of the picking season in mid-September were regarded as having *terminated positively* and were recruited to participate in the Illinois Migrant Council's full-time winter classes as a first step in the process of settling out of the migrant stream and joining the mainstream labor force of the United States.

But in 1980 normal conditions were not met. By May 1980, the Illinois Migrant Council's central office in Chicago found it was "over budget" and therefore no one would be receiving CETA stipends ($27.90 per 9 hr week) to attend the summer class in Cobden. Hitherto the stipend had been perceived by Illinois Migrant Council personnel as an incentive, without which it would be difficult to persuade pickers to put in three evenings a week after picking apples and peaches all day long. Would anyone attend classes on a regular basis for free?

The central office, however, wanted formal documentation to be submitted as if conditions were normal. In particular, they wanted to report to the Department of Labor, for the sake of appearance, ten names of legal and eligible migrant workers in the region—as if the ten were receiving stipends. Simply put, they wanted to document a fiction as if it were fact.

As Education Coordinator for the local (Delta) region of the Illinois Migrant Council, it was my responsibility to compile the necessary formal documentation. My strategy for dealing with this situation was two-fold. On the one hand, I maintained, through thick and thin, that I was under no obligation to report to the Federal Government, or any other authority, the names of people, anglos or Mexicans, "legal" or "illegal," who chose, for whatever private reason, to assemble freely in Cobden, at the grocery store or in the park. I therefore refused to produce the formal but fictitious documentation requested by the central office. On the other hand, I maintained it was in everyone's best interest to be up front about what was really happening in Cobden, and as the summer progressed, I circulated, within and without the Illinois Migrant Council, various informal working papers, reporting on what I saw as a collective effort by locals and migrants to lower the language barrier that was preventing communication on shared concerns.

It seemed to me immoral to pretend that ten migrant workers were sitting in a classroom doing classroom exercises when in fact well over two hundred people,[3] all told, including many local anglos who would never have come to a regular ESL class, were engaged in a freewheeling, unstructured give-and-take in the informal gatherings in Cobden.

Much more went on at the meetings than merely "teaching a little Spanish, learning a little English." Of those who came regularly, Alfonso and Cipriano were two who enjoyed playing the role of student for free, at least when Renée did not show up. Renée was a white migrant worker in her early teens.[4] She and her mother had, in May and June, frequently joined the meetings. Her mother had stopped coming after a while, but Renée had formed a close friendship with Alfonso and Cipriano, and the three of them would go off into a corner, or walk outside, and have long conversations in Spanish and English, which they were picking up from each other *líricamente* (i.e., without writing anything down). Renée had picked up quite a lot of Spanish in the field, while picking the apples and peaches. Alfonso and Cipriano were not Tarascans. They were cousins, part of the Gomez clan from Los Altos de Jalisco. Alfonso was the only Mexican in the area who had stayed in school past sixth grade. (Many had not made it past second or third grade.) Alfonso was the most literate member of the group: he had recently graduated from high school in Mexico.

On the nights when Renée did not show up, Alfonso and Cipriano, and a varying group of other young men, had enjoyed playing the role of student for free, with Martha, who enjoyed playing the role of teacher for free. It was Martha who under normal circumstances would have been the teacher of the part-time summer class, receiving a modest salary. This year, however, she came, from time to time, of her own free will, as a private individual like anyone else (including me). Whenever Martha arrived, she would soon be surrounded by a group of young men doing traditional classroom exercises out of a book under her guidance, while other people engaged in other activities.

On August 6, neither Renée nor Martha had come. As I followed Bridget, Danon, Constantino, and the others into the dark basement with the dirt floor and the bare light bulb, neither I nor, as far as I could tell, anyone else was in control. I felt, as often before, that we were entering a learning environment situated in no-man's land. Anything could happen. I was prepared to go with the flow.

Un silencio muy largo

Everyone sat down. Some on milk crates, others on the row of seats that had once belonged to a movie theater. Above our heads, as usual, the loud hum of the refrigerator in the grocery store. Otherwise, silence. No one spoke. I felt that I should be translating the mojado silence into English for the anglos, and maybe the anglo silence into Spanish for the mojados. But I preferred the silence and had no desire to break it.

The silence with which this meeting began, or now began again, may carry within it the true answer to my questions: why did these men, gathered together on this night, decide to produce their own diccionarios?

One of the hardest things to interpret about cultures is, surely, their silences. And yet, of all that we observe, silences often seem the most pregnant, charged with meaning, crying out to be interpreted.

Meditating and reflecting on language, one tends to forget, over and over again, that silence is the background, the vanishing point of the landscape in which language (as Halliday[5] would say) *does its job*. Or, as Quakers say, silence is *where words come from*. Silence is not a given, it calls for interpretation. Silence, too, is socially constructed.

And on that night, in that basement, we shared a silence which we ourselves "socially constructed," a bilingual, hybrid silence situated simultaneously in two languages at the same time—and in the no-man's land between the two languages, the unmarked grave.

A legal and an illegal silence.

A male and a female silence.

We sat waiting to see what words would come from that untranslatable, unspeakable void what job that situation called what language to do.[6]

Breaking the Silence

None of the previous gatherings had begun with a long, spontaneous silence. But then none had begun with a funeral either. Martha would probably have felt comfortable playing the teacherly role and initiating some activity to break the silence. But Martha was not there, and no one took her place.

The silence went on and on. It lasted ten, fifteen, maybe twenty minutes. Whose voice would finally break it?

It was an anglo voice that, at last, broke the silence—Rob Tate's. "What are we going to do?" It was not immediately clear whom he was addressing: who was included, who excluded, in his *we*.

An innocuous question, asked often enough on other nights, in other situations, in Spanish as often as in English. But on this night, on this occasion, the question rang out in the silence with new force. To my ears it resonated with Lenin's "What is to be done?"

What Is to Be Done?

Silence followed Rob Tate's question. Silence followed, at first, each subsequent utterance. One at a time, people broke their personal, individual silence, and said something—in Spanish. Gradually various themes emerged, various topics, a line of argument. It was not, at first, clear whether this was in response to Rob's question, suggesting possible things to do.

One of the first topics: tenemos que dominar el inglés, *we have to master English*. On previous nights it had been "let's learn *each other's* language." Tonight Juan said that, in his opinion, helping gringos speak Spanish was futile, and others agreed with him. "We've got to concentrate on mastering *their* way of speaking."

Constantino said, "Tenemos que razonar."

I translated this for Danon and Bridget as "we've got to strategize." *Razonar* is a normal Spanish word, cognate, of course, with *reason*. Constantino tended to use this word to name the activity of sitting or standing around in a group, thinking things out collectively, proposing a course of action, arguing the pros and cons, and coming to some shared conclusion.

Esequiel introduced another topic: yo sí conozco palabras sueltas, lo que no me lo sé es pegarlas. [I do know isolated words, what I can't do is stick 'em together.] Others agreed that this was their main problem with English. (To help me translate this idiom for Bridget, Danon and Rob, Juan explained that when you ask a girl to dance in Mexico, she can choose whether to dance suelta or pegada: unattached or clasped in your arms.)

The main difficulty with learning English, said Constantino, was *la escritura de inglés*. (I still didn't grasp that by *escritura*, Constantino meant, not only what English teachers means by *spelling* but also what the French mean by *écriture*—writing "in the larger sense.") Constantino wanted his compañeros to understand that the escritura of English was quite unlike what they imagined, quite different from the escritura of Spanish,[7] quite unlike what they thought of as escritura, period. Constantino said the challenge was to *alfabetizar los sonidos*. No one seemed to understand what he was talking about.

He appealed to me to help him make his point. Implicitly he invoked the series of conversations he and I had had at previous meetings. He would take me aside and ask me to please just tell him *el abecedario de inglés*. Thinking he was referring to the alphabet, I would always reply that the abecedario of English and the abecedario of Spanish were one and the same, *igualitos*. The only difference was little details like the *ñ* and the *ll*. After the meetings in the park, however, Constantino had argued with me. The abecedarios of English and Spanish, he had claimed, are not at all the same: the alfabetos are, but the abecedarios are not.

By *alfabeto*, Constantino meant a set of letters, by *abecedario* a set of sounds. The letters of the alphabet are the same for English and Spanish, but the relation between letters and sounds, between script and speech are very different. I had finally got it, and I had told him that I'd been to university, but I could not stand there and alfabetizar los sonidos de inglés: I could not recite the abecedario of English, the phonemes in lexical order. Nor did I know anyone who could.

Breaking the Ice: JUELLULIB

Thinking about the problem of making words stick, and the way the escritura of English misrepresents the blank spaces between words, and trying to explain to Bridget and Danon what the heated conversation in Spanish was all about, I walked to the easel and wrote down, with no comment, the first English words that Panchito had written, in the park, two days after he arrived from Cherán:

JUELLULIB

Cipriano asked me to say it. I didn't want to. I told him: you can read, *you* say it. They laughed. Danon asked, "Why're they laughing? What's it say?" Cipriano asked me to ask Danon to say it. She looked at it and said, "I can't read this." I translated her response into Spanish. They asked, "why can't she read this?" I said, "Tal vez es analfabeta"—maybe she's illiterate. More laughter, at the notion that a newspaper reporter is analfabeta and can't read as simple a phrase as JUELLULIB.

Tomás (in English): They want to know why you can't read this—are you illiterate?

Now the gringuitas laughed. The joke was shared.

Danon: I don't know Spanish—that's why I can't read it!

When I translated this, there was more laughter at the notion that JUELLULIB is Spanish.

As people wrestled more and more seriously with the paradox that was actually no joke, the conversation became even more lively. Juan and others called JUELLULIB a rompecabezas—a mind-bender, a brain-teaser. Someone else called it a trabalenguas, a tongue-twister. Neither Cipriano nor Danon are analfabetas yet neither can read this word, Cipriano because it's English, and he doesn't speak English, Danon because it's Spanish and she doesn't speak Spanish.

What is this word? ¿Es inglés? ¿Es español? Both? Neither?

More and more laughter was shared as people conversed in twos and threes, trying to solve this puzzle, this riddle. I heard Constantino's terms—escritura, abecedario, alfabeto, ortografía—being taken up and explored by one group after another. Finally, after much teasing, Cipriano got his nerve up and risked reading the word aloud (sightreading the score.) He pronounced the LL (correctly) as [dʒ] but did not pronounce the final B. Alfonso understood what Cipriano was saying, and smiled. Alfonso turned to Bridget and repeated what Cipriano had just said (i.e. without looking at the easel), addressing it as a bona fide question to Bridget: he really wanted to know where she lived. She in turn had no trouble understanding his question and replied, "In Carbondale. Where do *you* live?"

It was the first face-to-face gringo–mojado exchange of the evening, unmediated by an interpreter. It broke the ice.

Inverting the Hierarchy: DONDEVIVIS

Bridget, Danon, and Rob now wanted to know how to say *where d'you live* in Spanish. People got up from their seats, and rapidly, as on many previous evenings, groups formed with one gringo per group. Cipriano and Alfonso helped Bridget practice *¿dónde vives?* Esequiel, Froilán, and Pascual, helped Danon; Constantino and Juan helped Rob (who really had learned this phrase in the past already—more than once).

When Constantino heard Bridget asking Cipriano to write it down, he intervened and suggested that Bridget learn the phrase *líricamente* (like Panchito in the park and like Alfredo and his song) and then write it down in her own *escritura.*

Bridget and Danon conferred, jotted down some attempts on paper and then Bridget wrote on the easel:

DONDEVIVIS[8]

First some men expressed polite surprise that two reporters could make such simple spelling errors. Others then said that although it was not correcto it was bueno. All the men (except Alfonso) had had less than six years of schooling in Mexico. But this was sufficient for them all to feel sure that there should be a space between E and V (DONDE + VIVES) *porque no es una sola palabra, sino dos*—because it's not just one word, it's two. And that the last vowel *se escribe con la e*—is written as E not I. Juan concluded that Bridget and Danon's problem with Spanish was the same as his problem with English: como se pegan las palabras, how words stick to one another.

Alfonso, who had so far said much less than usual and had been watching the proceedings pensively, now explained that there are five vocales (vowels) in Spanish but that there are many more in English and they're not the same as the Spanish vocales, and that this was probably why Bridget and Danon failed to distinguish between the first and second sílabas (syllables) of *vives*. Constantino said no, it's the other way around, VIVIS had two few vocales, not too many. The problem, he argued, was that the escrituras of English and Spanish are dos sistemas distintos, two different systems. He asked Bridget and Danon how many vowels there are in English. Bridget and Danon said they didn't know. Rob said he didn't either. Constantino looked at me and I felt that I could read in his eyes that he finally believed me that gringos, even newspaper reporters, could not recite the abecedario of English.

Constantino was Alfonso's *tío político* (roughly, uncle-in-law as distinct from *tío carnal*, uncle by blood). Alfonso had finished high school but he maintained a modest demeanor of *respeto* in Constantino's presence. The two of them now had a quiet conversation together and then Alfonso asked Bridget, in English, "how many words?" pointing to JUELLULIB.

Bridget wrote down WHERE DO YOU LIVE under JUELLULIB.

JUELLULIB
WHERE DO YOU LIVE?

"Cuatro palabras," said Alfonso to Constantino. Everyone stared in silence at the surprising contrast between two escrituras, two ways of writing the same thing, one bueno but not correcto, the other correcto but not bueno.

The Dictionary is Useless

At this point, Juan pulled out a paperback Spanish–English dictionary. Half a dozen people started talking at once, telling Juan he was wasting his time. They were part of a group that, back in June, had looked pretty systematically at five different paperback dictionaries, brought in by various people, including anglos. They had finally concluded that el diccionario no sirve, the dictionary doesn't work.

Every time Juan tried to speak someone interrupted him. There are too many words in the dictionary. If you do find a Spanish word, you still don't know how to say it, you only know how to write it. Speaking English is one thing, writing it is something else. And if you know how to say a word in English, *líricamente*, you still can't find it in the dictionary. Alfonso pointed to JUELLULIB and said "Así se oye." It sounds like this. He pointed to WHERE DO YOU LIVE? and said "Y así se escribe en el diccionario." And in the dictionary it's written like this.

While all this was going on, Rob was showing Bridget and Danon Juan's dictionary. It had no pronunciation guide at all. Rob explained that few dictionaries had pronunication guides and these were all written in a special code, not the same for each dictionary. He told Bridget and Danon how everyone had decided it was useless to try and learn a special alphabet, with weird symbols, that was used nowhere except in this or that dictionary and which he, Rob, certainly couldn't read.

Constantino Calls for a Show of Hands

By now Constantino was standing up and addressing the whole group. Like many of the men, he had a mode of speech (a register, a tone of voice) which he used to reason in public (razonar.) His oratory was sometimes pretty fancy, but always directed and focused. The gist of his discourse was as follows:

> We need to find our own way out of this situation. Nos hace muy trabajoso aprender las dos cosas de un solo viaje, la nueva pronunciación y la nueva escritura: it's a lot of work for us to learn the two things at the same time, the new pronunciation and the new spelling system. There are 26 letters in the alphabet, but English has more than 26 sounds. So a letter is worth (vale) more than one sound. And that's why you don't know how to say it.
>
> Forget the dictionary. And forget la escritura. What we need to study is the abecedario of English. We need to figure it out for ourselves, our way. Otherwise they'll never understand us, even when we speak English. If you, Juan, want to stick words together you need to know the abecedario, not the escritura, of English. For us, this (pointing to JUELLULIB) is better than that (pointing to WHERE DO YOU LIVE?) Son dos sistemas distintos, they two different systems. We cannot study both at the same time. O la una o la otra, it's one or the other. We have to decide which of the two comes first for us.

Constantino ended his speech by proposing that everyone work together to study primero la pronunciación, luego la escritura, first the pronunciation, then the [correct] spelling-system. And he called for a vote. Those who want to start with the escritura, raise your hand. Only one hand went up—Alfonso's. Those who want to start with la pronunciación. Everyone's hand went up, including Alfonso's. People laughed. Alfonso explained that he had spent years studying English in high school in Mexico and already knew mucha escritura—a lot of spelling—but that none of his teachers had ever pronounced English the way gringos spoke in Cobden, and he, Alfonso, wanted to study both ortografías at the same time. People replied fine, be that way, we'll stick to la ortografía mexicana, the Mexican way of writing.

EVRI BARI GUANTS TULEM

I stepped out of the room for a cigarette and a breath of fresh air. When I came back someone was saying "La cosecha empieza con la primera uva." The harvest starts with the first grape.

They chose *todo el mundo quiere estudiar* (everybody wants to study) as their "first grape," their first attempt to write English como de veras se oye, the way it really sounds. The bet was that *todo el mundo quiere estudiar* could be written in English using la ortografía mexicana, one letter one sound. A couple of people already knew how to say *todo el mundo* in English. Everybody said it well, intelligibly, with only a slight accent. Rob, Danon, and Bridget understood, and practiced saying *todo el mundo*, but couldn't get the vowels right, and couldn't get the first *d* right. They had a thick gringo accent. Everyone smiled. They wanted me to pronounce *everybody* correctly. I alluded to the recurrent motif at these meetings: that my pronunciation of English tended to sound *británico*. "¿Quieren hablar como la reina de inglaterra?" I asked them— do you want to speak like the Queen of England? Laughter. They got the joke.

"Cada región tiene su propia musiquita, su propio ritmo," said Juan—every region has its own intonation, its own rhythm. "Su propio tiple," added Constantino—its own twang.

Rob, Bridget, and Danon agreed to serve as models for the local pronunciation. Everyone (including me) echoed them to get the tiple right: the Southern drawl, the rhythm, the intonation, and the allophones.

People worked on writing down the sounds that they themselves were saying. Everyone except Juan (who was there for the first time) had his little notebook and pen in their back pocket.

Froilán went to the easel and wrote EVRI. Underneath it, Cipriano wrote EBRI. Above these two words Alfonso wrote EVERY

EVERY

EVRI

EBRI

As discussion proceeded, Alfonso stood in front of the group like a teacher and noted the main points on the easel. He circled the two V's and the B, because in Mexico these are two ways of writing the same sound. He put a line through the second E in EVERY, because "así se escribe pero no se oye"— that's how it's written, but it's not heard (i.e., it's "silent"). And he circled the Y and the I's because, according to him, in English spelling, Y can be a vowel, the same as I.

The consensus was that EVRI was the best of the three. There was no discussion about *body*, because it turned out everyone had written it the same way: BARI.

The second half of the sentence, *quiere estudiar*, caused a lot of trouble and laughter. The translation was easy, *wants to study*,[9] but the pronunciation was a tongue twister. *Se traba la lengua.* The cluster of consonants around the neutral vowel (*wants to study*) stumped everyone. And no one could stop themselves from saying "estudi" (inserting an [e] before the initial *st* and saying [u] instead of [ʌ].) (The pronunciation of a cognate is often trickier than that of a non-cognate.)

Someone called out "¡Todos quieren aprender, pero muchos no quieren estudiar!"—everyone wants to learn but no one wants to study.

The target sentence was changed to *todo el mundo quiere aprender* (i.e., from *everybody wants to study* to *everybody wants to learn*.)

But *wants to learn* caused further headaches. They didn't like the way I said *to learn*. They wanted to hear Rob say it, over and over, because he had the local *tiple*, the local dialect. They worked hard on mimicking his vowels, his "dark" /l/, his very liquid, semi-vowel /r/ and his final /n/.

People worked in small groups, or alone. Some wandered around looking at what others were writing. When everyone was done, it turned out that *wants* and *to learn* had each been transcribed in three different ways. In *wants* the only question was what to do about the initial /w/.

GUANTS
HUANTS
UANTS

Each version had its advocates. They wanted me to referee, to say which was the best. Not the most correct, but the closest to the way it really sounds. I declined. But I wrote WANTS underneath the three versions on the easel. Rob Tate suggested a vote. Almost everyone voted for GUANTS.

The three transcriptions of *to learn* surprised Rob, Bridget, Danon, and me:

TULONT
TULEM
TULURN

I expected everyone to choose the third version, TULURN, but in fact they all said the second one was the shortest, and therefore the best, even though (as far as I could hear) no one was pronouncing the word with a final /m/.

So everyone had learned, everyone was very happy and very tired. By now it was about 10:30 p.m. Everyone was writing down the complete sentence in their little notebooks,

EVRI BARI GUANTS TULEM

TODO EL MUNDO QUIERE APRENDER.

Murder

There came a lull.

It was time to call it a day.

Danon looked at her watch.

No one moved.

Quiet conversations ended. Silence. An echo of the silence with which the evening had begun.

Suddenly, Juan spoke one word, loudly and clearly, in English: "murder."

"¿Y qué?" said Esequiel.

"The law," said Juan, again in English.

"La ley," said Froilán.

"Siempre nos busca la ley,"[10] sang Esequiel.

And Antonio, who had not spoken up all night, said "La ley no nos ampara."

The law does not protect us. This sentence promptly became the second grape of the harvest. They followed the same process as for the first sentence. The variant transcriptions for each part of the sentence were as follows:

(the law	doesn't	protect	us)
DOLOR	DATSUN	PORTEX	AS
DOLOD	DASUNT	PORTEEX	
DOLOC	DATSNT	PROTKT	
DOLÓ	DANTS	PROTEKT	
TOLOON	DASN'T	PROTECT	
	DSNT		

155

And the final vote was for

DOLÓ   DASN'T   PROTECT   AS

And we called it a day.

One grower says they're the best in the business

SEP 6 - 1980

By JIM ORSO
Globe-Democrat Staff Writer

COBDEN, Ill. — Three dozen Mexicans moved silently but at a blistering pace — among the peach trees that dotted a gentle hillside near Cobden, about 100 miles southeast of St. Louis.

Grower Ed Flamm looked on in fascination.

"It started as a gradual thing, the Mexicans doing the work. And then it went completely that way, because these boys are just natural at this. It would take 60 people to do what 30 of these boys are doing," Flamm said.

"All you have to do is keep them in water."

Down among the rows of trees, deep-brown Mexican men stooped and reached to fill their half-bushel canvas bags with fruit, then rushed to a nearby wagon to dump the load.

As their bags emptied, the men reached quickly for a white chip issued by a worker and representing 30 cents.

Words were rarely exchanged. The language barrier here between Spanish-speaking workers and their English-speaking bosses seems to add to the quickened pace. No one can ask questions.

"I know 'mucho verde' (too green) and 'rojo' (red). That's all I need," Flamm said.

The need for bilingualism is only one of many sides of the phenomenon as Southern Illinois' multimillion dollar fruit industry grows increasingly dependent on Spanish-speaking migrant workers.

There is also the issue of the state's huge employment rates in this territory where thousands of migrant workers come each

summer.

And cultural differences between migrants and residents in small towns near the orchards sometimes produce clashes.

Finally, there is the matter of illegal aliens among Illinois' 32,000 migrant workers. No one knows for sure how many of the the Mexican laborers are not registered to work here legally, but many assume the number is very high.

"The wages the guy accepts are prima facie evidence that he is in the U.S. illegally," said Jack Parks, an agent with the U.S. Immigration and Naturalization Service at St. Louis.

"No one else would work for the wages set by some of the growers," he said.

FOR MANY GROWERS, illegal aliens answer the need for a stable yet temporary work force to meet the needs of high demands of fruit picking in the heat of summer.

"Why should I ask the workers about their legal status?" Flamm said, adding that it makes no difference to him if his workers are registered.

For Cobden Police Chief Art Pender, illegal aliens are a minor nuisance, only because some of them are unlicensed drivers.

"The one area that they're really deficient in is driver licenses. They just plain don't have 'em," Pender said of the Mexicans sometimes cited for traffic violations as they travel to and from Cobden from nearby camps.

U.S. Rep. Paul Simon, D-Illinois, said illegal aliens in the farm labor force are both a "liability and an asset" to the economy of the region.

Simon said he would favor legislation creating "temporary work cards" for non-U.S. citizens who cross the border in search of work.

Simon said high unemployment rates in Southern Illinois are not eased by farm jobs partly because "our present employment policies do not encourage good work habits,

156

and the migrant workers are willing to put in long hours and do some of the work that others might not do."

Those who work closely with the migrants say there are more "local" laborers than normal this year because of lack of work elsewhere. But there also are more migrant workers in Illinois — because of crop failures elsewhere, according to Illinois Job Service officer Virginia Ortega Avery.

Mrs. Avery's employment office in the Union-Jackson Farm Labor Camp near Cobden functions somewhat like a trade union hall. Area growers come to the office looking for prospective workers who have registered with Mrs. Avery in search of employment.

Most migrant workers live in camps on the growers' property that must be licensed by the Illinois Department of Public Health. But the Union-Jackson camp was opened about 10 years ago to provide housing for laborers whose employers were attempting to cut out the high cost of state-approved housing.

THE CAMP HOUSES ABOUT 180 persons and includes a day care center and health clinic funded by federal grants.

Mrs. Avery said about 80 percent of the nearly 1,000 workers in Union and Jackson Counties speak Spanish as their native language — as their only language, usually.

At the Su Casa grocery store in Cobden, an education coordinator for the Illinois Migrant Council has been bringing the Mexicans and local residents together in recent months for dialogue that he hopes will lead to much more than verbal understanding between the groups.

"It's time to face the fact that the Mexicans are here to stay," Tomas Kalmar said over coffee in Flamm's Cafe at Cobden.

Kalmar started the language exchange program in part to bring Mexicans and Cobden residents together on a common footing.

He hopes the program will bring a better understanding of the Mexican migrant workers. But Cobden isn't expected to transform into a bilingual haven over night.

Pender said he and other police officers have enrolled in fall courses in the Spanish language at the local college. They bypassed the weekly Su Casa dialogue, Pender said, because "it's for the Mexicans."

At a recent dialogue session in Cobden, about a dozen Mexicans and about three "Anglos" came to Kalmar's class.

One of them, Eduardo, told a reporter that "trust" is the byword for Mexicans on the road year-round in an alien country.

"I am always working some place, then I go to the next place," he said, saying his next stop will be the orange groves of Florida.

"The travelers have a knack for establishing trust quickly, because you need to make good friends," he said through an interpreter. "The people who grow up together, in one place, do not make friends so fast."

Eduardo, 35, said "the money I earn here and there" is sent to his family in Mexico City, to benefit his parents, two brothers and three sisters he last saw in 1973 when he left Mexico for the life of the migrant worker.

It is simple economics, said Eduardo. "The pay is better here for the same work." But the life is hard, he said, and many Mexicans return home soon.

"Some Mexicans can do this, some can't stand it any more an go back, others stay and forget their families."

Eduardo said he returns each year to work for Flamm, who he said "is good for me."

And Flamm says the Mexicans are good for him. His peach pickers can make up to $60 a day, he said, when the conditions are right for picking 100 bushels in a day.

"You just can't get pickers around here that will work like this" he said, as the silent men marched relentlessly to the wagon that began to fill with tree-ripened peaches.

"You ought to see 'em when I really get 'em going."

Notes

1. For these, and for corridos in general, see the classic work by Mendoza 1984.

2. Versions of this song are popular on both sides of the U.S.–Mexican border, and are sung—not often in public—as a sort of unofficial "national anthem" by Mexican migrant workers in the United States.

3. Counting those who only came once or twice.

4. Renée and her friend Stephanie were socializing with Alfonso and Cipriano at the Village Park on Monday, July 7.

5. Halliday, M.A.K., 1975. *Learning How to Mean: Explorations in the Development of Language*. London: Edward Arnold.

    ———1978. *Language as Social Semiotic: The Social Interpretation of Language and Meaning*. London: Edward Arnold.

    ———1989. *Spoken and Written Language*. Oxford: Oxford University Press.

6. Tyler, S., 1987. *The Unspeakable: Discourse, Dialogue and Rhetoric in the Postmodern World*. Madison: University of Wisconsin Press.

7. Or the escritura of Tarascan.

8. That is, they wrote it as one word, not two, and although the **E** in DOND **E** and the **E** in VIV**ES** represent allophones of one Spanish phoneme, Bridget and Danon represented the first and second vowels in VIVIS as allophones of the phoneme represented by **I**.

9. Too easy. *Estudiar* means more than study.

10. The second line of the song *Los mojados*, see above, where I translate it as *the law is always after us*.

All Souls' Night

MICHAEL PATRICK macDONALD

"All Souls's Night" is an excerpt from the first chapter of Michael Patrick MacDonald's memoir, All Souls: A Family Story from Southie. *Here, he writes about growing up in the context of a public housing project in South Boston, a white Irish American working class community, in the 1970s and 1980s, a time when the city of Boston was deeply and violently divided on desegregation. Contending with competing representations of this community, MacDonald introduces readers to the tension he feels as both an insider and an outsider in a neighborhood that continues to shape his identity even though he is no longer a resident.*

I was back in Southie, "The best place in the world," as Ma used to say before the kids died. That's what we call them now, "the kids." Even when we want to say their names, we sometimes get confused about who's dead and who's alive in my family. After so many deaths, Ma just started to call my four brothers "the kids" when we talked about going to see them at the cemetery. But I don't go anymore. They're not at the cemetery; I never could find them there. When I accepted the fact that I couldn't feel them at the graves, I figured it must be because they were in heaven, or the spirit world, or whatever you want to call it. The only things I kept from the funerals were the mass cards that said, "Do not stand at my grave and weep, I am not there, I do not sleep. I am the stars that shine through the night," and so on. I figured that was the best way to look at it. There are seven of us kids still alive, and sometimes I'm not even sure if that's true.

I came back to Southie in the summer of 1994, after everyone in my family had either died or moved to the mountains of Colorado. I'd moved to downtown Boston after Ma left in 1990, and was pulled one night to wander through Southie. I walked from Columbia Point Project, where I was born, to the Old Colony Project where I grew up, in the "Lower End," as we called it. On that August night, after four years of staying away, I walked the streets of my old neighborhood, and finally found the kids. In my memory of that night I can see them clear as day. *They're right here*, I thought, and it was an ecstatic feeling. I cried, and felt alive again myself. I passed by the outskirts of Old Colony, and it all came back to me—the kids were joined in my mind by so many others I'd last seen in caskets at Jackie O'Brien's Funeral Parlor. They were all here now, all of my neighbors and friends who had died young from violence, drugs, and from the other deadly things we'd been taught didn't happen in Southie.

We thought we were in the best place in the world in this neighborhood, in the all-Irish housing projects where everyone claimed to be Irish even if his name was Spinnoli. We were proud to be from here, as proud as we were to be Irish. We didn't want to own the problems that took the lives of my brothers and of so many others like them: poverty, crime, drugs—those were black things that happened in the ghettos of Roxbury. Southie was Boston's proud Irish neighborhood.

On this night in Southie, the kids were all here once again—I could feel them. The only problem was no one else in the neighborhood could. My old neighbors were going on with their nightly business—wheeling and dealing on the corners, drinking on the stoops, yelling up to windows, looking for a way to get by, or something to fight for. Just like the old days in this small world within a world. It was like a family reunion to me. That's what we considered each other in Southie—family. There was always this feeling that we were protected, as if the whole neighborhood was watching our backs for threats, watching for all the enemies we could never really define. No "outsiders" could mess with us. So we had no reason to leave, and nothing ever to leave for. It was a good feeling to be back in Southie that night, surrounded by my family and neighbors; and I remember hating having to cross over the Broadway Bridge again, having to leave the peninsula neighborhood and go back to my apartment in downtown Boston.

Not long after, I got a call at Citizens for Safety, where I'd been working on antiviolence efforts across Boston since 1990. It was a reporter from *U.S. News & World Report* who was working on an article about what they were calling "the white underclass." The reporter had found through demographic studies that Southie showed three census tracts with the highest concentration of poor whites in America. The part of Southie he was referring to was the Lower End, my own neighborhood at the bottom of the steep hills of City Point, which was the more middle-class section with nicer views of the harbor. The magazine's findings were based on rates of joblessness and single-parent female-headed households. Nearly three-fourths of the families in the Lower End had no fathers. Eighty-five percent of Old Colony collected welfare. The reporter wasn't telling me anything new—I was just stunned that someone was taking notice. No one had even seemed to believe me or to care when I told them about the amount of poverty and social problems where I grew up. Liberals were usually the ones working on social problems, and they never seemed to be able to fit urban poor whites into their world view, which tended to see blacks as the persistent dependent and their own white selves as provider. Whatever race guilt they were holding onto, Southie's poor couldn't do a thing for their consciences. After our violent response to court-ordered busing in the 1970s, Southie was labeled as the white racist oppressor. I saw how that label worked to take the blame away from those able to leave the city and drive back to all-white suburban towns at the end of the day.

Outsiders were also used to the image, put out by our own politicians, that we were a working-class and middle-class community with the lowest rates of social problems anywhere, and that we wanted to keep it that way by not letting blacks in with all their problems. Growing up, I felt alone in thinking this attitude was an injustice to all the Southie people I knew who'd been murdered. Then there were all the suicides that no one wanted to talk about. And all the bank robberies and truck hijackings, and the number of addicts walking down Broadway, and the people limping around or in wheelchairs, victims of violence.

The reporter asked me if I knew anyone in Southie he could talk to. He wanted to see if the socioeconomic conditions in the neighborhood had some of the same results evident in the highly concentrated black ghettos of America. I called some people, but most of them didn't want to talk. We were all used to the media writing about us only when something racial happened, ever since the neighborhood had erupted in antibusing riots during the seventies. Senator Billy Bulger, president of the Massachusetts Senate, had always reminded us of how unfair the media was with its attacks on South Boston. He told us never to trust them again. No news was good news. And his brother, neighborhood drug lord James "Whitey" Bulger, had liked it better that way. Whitey probably figured that all the shootings in the nearby black neighborhood of Roxbury, and all the activists willing to talk over there, would keep the media busy. They wouldn't meddle in Southie as long as we weren't as stupid and disorganized as Roxbury's drug dealers. And by the late eighties, murders in Southie had started to be less visible even to us in the community. Word around town was that Whitey didn't allow bodies to be left on the streets anymore; instead, people went missing, and sometimes were found hog-tied out in the suburbs, or washed up on the shores of Dorchester Bay. The ability of our clean-cut gangsters to keep up appearances complemented our own need to deny the truth. Bad guy stuff seemed to happen less often within the protected turf of South Boston. Maybe a few suicides were here and there, or maybe an addict "scumbag," but that was the victim's own problem. Must have come from a bad family—nothing to do with "Our Beautiful World," as the *South Boston Tribune* was used to calling it, above pictures of church bazaars, bake sales, christenings, and weddings.

I agreed to take the reporter on a tour through Southie. We stayed in the car because I was too nervous to walk around with an "outsider" in a suit. It was bad enough that I was driving his rented sports car. People in Southie usually drove big Chevys, or when they were in with "the boys," as we called our revered gangsters, they'd upgrade to an even bigger Caddy or Lincoln Continental. I wore sunglasses and a scally cap, the traditional local cap once favored by hard-working Irish immigrants and longshoremen, and more recently made popular by tough guys and wannabes. I disguised myself so I wouldn't be identified collaborating with an outsider. Everyone knew I was an activist working to reduce violence and crime. But when they saw me on the news, I was usually organizing things over in Roxbury or Dorchester, the black places that my neighbors thanked God they didn't live in. "That stuff would never happen in Southie," a mother in Old Colony once told me. Her own son had been run over by gangsters for selling cocaine on their turf without paying up.

When I rode around the Lower End with the reporter, I pointed to the land-marks of my childhood: St. Augustine's grammar school, where Ma struggled to keep up with tuition payments so we wouldn't be bused to black neigh-borhoods; the Boys and Girls Club, where I was on the swim team with my brother Kevin; Darius Court, where I played and watched the busing riots; the liquor store with a giant green shamrock painted on it, where Whitey Bulger ran the Southie drug trade; the sidewalk where my sister had crashed from a project rooftop after a fight over drugs; and St. Augustine's Church, down whose front steps I'd helped carry my brothers' heavy caskets. "I miss this place," I said to him. He looked horrified but kept scribbling notes as I went on about this being the best place in the world. "I always had a sense of security here, a sense of belonging that I've never felt anywhere else," I explained. "There was always a feeling that someone would watch your back. Sure, bad things happened to my family, and to so many of my neighbors and friends, but there was never a sense that we were victims. This place was ours, it was all we ever knew, and it was all ours."

Talking to this stranger, driving through the streets of Southie, and saying these things confused me. I thought about how much I'd hated this place when I'd learned that everything I'd just heard myself say about Southie loyalty and pride was a big myth, one that fit well into the schemes of career politicians and their gangster relatives. I thought about how I'd felt betrayed when my brothers ended up among all the other ghosts in our town who were looked up to when they were alive, and shrugged off when they were dead, as punks only asking for trouble.

I didn't know now if I loved or hated this place. All those beautiful dreams and nightmares of my life were competing in the narrow littered streets of Old Colony Project. Over there, on my old front stoop at 8 Patterson Way, were the eccentric mothers, throwing their arms around and telling wild stories. Standing on the corners were the natural-born comedians making everyone laugh. Then there were the teenagers wearing their flashy clothes, "pimp" gear, as we called it. And little kids running in packs, having the time of their lives in a world that was all theirs. But I also saw the junkies, the depressed and lonely mothers of people who'd died, the wounded, the drug dealers, and a known murderer accepted by everyone as warmly as they accepted anything else in the familiar landscape. "I'm thinking of moving back," I told the reporter.

I moved back to Southie after four years of working with activists and victims of violence, mostly in Roxbury, Dorchester, and Mattapan, Boston's largely black and Latino neighborhoods. In those neighborhoods I made some of the closest friends of my life, among people who too often knew the pain of losing their loved ones to the injustices of the streets. Families that had experienced the same things as many of my Southie neighbors. The only difference was that in the black and Latino neighborhoods, people were saying the words: *poverty, drugs, guns, crime, race, class, corruption.*

Two weeks after I moved back home, every newsstand in town had copies of *U.S. News & World Report* with a picture of me, poster boy for the white underclass, leading the article, and demographic evidence telling just a few of Southie's dirty little secrets. South Boston's Lower End was called the white underclass capital of America with a report showing all the obvious social problems that usually attend concentrated poverty in urban areas. The two daily papers in Boston wrote stories about the article's findings, with their own interviews of housing project residents, politicians, and a local priest, mostly refuting the findings. A group of women sitting on a stoop in the housing development laughed at the article. "We're not poor," one said. "We shop at Filene's and Jordan Marsh." I remembered how I spent my teenage years, on welfare, making sure that I too had the best clothes from those department stores, whether stolen or bought with an entire check from the summer jobs program. I thought I looked rich, until I saw that all the rich kids in the suburbs were wearing tattered rags.

A local politician said that the article in *U.S. News* was a lie, that it was all about the liberal media attacking South Boston's tight-knit traditional community. A local right-wing community activist called the magazine a "liberal rag." And a *Boston Herald* columnist who'd grown up in one of the census tracts wrote that he was better off not knowing he was poor. But he grew up long before the gangsters started opening up shop in liquor stores on the edge of the housing projects, marketing a lucrative cocaine trade to the children of single women with few extended family support structures or men around.

Our local priest said that it was terrible to stigmatize Southie children with such findings, labeling them "underclass." I didn't like the term either, but I thought at least now some of the liberal foundations might begin to offer real support for social service agencies struggling to keep up with the needs of Southie families in crisis. People from Southie nonprofits had told me that they were constantly denied funding because their population was not diverse, and probably also because the name "Southie" automatically brings "racists" to mind—the same kind of generalizing that makes all black children "gang bangers" in the minds of bigots. One thing growing up in Southie taught me is that the right wing has no monopoly on bigotry. Eventually, I saw, the priest and other local social service agencies started to refer to the article when they looked for funding or other support.

When I first moved back to Southie, I was always looking over my shoulder. I wasn't sure if anyone minded all the stuff I'd been saying to the press. Instead, people I didn't even know started coming up to me, telling me their own stories. It was as if they felt it was safe to come out, and they wanted to take the tape off their mouths. Before this, I would walk through the main streets of Southie and see so many people who had experienced drug- and crime-related catastrophes, but who didn't connect with others who'd suffered in similar ways, the way I'd been doing with people in Roxbury. It seemed that people wanted to talk after years of silence.

I knew we could do it in Southie once I'd seen how a group of families from Charlestown had banded together when their children were murdered, to break that neighborhood's own infamous code of silence. When I was organizing a citywide gun buyback, getting people in Boston to turn in their working firearms to be destroyed, I met Sandy King and Pam Enos. They had founded the Charlestown After Murder Program. Sandy's son Chris had been murdered in 1986 in front of a hundred people who remained silent. Then in 1991, her son Jay was murdered. Pam's son Adam was murdered in 1992 by the same person who'd murdered Jay. The women organized other mothers of the tight-knit one-square-mile Irish American neighborhood, which had experienced up to six public executions a year, to speak out against the gangsters who controlled the town. They assisted in their neighborhood's gun buy-back, which brought in the most guns citywide in 1994 and 1995, and they built close bonds with mothers of murdered children in neighborhoods of color. They pressured law enforcement to pay attention to murder in Charlestown, put a media spotlight on "the town," exposed corruption, and organized an annual vigil to bring neighbors out of isolation and fear. When I went to Charlestown's vigil, I saw mothers' faces that looked so much like Southie faces, pictures of murdered children who looked so much like Southie kids, and I looked around at the symbols of a community so much like our own: shamrocks and claddaghs, symbolizing "friendship, loyalty, and love." Their vigil took place at St. Catherine's Church, just outside Charlestown's mostly Irish housing projects. By the time I moved back to Southie, I knew what we could do with all the people who at last seemed ready to tell their painful stories.

Untitled Op-Art

MARJANE SATRAPI

Marjane Satrapi is a writer and artist whose graphic novels Persepolis *and* Persepolis 2 *(originally published as four volumes in France) have circulated widely. Having grown up in Iran and lived in France, she has offered critical insight on political oppression, war, and imperialism. The following text was published as an op-art piece in the* New York Times. *The op-art genre, like other op-ed pieces, typically comments on public and newsworthy issues in the world. Here, Satrapi—who has been vocal against both war in general and former President Bush's approach to the Middle East—creates a verbal and visual text that demonstrates how she enters a context that seems antithetical to her political views.*

Hejira

DAVID SEDARIS

As an American humorist, comedian writer, and National Public Radio con-
tributor, David Sedaris draws much of his material from his own life. From
his essay collection, Dress Your Family in Corduroy and Denim *(2004),*
this short piece focuses on the time in Sedaris's life when, as a young college
drop-out, his father kicked him out of the house. Through his description of
and reflection on the events leading up to this moment, Sedaris shows us how,
depending on our own understanding of our contexts, we can fail to recognize
the defining moments of our lives and, even more importantly, misread and
misinterpret one another's reasons and actions within those moments.

It wasn't anything I had planned on, but at the age of twenty-two, after dropping out of my second college and traveling across the country a few times,
I found myself back in Raleigh, living in my parents' basement. After six
months spent waking at noon, getting high, and listening to the same Joni
Mitchell record over and over again, I was called by my father into his den and
told to get out. He was sitting very formally in a big, comfortable chair behind
his desk, and I felt as though he were firing me from the job of being his son.

I'd been expecting this to happen, and it honestly didn't bother me all that
much. The way I saw it, being kicked out of the house was just what I needed
if I was ever going to get back on my feet. "Fine," I said, "I'll go. But one day
you'll be sorry."

I had no idea what I meant by this. It just seemed like the sort of thing a person should say when he was being told to leave.

My sister Lisa had an apartment over by the university and said that I could
come stay with her as long as I didn't bring my Joni Mitchell record. My
mother offered to drive me over, and after a few bong hits I took her up on
it. It was a fifteen-minute trip across town, and on the way we listened to
the rebroadcast of a radio call-in show in which people phoned the host to
describe the various birds gathered around their backyard feeders. Normally
the show came on in the morning, and it seemed strange to listen to it at night.

The birds in question had gone to bed hours ago and probably had no idea they were still being talked about. I chewed this over and wondered if anyone back at the house was talking about me. To the best of my knowledge, no one had ever tried to imitate my voice or describe the shape of my head, and it was depressing that I went unnoticed while a great many people seemed willing to drop everything for a cardinal.

My mother pulled up in front of my sister's apartment building, and when I opened the car door she started to cry, which worried me, as she normally didn't do things like that. It wasn't one of those "I'm going to miss you" things, but something sadder and more desperate than that. I wouldn't know it until months later, but my father had kicked me out of the house not because I was a bum but because I was gay. Our little talk was supposed to be one of those defining moments that shape a person's adult life, but he'd been so uncomfortable with the most important word that he'd left it out completely, saying only, "I think we both know why I'm doing this." I guess I could have pinned him down, I just hadn't seen the point. "Is it because I'm a failure? A drug addict? A sponge? Come on, Dad, just give me one good reason."

Who wants to say that?

My mother assumed that I knew the truth, and it tore her apart. Here was yet another defining moment, and again I missed it entirely. She cried until it sounded as if she were choking. "I'm sorry." she said. "I'm sorry, I'm sorry, I'm sorry."

I figured that within a few weeks I'd have a job and some crummy little apartment. It didn't seem insurmountable, but my mother's tears made me worry that finding these things might be a little harder than I thought. Did she honestly think I was that much of a loser?

"Really," I said, "I'll be fine."

The car light was on and I wondered what the passing drivers thought as they watched my mother sob. What kind of people did they think we were? Did they think she was one of those crybaby moms who fell apart every time someone chipped a coffee cup? Did they assume I'd said something to hurt her? Did they see us as just another crying mother and her stoned gay son, sitting in a station wagon and listening to a call-in show about birds, or did they imagine, for just one moment, that we might be special?

Toward a Civil Society:
Memory, History, and the *Enola Gay*

ANDREA USEEM

In "Toward a Civil Society: Memory, History, and the Enola Gay*," Andrea Useem examines the complications inherent to discussing and portraying historical context. Specifically, she looks at a Smithsonian exhibit of the plane that dropped an atomic bomb on Hiroshima, Japan, and the various factions that debate the bomb's role and necessity in World War II. Published in the anthology* An Ethical Compass: Coming of Age in the 21st Century *when Useem was an undergraduate, this essay won the 1995 Ethics Prize from the Elie Wiesel Foundation for Humanity.*

The United States is a nation that has always had a particular sense of destiny. From the religious reformers who carved a life out of the New England forests to modern voices who call for foreign intervention, the American people have believed that the United States has a special mission to be a lighthouse of freedom and hope for other nations.[1] This mission is revealed in history and is especially clear in conflicts; the national vision was articulated in the Revolutionary War, tested and strained during the Civil War, undermined during Vietnam. World War II, a war fought to "save civilization," was another time to put values to ultimate tests and live with the sacrifices. The conflict is woven into our national identity like a star on the flag.

Fifty years have since passed and—though memories never sank far beneath conscious thought—the anniversary is a chance to pull up stories and memories from the deep past. The power and resonance of a fifty years' memorial was clear on June 6, 1994, when D-Day made headlines again, this time not for war cries or the thunder of guns but for speeches and the thunder of applause. Men and women who survived the fire of war in their youth have raised children and seen them through Vietnam, witnessed the unfolding of the arms race, the fall of the Berlin Wall, and the phoenix-like growth of Japan. As they begin to tell war stories to their great-grandchildren, they realize that World War II will soon pass into history. Their memory will be entrusted to their children. This anniversary, then, is a national ritual for telling and listening, as well as a dynamic moment for questioning and reflecting.

But as we exhume conflicts fifty years gone, we find they were never laid to rest, only buried alive as the rest of the twentieth century bulldozed past. We find the passions and convictions of fifty years ago living quietly in those who were there. Then we find, buried beneath volumes of historical text, breathing softly beneath the rationalizations and justifications, the deep moral ambiguities of wartime. And as we look at history through our only lens, the present, we gain new information and insights, which translate into new conflicts. The current generation of scholars and students are inheritors of World War II, and where past and present overlap is where new conflicts burn most brightly. No legacy is more loaded than that of the atomic bomb. Freeman Dyson compares the legacy with the rules of an imaginary city he recalls from a childhood book: "It is a law of life in the magic city that if you wish for anything you can have it. But with this law goes a special rule about machines. If anyone wishes for a piece of machinery, he is compelled to keep it and go on using it for the rest of his life."[2] As any newspaper will tell, the Smithsonian's upcoming display of the *Enola Gay* is the epicenter of the conflict.

"The Nation's Attic"

The U.S. government placed the stewardship of national memory in the hands of the Smithsonian Institution in 1826. Funded through private endowment and federal money, the white stone buildings flank the Mall in Washington, D.C. They are intellectual and cultural corridors connecting the Washington, Lincoln, and Vietnam memorials, where American history is enshrined, to the Capitol, where today's history happens. An act of Congress in 1946 created the National Air Museum. The 1966 statute—amended to include the space program—charged the museum to "memorialize the national development of aviation and space flight; collect, preserve and display aeronautical and space flight equipment…; serve as a repository for science equipment and data; and provide educational material for the historical study of aviation and space flight."[3] National achievements in the air hold a special place in American consciousness; the Wright brothers and the Apollo 11 mission have become symbols of American ingenuity. The museum itself is a unique experience. For my own family and thousands of others, our annual pilgrimage there is as much a part of Christmas as the tree. I recall my own dizzy awe walking beneath the wheeling planes and towering rockets.

With the fifty-year anniversary coming up in 1995, the National Air and Space Museum (NASM) decided to display the B-29 Super Fortress that dropped the first atomic bomb. The Smithsonian has been the *Enola Gay*'s legal guardian since July 1949, though the museum asked the air force to house it. With limited hangar space, new technology, and an assignment in

Korea, the air force squeezed the *Enola Gay* out into the rain and wind. Its restoration, started ten years ago, has taken twenty-five workers and a million dollars to complete. Museum visitors will see a shiny sixty-foot section of the front fuselage hanging in the gallery. Curators worked simultaneously on an exhibit to explain the role of the *Enola Gay* in the end of World War II. Following standard operating procedures, the museum staff submitted their work-in-progress, originally titled "The Crossroads: The End of World War II, the Atomic Bomb and the Origins of the Cold War," to an advisory committee.[4] The panel of experts includes well-known historians from the military, government, science, and academe. During that same period, NASM directors met with officials of the Air Force Association to discuss the exhibit and—on request—to provide a copy of the script. John Correll, the editor-in-chief of *Air Force Magazine*, wrote an article in the April 1 issue that was harshly critical of the exhibit, thereby bringing the issue to broad public attention.

The April article ("War Stories at Air and Space") and follow-up articles articulate the veteran's criticisms both specific and sweeping. Correll claims that the exhibit takes the Pacific war out of context, depicting "the Japanese in defense of their home islands, saying little about what had made such a defense necessary" and thereby making American offensive moves appear "brutal, vindictive and racially motivated." Second, the article accuses the exhibit of "imbalance," meaning that the exhibit is designed to evoke more empathy for the Japanese than for the Americans. He noted, for example, that a greater number of photos were devoted to Japanese war dead than American. The article also describes how the "emotional center" of the exhibit—artifacts, pictures, and text from "ground zero"—is designed for "shock effect" and will leave the most lasting impression on the visitor. Finally, he blasts the museum for its handling of perhaps the most contentious detail: the number of casualties projected for the invasion of Japan. Correll also saves a good deal of artillery for the current Smithsonian administration, whom he accuses of "politically correct curating."[5]

Due in part to grass-roots organizing by veterans, the controversy crossed the street to Capitol Hill. On August 10, 1994, a bipartisan group of twenty-four House members signed a letter to Robert McCormick Adams, the Smithsonian's executive secretary, calling the exhibit a "historically narrow revisionist view." On that same day a group of six House Republicans met with Martin Harwit, NASM's director, to voice similar complaints. Congressional pressure reached a pitch when the Senate passed a resolution threatening to cut congressional appropriations, which currently make up 85 percent of the museum's budget. Pressure to change the exhibit continued from the press and veterans' groups. By late September, the museum officials sat down behind closed doors with the American Legion and sandpapered the script. Then it was the historians who were outraged: they, too, flung the accusation of "revisionism."

The treatment of the debate to drop the atomic bomb was at the center of their criticism. The earlier scripts contained historical documents that questioned the necessity of dropping the bomb. The newly edited script, however, reflected the "inaccurate but understandable belief that the atomic bomb saved [American soldiers] from being sacrificed in an invasion of Japan." According to the historians, the Smithsonian exhibit was propagating "feel good national myths."[6]

The historians attacked the Smithsonian and the veterans' pressure groups in evocative terms. "It was a humiliating spectacle, scholars being forced to recant the truth," wrote Kai Bird in a *New York Times* column, calling up the tragic specter of Galileo. Similarly, more than a hundred historians signed a letter to the new secretary of the Smithsonian that likened the recent script changes to "historical cleansing."

The use of this phrase draws a subtle link to the "ethnic cleansing" in Bosnia, implying that historical truths—like the Croats—are being wiped out in an internationally criminal act.[7] Finally, the historians accuse the Smithsonian of being "PC," that is, "patriotically correct."

Although the threads of the past intimately bind those who remember the past and those who study it, the two camps are no longer in dialogue with each other. The debate has ceased to be a debate. The rhetoric has reached a strident pitch, and both sides are mobilizing; witness the resolutions passed by the Senate and the Organization of American Historians. Both sides find the values most central to their identity at stake. For a historian, what could be more important than intellectual integrity? For a veteran, what could be more essential than defending the values for which they risked their lives? To sound the depths of the conflict, we must look beneath the media rhetoric.

"Thank God for the Bomb"

What do the veterans mean when they ask the museum to display the *Enola Gay* in its proper context? How would they tell the story? Many would begin their story some years before the war, when the country was reflecting on the empty victory of the Great War and pacifism was in vogue.

Suddenly, bombs, fire, smoke, and lolling ships: Pearl Harbor. Two thousand Americans, eighteen ships, and 292 aircraft were destroyed in the Japanese sneak attack.[8] Though the military losses were far from crippling, the event was a profound psychological turning point of which we are constantly reminded. President Franklin D. Roosevelt, in his speech to Congress asking for a declaration of war, forever tied Pearl Harbor to the terms of Japanese surrender: "unconditional." Pacifism blew away like a feather in a tornado, and the country mobilized for war. A desire for revenge burned brightly among other motivations: the Japanese would pay a hundredfold for catching America with its pants down. It was a playground morality, for all of its depth and seriousness.

Other Japanese military actions incited the emotions of wartime America. A nation with colonial ambitions, the Japanese were aggressively pursuing their goals in East Asia, invading China, Manchuria, and several South Pacific islands. They often treated their newest imperial subjects ruthlessly, and the American press covered the events. Americans were horrified by the "rape of Nanking," in which the Japanese looted, burned, raped, and murdered freely in the Chinese city.

The sense of outrage became all the more intense when American soldiers came face to face with Japanese military strategy. Because of practices such as *kamikaze* missions (a suicidal flight into an enemy ship) and *hara-kiri* (ritual suicide chosen over dishonor), many Americans considered the Japanese to be "fanatics" who would never surrender. Surrender was dishonorable for Japanese soldiers; they held Allied soldiers to the same standards and treated them brutally. In short, the Japanese pursued the battle with a total commitment to victory and a complete disregard for what the Western world accepted as "rules of warfare." This strategy was powerful. Where the Japanese did not win, they forced Allied troops to pay in blood for every inch gained.

Hatred for Japan was strong. The press filled the national vacuum of understanding for this Eastern culture, often portraying the Japanese as less than human. Polls from the era reveal that 10 to 13 percent of the American people wanted to see them wiped out as a race.[9] This psychological tactic is as old and as common as warfare. When the enemy is perceived inhuman, annihilation of the enemy becomes acceptable, even justified.

As hatred and contempt for the Japanese evolved, so too did American bombing policy. During the European war, the United States refused to join England in the policy of area or "morale" bombing, in which noncombatants became targets. Instead, the U.S. Air Force established a doctrine of precision bombing, based on both ethical and military considerations.[10] In the Pacific theater this doctrine began to crumble under new pressures and new leadership. Weather and geographical considerations made daylight precision bombing less effective than nighttime area bombing. On his own authority, General Curtis LeMay, the results-oriented head of XXI Bomber Command, ordered the firebombing of Tokyo on March 9, 1945. When the mission's success became clear, the war machine in Washington applauded his bold action. Bomber Command swept ethical considerations for noncombatants under the carpet with a simple reclassification: Japan had no civilians. Said LeMay, "All you had to do was visit one of those targets after we'd roasted it, and see the ruins of a multitude of tiny houses, with a drill press sticking up through the wreckage of every home.... Had to be done."[11] By the summer of 1945, key military decision makers were comfortable with ninety thousand to a hundred thousand civilian casualties in one night. The most immediate "context" of the atomic bomb was the situation in early August 1945.

Thousands of servicemen were preparing to invade Japan in November. Many came directly from the European theater, while the others were already initiated into the terrors of Pacific warfare. The conflict had reached a grim plateau; it would clearly be a fight to the finish. The American military men were determined to whip Japan into unconditional surrender, though they knew they would die in the process. "We were living under a death sentence," said John Useem, a Navy lieutenant scheduled for the fourth wave of the invasion. Useem describes taking a thirty-day leave in the summer of 1945. "I went back to the University of Wisconsin, where I got my degree. Someone offered me a job when the war ended. I laughed because I knew I wasn't coming back."[12] On August 7, when news of the atomic explosion over Hiroshima reached American troops, they were ecstatic.

The sense of relief was tremendous. Surely the war would end! Eight days and one plutonium bomb later, the Japanese surrendered. The apparent cause-and-effect relationship was enormously powerful, burning into the hearts of American servicemen and their families. Harry Truman reinforced this connection, announcing in his radio broadcast of December 9 that he had dropped the bomb to save American lives. The atomic bomb appeared to graciously restore the lives Americas were preparing to sacrifice, just as God had restored Isaac to Abraham. "Thank God for the bomb."

Why would the veterans want to see the museum tell this story? They want to invite the listener (in this case, the museum visitor) to walk in the shoes of a young G.I. stationed in the Pacific. As the events of the war unfold, the visitor is moved along with them. A veteran-designed exhibit would evoke shock at Pearl Harbor and outrage at the treatment of American POWs in Japan. Historical displays, then, become tools for drawing out particular emotions. When listeners become emotionally involved in a narrative, they are leaving themselves open for the story to *change* them.[13]

This process of listening and transformation is a major function of narrative. Clearly, then, when the historians make ground zero the "emotional center" of the exhibit, the veterans are deeply uncomfortable. According to their experience, the listener should feel enormously relieved on August 6. The "emotional center" should be an impromptu barracks celebration as G.I.s realize they will live to see their families again.

Displaying the *Enola Gay* in a veterans' "context" would serve a moral. The exhibit would explain how decent American citizens could be overjoyed that sixty thousand Japanese civilians had perished in an instant. If visitors are successfully emotionally involved, they will perceive how, if *they* were in a similar situation, they might also say, "Thank God for the bomb."

For the Record

One asks the question: "Why did the United States drop an atomic bomb on Hiroshima?"

The most common answer is: "To save a million American lives." Historians have probed this question and found answers very different from the one above. The final decision to drop the bomb lay with President Truman. Therefore, they have examined the criteria by which he made his decision. When military advisers briefed Truman about a possible invasion of Japan, how high were the casualty estimates they quoted? Archival research revealed that the figures discussed in the Oval Office never exceeded forty-six thousand.[14] The historians want to clear the historical record. They traced the etymology of the phrase "a million American lives" to a 1946 *Harper's* article by Henry Stimson, secretary of war, and found no factual evidence beneath it.[15] Truman's memoirs, too, exaggerated the casualty estimates. Some veterans imagine that this clarification implies a judgment that, if only forty-six thousand were going to perish, then Truman should have chosen invasion over bombing. No historian has ever made this claim. Rather, the historians are interested in the questions behind the numbers: Were Truman and Stimson laboring to relieve their guilt and justify the bombings to themselves and to the public?

The historians leave behind the question "How many American lives did Truman believe the bomb would save?" to ask, "Was saving American lives his primary interest in dropping the bomb?"

Those who would answer "yes" to this question must prove that Truman believed the war could end *only* through invasion. The historical record will not back them up. Or the contrary, Truman seemed to have thought peace was at hand; he was aware of Japanese diplomatic interest in peace, the possibility of continued firebombing over Japan and entry of Russia into the war. Why, then, did he need the bomb? Historians have concluded that a host of concerns motivated Truman in his authorization of the bomb. Some scholars focus on his relatively weak position as president. As of August 1945 he had yet to emerge from Roosevelt's awesome shadow; using the atomic bomb would show his allegiance to FDR's "unconditional surrender" doctrine. Historians tick off the other motivations: to intimidate Russia, to establish U.S. power in the postwar world, to allow for the bureaucratic momentum of the Manhattan Project, to use a God-given weapon. Besides establishing these motivations, historians want to present the voices of dissent from the Truman administration and the Manhattan Project.

The historians have an enormously difficult task in helping the veterans and the public incorporate this newly articulated information into their understanding of the war. Many read it as an affront, an accusation, a judgment. If historians dug up a wealth of factual information on the life of Jesus, some of which seemed to contradict the Gospel, surely Matthew, Mark, Luke, and John would be angry. For fifty years the Americans of World War II have arranged the facts in a certain way. Over time the disparate voices and memories have become more unified, and the veterans tell their story with the power of a collective voice. Bound up within this traditional narrative are historical events, strong emotions, and moral justifications. The story represents the veterans' self-understanding.

It is their identity, which they, in turn, have identified with the sacred destiny of the United States. And when historians give the whole story a shake, to test its factual foundation, the storytellers fear they want to tip over the whole structure.

What do the historians want the visitors to experience? In keeping with their professional values, the historians want to create in visitors an attitude of objectivity, of questioning. When the historians researched World War II, they tried not to identify themselves with a particular nationality; according to the rules of objectivity, history written solely from an "American" perspective would be propaganda. Thus, the historians invite the visitors to suspend their own national or political identity to consider the events. With evidence from both Japanese and American perspectives, visitors can make rational, objective judgments. If visitors become successfully involved in this exhibit, they will lose any preconceptions they may have had about the *necessity* of historical events. In this creative state of questioning, the visitors may arrive at new understandings or judgments about the role of the *Enola Gay* in the end of World War II. This opportunity for questioning, however, comes at the cost of an empathetic understanding of the American experience in the Pacific.

Values in Conflict

A deep division at the heart of this conflict separates moral experience from moral reasoning. Veterans want new generations of Americans to learn *why* they believed their actions were right. Historians ask visitors to consider *whether* historical decisions were right. Both perspectives are firmly grounded in valid human experience. The veterans' stories have a stamp of authenticity that comes from life lived. Their words are forged in blood and mud, sleepless nights and letters home.

The historians speak from the authority of rationality and luxury of detached reflection. These two perspectives are in conflict, as the words of my grandfather show clearly. When I asked him if the historians' new numbers and theories were true, he said, "Yes, the evidence is correct, but I can't agree with it, because of my experience. For the historians, the facts are absolute truth and again, I can't agree."[16]

If we look at this dispute carefully, we find serious challenges to any ideal we may have about universal truth. The veterans make the case that the bombing of Hiroshima was subjectively right.

The historians argue that it is objectively questionable. We cannot escape either perspective. We are bound to enter the emotional world of a combat soldier *and* face these two questions: Was the use of the bomb a military necessity? Is the deliberate targeting of noncombatants morally acceptable in any situation? How can we reconcile the two points of view? Moral relativism is an easy and unacceptable solution that prematurely seems to resolve the conflict. A more rigorous view of the conflict asks us to grasp the paradox and internalize it. Living with paradox requires careful thought and constant energy. By allowing ourselves to be "caught in the middle," we see more clearly the moral possibilities within ourselves as human beings.

It seems a small thing to ask of people: to recognize and learn from conflicts over values. Yet it is an exercise in which American society is out of shape. If we consider the venom of the last elections or the protests that lead to body bags in Planned Parenthood, we see individuals and groups unable to resolve value conflicts in peaceful ways. In the Smithsonian debate we are disappointed to find similar symptoms: two sides no longer listening to one another.

Given the diversity of human experience, we will always find ourselves among people who hold conflicting values. Living in a democratic society means that we agree to resolve those conflicts peacefully. Isn't that the civilization Americans fought to save fifty years ago? Didn't those veterans risk their lives to preserve a society that produced people who disagree with them? Listening and learning from other value systems, allowing for complexity and depth, are vital skills. This debate, then, is an opportunity to sharpen our sensitivities. It challenges our historical sense, sparks careful study, and prompts us to recognize the ultimate well-spring of moral judgment: our own awareness.

Notes

1. Robert Bellah and William McLoughlin, eds., *Religion in America* (Boston: Houghton Mifflin, 1968).

2. Freeman Dyson, *Disturbing the Universe* (New York: Basic Books, 1979), 4.

3. John Correll, "War Stories at Air and Space," *Air Force Magazine*, April 1994, 29.

4. Martin Harwit, "*Enola Gay* and a Nation's Memory," *Air and Space Magazine*, August-September 1994, 20.

5. Correll, "War Stories at Air and Space," 24-27.

6. Kai Bird, "The Curators Cave In," *New York Times*, October 9, 1994, 15.

7. Martin Sherwin and Kai Bird to Ira Michael Heyman, unpublished letter, November 16, 1994.

8. Richard Rhodes, *The Making of the Atomic Bomb* (New York: Simon and Schuster, 1986), 392.

9. John Dower, *War Without Mercy* (New York: Pantheon, 1986), 53.

10. Recent scholarship, particularly that of Ronald Schaffer and Michael Sherry, implies that this doctrine, often cited to lend moral superiority to the AAF, is little more than a myth. Conrad Crane, *Bombs, Cities and Civilians* (Lawrence: University Press of Kansas, 1993), 4.

11. Crane, *Bombs, Cities and Civilians*, 133.

12. Interview, John Useem, December 26, 1994, Washington, DC.

13. Walter Davis, a scholar who studies Vietnam veterans, noted the importance of the relationship between a veteran and his audience. "The healing of the combat veteran is inextricably connected to our capacity as a community to hear what the veteran has to tell us and to be changed by it." Jonathan Shay, "Binding Up the Wounded National Theology," *Religion and Values in Public Life* (Fall 1994): 1.

14. Martin Sherwin, *A World Destroyed* (New York: Random House, 1987), Appendix U: "War Planners Casualty Estimates," 342.

15. Bird, "Curators Cave In," 15.

16. Bird, "Curators Cave In," 15.

My Life as an Undocumented Immigrant

JOSE ANTONIO VARGAS

Jose Antonio Vargas, a Pulitzer Prize-winning journalist and founder of the Define American organization, chronicles his lifelong pursuit of the American Dream while reconciling his sense of self with his status as an undocumented immigrant. Published both in print and online in the New York Times *in 2011, this text eloquently points to the complexities of immigration policies and social systems that affect the lives of many individuals living in the United States.*

One August morning nearly two decades ago, my mother woke me and put me in a cab. She handed me a jacket. *"Baka malamig doon"* were among the few words she said. ("It might be cold there.") When I arrived at the Philippines' Ninoy Aquino International Airport with her, my aunt and a family friend, I was introduced to a man I'd never seen. They told me he was my uncle. He held my hand as I boarded an airplane for the first time. It was 1993, and I was 12.

My mother wanted to give me a better life, so she sent me thousands of miles away to live with her parents in America—my grandfather (*Lolo* in Tagalog) and grandmother (*Lola*). After I arrived in Mountain View, Calif., in the San Francisco Bay Area, I entered sixth grade and quickly grew to love my new home, family and culture. I discovered a passion for language, though it was hard to learn the difference between formal English and American slang. One of my early memories is of a freckled kid in middle school asking me, "What's up?" I replied, "The sky," and he and a couple of other kids laughed. I won the eighth-grade spelling bee by memorizing words I couldn't properly pronounce. (The winning word was "indefatigable.")

One day when I was 16, I rode my bike to the nearby D.M.V. office to get my driver's permit. Some of my friends already had their licenses, so I figured it was time. But when I handed the clerk my green card as proof of U.S. residency, she flipped it around, examining it. "This is fake," she whispered. "Don't come back here again."

Confused and scared, I pedaled home and confronted Lolo. I remember him sitting in the garage, cutting coupons. I dropped my bike and ran over to him, showing him the green card. *"Peke ba ito?"* I asked in Tagalog. ("Is this fake?") My grandparents were naturalized American citizens—he worked as a security guard, she as a food server—and they had begun supporting my mother and me financially when I was 3, after my father's wandering eye and inability to properly provide for us led to my parents' separation. Lolo was a proud man, and I saw the shame on his face as he told me he purchased the card, along with other fake documents, for me. "Don't show it to other people," he warned.

I decided then that I could never give anyone reason to doubt I was an American. I convinced myself that if I worked enough, if I achieved enough, I would be rewarded with citizenship. I felt I could earn it.

I've tried. Over the past 14 years, I've graduated from high school and college and built a career as a journalist, interviewing some of the most famous people in the country. On the surface, I've created a good life. I've lived the American dream.

But I am still an undocumented immigrant. And that means living a different kind of reality. It means going about my day in fear of being found out. It means rarely trusting people, even those closest to me, with who I really am. It means keeping my family photos in a shoebox rather than displaying them on shelves in my home, so friends don't ask about them. It means reluctantly, even painfully, doing things I know are wrong and unlawful. And it has meant relying on a sort of 21st-century underground railroad of supporters, people who took an interest in my future and took risks for me.

Last year I read about four students who walked from Miami to Washington to lobby for the Dream Act, a nearly decade-old immigration bill that would provide a path to legal permanent residency for young people who have been educated in this country. At the risk of deportation—the Obama administration has deported almost 800,000 people in the last two years—they are speaking out. Their courage has inspired me.

There are believed to be 11 million undocumented immigrants in the United States. We're not always who you think we are. Some pick your strawberries or care for your children. Some are in high school or college. And some, it turns out, write news articles you might read. I grew up here. This is my home. Yet even though I think of myself as an American and consider America my country, my country doesn't think of me as one of its own.

∼

My first challenge was the language. Though I learned English in the Philippines, I wanted to lose my accent. During high school, I spent hours at a time watching television (especially "Frasier," "Home Improvement" and reruns of "The Golden Girls") and movies (from "Goodfellas" to "Anne of Green Gables"), pausing the VHS to try to copy how various characters enunciated their words. At the local library, I read magazines, books and newspapers—anything to learn how to write better. Kathy Dewar, my high-school English teacher, introduced me to journalism. From the moment I wrote my first article for the student paper, I convinced myself that having my name in print—writing in English, interviewing Americans—validated my presence here.

The debates over "illegal aliens" intensified my anxieties. In 1994, only a year after my flight from the Philippines, Gov. Pete Wilson was re-elected in part because of his support for Proposition 187, which prohibited undocumented immigrants from attending public school and accessing other services. (A federal court later found the law unconstitutional.) After my encounter at the D.M.V. in 1997, I grew more aware of anti-immigrant sentiments and stereotypes: *they don't want to assimilate, they are a drain on society.* They're not talking about me, I would tell myself. I have something to contribute.

To do that, I had to work—and for that, I needed a Social Security number. Fortunately, my grandfather had already managed to get one for me. Lolo had always taken care of everyone in the family. He and my grandmother emigrated legally in 1984 from Zambales, a province in the Philippines of rice fields and bamboo houses, following Lolo's sister, who married a Filipino-American serving in the American military. She petitioned for her brother and his wife to join her. When they got here, Lolo petitioned for his two children—my mother and her younger brother—to follow them. But instead of mentioning that my mother was a married woman, he listed her as single. Legal residents can't petition for their married children. Besides, Lolo didn't care for my father. He didn't want him coming here too.

But soon Lolo grew nervous that the immigration authorities reviewing the petition would discover my mother was married, thus derailing not only her chances of coming here but those of my uncle as well. So he withdrew her petition. After my uncle came to America legally in 1991, Lolo tried to get my mother here through a tourist visa, but she wasn't able to obtain one. That's when she decided to send me. My mother told me later that she figured she would follow me soon. She never did.

The "uncle" who brought me here turned out to be a coyote, not a relative, my grandfather later explained. Lolo scraped together enough money—I eventually learned it was $4,500, a huge sum for him—to pay him to smuggle me here under a fake name and fake passport. (I never saw the passport again after the flight and have always assumed that the coyote kept it.) After I arrived in America, Lolo obtained a new fake Filipino passport, in my real name this time, adorned with a fake student visa, in addition to the fraudulent green card.

Using the fake passport, we went to the local Social Security Administration office and applied for a Social Security number and card. It was, I remember, a quick visit. When the card came in the mail, it had my full, real name, but it also clearly stated: "Valid for work only with I.N.S. authorization."

When I began looking for work, a short time after the D.M.V. incident, my grandfather and I took the Social Security card to Kinko's, where he covered the "I.N.S. authorization" text with a sliver of white tape. We then made photocopies of the card. At a glance, at least, the copies would look like copies of a regular, unrestricted Social Security card.

Lolo always imagined I would work the kind of low-paying jobs that undocumented people often take. (Once I married an American, he said, I would get my real papers, and everything would be fine.) But even menial jobs require documents, so he and I hoped the doctored card would work for now. The more documents I had, he said, the better.

While in high school, I worked part time at Subway, then at the front desk of the local Y.M.C.A., then at a tennis club, until I landed an unpaid internship at The Mountain View Voice, my hometown newspaper. First I brought coffee and helped around the office; eventually I began covering city-hall meetings and other assignments for pay.

For more than a decade of getting part-time and full-time jobs, employers have rarely asked to check my original Social Security card. When they did, I showed the photocopied version, which they accepted. Over time, I also began checking the citizenship box on my federal I-9 employment eligibility forms. (Claiming full citizenship was actually easier than declaring permanent resident "green card" status, which would have required me to provide an alien registration number.)

This deceit never got easier. The more I did it, the more I felt like an impostor, the more guilt I carried—and the more I worried that I would get caught. But I kept doing it. I needed to live and survive on my own, and I decided this was the way.

Mountain View High School became my second home. I was elected to represent my school at school-board meetings, which gave me the chance to meet and befriend Rich Fischer, the superintendent for our school district. I joined the speech and debate team, acted in school plays and eventually became co-editor of The Oracle, the student newspaper. That drew the attention of my principal, Pat Hyland. "You're at school just as much as I am," she told me. Pat and Rich would soon become mentors, and over time, almost surrogate parents for me.

After a choir rehearsal during my junior year, Jill Denny, the choir director, told me she was considering a Japan trip for our singing group. I told her I couldn't afford it, but she said we'd figure out a way. I hesitated, and then decided to tell her the truth. "It's not really the money," I remember saying. "I don't have the right passport." When she assured me we'd get the proper documents, I finally told her. "I can't get the right passport," I said. "I'm not supposed to be here."

She understood. So the choir toured Hawaii instead, with me in tow. (Mrs. Denny and I spoke a couple of months ago, and she told me she hadn't wanted to leave any student behind.)

Later that school year, my history class watched a documentary on Harvey Milk, the openly gay San Francisco city official who was assassinated. This was 1999, just six months after Matthew Shepard's body was found tied to a fence in Wyoming. During the discussion, I raised my hand and said something like: "I'm sorry Harvey Milk got killed for being gay.... I've been meaning to say this.... I'm gay."

I hadn't planned on coming out that morning, though I had known that I was gay for several years. With that announcement, I became the only openly gay student at school, and it caused turmoil with my grandparents. Lolo kicked me out of the house for a few weeks. Though we eventually reconciled, I had disappointed him on two fronts. First, as a Catholic, he considered homosexuality a sin and was embarrassed about having "ang apo na bakla" ("a grandson who is gay"). Even worse, I was making matters more difficult for myself, he said. I needed to marry an American woman in order to gain a green card.

Tough as it was, coming out about being gay seemed less daunting than coming out about my legal status. I kept my other secret mostly hidden.

~

While my classmates awaited their college acceptance letters, I hoped to get a full-time job at The Mountain View Voice after graduation. It's not that I didn't want to go to college, but I couldn't apply for state and federal financial aid. Without that, my family couldn't afford to send me.

But when I finally told Pat and Rich about my immigration "problem"—as we called it from then on—they helped me look for a solution. At first, they even wondered if one of them could adopt me and fix the situation that way, but a lawyer Rich consulted told him it wouldn't change my legal status because I was too old. Eventually they connected me to a new scholarship fund for high-potential students who were usually the first in their families to attend college. Most important, the fund was not concerned with immigration status. I was among the first recipients, with the scholarship covering tuition, lodging, books and other expenses for my studies at San Francisco State University.

As a college freshman, I found a job working part time at The San Francisco Chronicle, where I sorted mail and wrote some freelance articles. My ambition was to get a reporting job, so I embarked on a series of internships. First I landed at The Philadelphia Daily News, in the summer of 2001, where I covered a drive-by shooting and the wedding of the 76ers star Allen Iverson. Using those articles, I applied to The Seattle Times and got an internship for the following summer.

But then my lack of proper documents became a problem again. The Times's recruiter, Pat Foote, asked all incoming interns to bring certain paperwork on their first day: a birth certificate, or a passport, or a driver's license plus an original Social Security card. I panicked, thinking my documents wouldn't pass muster. So before starting the job, I called Pat and told her about my legal status. After consulting with management, she called me back with the answer I feared: I couldn't do the internship.

This was devastating. What good was college if I couldn't then pursue the career I wanted? I decided then that if I was to succeed in a profession that is all about truth-telling, I couldn't tell the truth about myself.

After this episode, Jim Strand, the venture capitalist who sponsored my scholarship, offered to pay for an immigration lawyer. Rich and I went to meet her in San Francisco's financial district.

I was hopeful. This was in early 2002, shortly after Senators Orrin Hatch, the Utah Republican, and Dick Durbin, the Illinois Democrat, introduced the Dream Act—Development, Relief and Education for Alien Minors. It seemed like the legislative version of what I'd told myself: If I work hard and contribute, things will work out.

But the meeting left me crushed. My only solution, the lawyer said, was to go back to the Philippines and accept a 10-year ban before I could apply to return legally.

If Rich was discouraged, he hid it well. "Put this problem on a shelf," he told me. "Compartmentalize it. Keep going."

And I did. For the summer of 2003, I applied for internships across the country. Several newspapers, including The Wall Street Journal, The Boston Globe and The Chicago Tribune, expressed interest. But when The Washington Post offered me a spot, I knew where I would go. And this time, I had no intention of acknowledging my "problem."

The Post internship posed a tricky obstacle: It required a driver's license. (After my close call at the California D.M.V., I'd never gotten one.) So I spent an afternoon at The Mountain View Public Library, studying various states' requirements. Oregon was among the most welcoming—and it was just a few hours' drive north.

Again, my support network came through. A friend's father lived in Portland, and he allowed me to use his address as proof of residency. Pat, Rich and Rich's longtime assistant, Mary Moore, sent letters to me at that address. Rich taught me how to do three-point turns in a parking lot, and a friend accompanied me to Portland.

The license meant everything to me—it would let me drive, fly and work. But my grandparents worried about the Portland trip and the Washington internship. While Lola offered daily prayers so that I would not get caught, Lolo told me that I was dreaming too big, risking too much.

I was determined to pursue my ambitions. I was 22, I told them, responsible for my own actions. But this was different from Lolo's driving a confused teenager to Kinko's. I knew what I was doing now, and I knew it wasn't right. But what was I supposed to do?

I was paying state and federal taxes, but I was using an invalid Social Security card and writing false information on my employment forms. But that seemed better than depending on my grandparents or on Pat, Rich and Jim—or returning to a country I barely remembered. I convinced myself all would be O.K. if I lived up to the qualities of a "citizen": hard work, self-reliance, love of my country.

At the D.M.V. in Portland, I arrived with my photocopied Social Security card, my college I.D., a pay stub from The San Francisco Chronicle and my proof of state residence—the letters to the Portland address that my support network had sent. It worked. My license, issued in 2003, was set to expire eight years later, on my 30th birthday, on Feb. 3, 2011. I had eight years to succeed professionally, and to hope that some sort of immigration reform would pass in the meantime and allow me to stay.

It seemed like all the time in the world.

~

My summer in Washington was exhilarating. I was intimidated to be in a major newsroom but was assigned a mentor—Peter Perl, a veteran magazine writer—to help me navigate it. A few weeks into the internship, he printed out one of my articles, about a guy who recovered a long-lost wallet, circled the first two paragraphs and left it on my desk. "Great eye for details—awesome!" he wrote. Though I didn't know it then, Peter would become one more member of my network.

At the end of the summer, I returned to The San Francisco Chronicle. My plan was to finish school—I was now a senior—while I worked for The Chronicle as a reporter for the city desk. But when The Post beckoned again, offering me a full-time, two-year paid internship that I could start when I graduated in June 2004, it was too tempting to pass up. I moved back to Washington.

About four months into my job as a reporter for The Post, I began feeling increasingly paranoid, as if I had "illegal immigrant" tattooed on my forehead—and in Washington, of all places, where the debates over immigration seemed never-ending. I was so eager to prove myself that I feared I was annoying some colleagues and editors—and worried that any one of these professional journalists could discover my secret. The anxiety was nearly paralyzing. I decided I had to tell one of the higher-ups about my situation. I turned to Peter.

By this time, Peter, who still works at The Post, had become part of management as the paper's director of newsroom training and professional development. One afternoon in late October, we walked a couple of blocks to Lafayette Square, across from the White House. Over some 20 minutes, sitting on a bench, I told him everything: the Social Security card, the driver's license, Pat and Rich, my family.

Peter was shocked. "I understand you 100 times better now," he said. He told me that I had done the right thing by telling him, and that it was now our shared problem. He said he didn't want to do anything about it just yet.

I had just been hired, he said, and I needed to prove myself. "When you've done enough," he said, "we'll tell Don and Len together." (Don Graham is the chairman of The Washington Post Company; Leonard Downie Jr. was then the paper's executive editor.) A month later, I spent my first Thanksgiving in Washington with Peter and his family.

In the five years that followed, I did my best to "do enough." I was promoted to staff writer, reported on video-game culture, wrote a series on Washington's H.I.V./AIDS epidemic and covered the role of technology and social media in the 2008 presidential race. I visited the White House, where I interviewed senior aides and covered a state dinner—and gave the Secret Service the Social Security number I obtained with false documents.

I did my best to steer clear of reporting on immigration policy but couldn't always avoid it. On two occasions, I wrote about Hillary Clinton's position on driver's licenses for undocumented immigrants. I also wrote an article about Senator Mel Martinez of Florida, then the chairman of the Republican National Committee, who was defending his party's stance toward Latinos after only one Republican presidential candidate—John McCain, the co-author of a failed immigration bill—agreed to participate in a debate sponsored by Univision, the Spanish-language network.

It was an odd sort of dance: I was trying to stand out in a highly competitive newsroom, yet I was terrified that if I stood out too much, I'd invite unwanted scrutiny. I tried to compartmentalize my fears, distract myself by reporting on the lives of other people, but there was no escaping the central conflict in my life. Maintaining a deception for so long distorts your sense of self. You start wondering who you've become, and why.

In April 2008, I was part of a Post team that won a Pulitzer Prize for the paper's coverage of the Virginia Tech shootings a year earlier. Lolo died a year earlier, so it was Lola who called me the day of the announcement. The first thing she said was, "*Anong mangyayari kung malaman ng mga tao?*"

What will happen if people find out?

I couldn't say anything. After we got off the phone, I rushed to the bathroom on the fourth floor of the newsroom, sat down on the toilet and cried.

~

In the summer of 2009, without ever having had that follow-up talk with top Post management, I left the paper and moved to New York to join The Huffington Post. I met Arianna Huffington at a Washington Press Club

Foundation dinner I was covering for The Post two years earlier, and she later recruited me to join her news site. I wanted to learn more about Web publishing, and I thought the new job would provide a useful education.

Still, I was apprehensive about the move: many companies were already using E-Verify, a program set up by the Department of Homeland Security that checks if prospective employees are eligible to work, and I didn't know if my new employer was among them. But I'd been able to get jobs in other newsrooms, I figured, so I filled out the paperwork as usual and succeeded in landing on the payroll.

While I worked at The Huffington Post, other opportunities emerged. My H.I.V./AIDS series became a documentary film called "The Other City," which opened at the Tribeca Film Festival last year and was broadcast on Showtime. I began writing for magazines and landed a dream assignment: profiling Facebook's Mark Zuckerberg for The New Yorker.

The more I achieved, the more scared and depressed I became. I was proud of my work, but there was always a cloud hanging over it, over me. My old eight-year deadline—the expiration of my Oregon driver's license—was approaching.

After slightly less than a year, I decided to leave The Huffington Post. In part, this was because I wanted to promote the documentary and write a book about online culture—or so I told my friends. But the real reason was, after so many years of trying to be a part of the system, of focusing all my energy on my professional life, I learned that no amount of professional success would solve my problem or ease the sense of loss and displacement I felt. I lied to a friend about why I couldn't take a weekend trip to Mexico. Another time I concocted an excuse for why I couldn't go on an all-expenses-paid trip to Switzerland. I have been unwilling, for years, to be in a long-term relationship because I never wanted anyone to get too close and ask too many questions. All the while, Lola's question was stuck in my head: What will happen if people find out?

Early this year, just two weeks before my 30th birthday, I won a small reprieve: I obtained a driver's license in the state of Washington. The license is valid until 2016. This offered me five more years of acceptable identification—but also five more years of fear, of lying to people I respect and institutions that trusted me, of running away from who I am.

I'm done running. I'm exhausted. I don't want that life anymore.

So I've decided to come forward, own up to what I've done, and tell my story to the best of my recollection. I've reached out to former bosses and employers and apologized for misleading them—a mix of humiliation and liberation coming with each disclosure. All the people mentioned in this article gave me permission to use their names. I've also talked to family and friends about my situation and am working with legal counsel to review my options. I don't know what the consequences will be of telling my story.

I do know that I am grateful to my grandparents, my Lolo and Lola, for giving me the chance for a better life. I'm also grateful to my other family—the support network I found here in America—for encouraging me to pursue my dreams.

It's been almost 18 years since I've seen my mother. Early on, I was mad at her for putting me in this position, and then mad at myself for being angry and ungrateful. By the time I got to college, we rarely spoke by phone. It became too painful; after a while it was easier to just send money to help support her and my two half-siblings. My sister, almost 2 years old when I left, is almost 20 now. I've never met my 14-year-old brother. I would love to see them.

Not long ago, I called my mother. I wanted to fill the gaps in my memory about that August morning so many years ago. We had never discussed it. Part of me wanted to shove the memory aside, but to write this article and face the facts of my life, I needed more details. Did I cry? Did she? Did we kiss goodbye?

My mother told me I was excited about meeting a stewardess, about getting on a plane. She also reminded me of the one piece of advice she gave me for blending in: If anyone asked why I was coming to America, I should say I was going to Disneyland.

How to Make a Slave

JERALD WALKER

"How to Make a Slave" puts the reader in the shoes of a African American man confronting his blackness over the course of his life. The stylistic choices of this text require the reader to consider the perspective of a man who confronts race and its effects on his relationships and life choices. This piece was published in the Southern Humanities Review *and was reprinted in* The Best American Essays 2014. *Jerald Walker is a widely published author and works as an Associate Professor in the Department of Writing, Literature, and Publishing at Emerson College.*

Gather, scissors, construction paper, crayons, popsicle sticks, and glue. Take them to the den, where your thirteen-year-old sister sits at the table thumbing through your schoolbook on black history. Smile when she notices you and turns to the pre-marked page with a photo of Frederick Douglass. It's one from his later years, when his Afro was white. Realize you need cotton balls. Leave and return with them a moment later to see that your sister has already cut from the construction paper a circle that will serve as Douglass's head. Start gluing popsicle sticks together to make his body. As you work silently, your sister tells you basic facts about slavery and abolition that you will present to your class. You'll end the presentation by saying with passion that Frederick Douglass is your hero, which will not be true because you are only ten and the things you are learning about black history make it difficult to feel good about his life, and sometimes yours.

But feel good about the beating he gave his master. Your classmates feel good about it too. They cheer when you describe it, as they cheered seconds earlier when you recited Douglass's famous line: *You have seen how a man was made a slave; you shall see how a slave was made a man.* "I wouldn't have taken that stuff either," one of your classmates says after school. Forget his name in a few years but remember his skin was so dark that you and your friends had no choice but to call him Congo. Congo explains how he would have gouged out his master's eyes, and then other boys break their masters' legs and amputate their arms, and when someone curls his fingers into a claw and twists off his master's balls everyone cups his crotch in agony before laughing. Enjoy how wonderful it feels to laugh at that moment, and as you walk home, with Douglass staring somberly out of your back pocket, wish black history had some funny parts.

Find a funny part. One has been captured on an FBI wiretap of Martin Luther King, Jr., in which he's in a hotel having sex and at the right moment yells, "I'm fucking for God!" The funniness is not immediately apparent, though, because you are twenty-five now and King is your hero and the woman with whom he is performing God's work is not his wife. Wonder with indignation how he could do such a thing, but while smoking the second of three bongs come to terms with the complexity of humankind and the idea of moral subjectivism. Now it is clear that the important thing here is not the messenger but rather the message. It is also clear that the message bears repeating.

After you repeat it, your girlfriend looks confused. She opens her mouth as if to respond but all she does is stare up at you, not even blinking when a bead of sweat falls from your forehead onto hers. Try to explain that you are only quoting some black history but be overtaken by the giggles and conclude that this is a conversation for a different time, when you have not smoked three bongs and are not doing God's work. And maybe it is a conversation for a different person too, because this one is white and does not like to talk about race. She does not even *see* race, she has said, having taught herself to judge individuals solely by their character and deeds. She is postracial, the first postracial person you have ever known, but because the term has not yet been invented you just think she's stupid. And because you are the first person she has ever known who has taught himself to see race in everything, she thinks you are stupid too. In time, you both seek and find smarter companions.

Yours, like Frederick Douglass, is, to use a phrase from that earlier era, a mulatto. This appeals to you a great deal because you know mulattos give race a lot of thought, and so this girlfriend probably will not mind helping you see it in places you might have missed. And maybe she can understand it in ways you cannot, since her perspective was not shaped by a stereotypical ghetto experience, like yours, but by a stereotypical suburban experience, like the Fonz's.

"It wasn't quite like his," she says.

The schools she attended were excellent; her neighborhood was safe; the parks and streets were pristine; racial diversity was negligible; the community had its own Fourth of July parade. As you remind her of these facts, sense her getting uptight, and diffuse her discomfort with a wide grin and a bad joke, something along the lines of her only run-in with the police being with an officer named Friendly.

She nearly smiles.

Give her two thumbs up at the hip and say, "Aeyyyyyyy!"

She does smile as she calls you a moron. "But seriously," she continues, and do not interrupt when she relates some of the challenges she faced as one of the few black kids in high school. You have been disappointed by how little she talks about race, to say nothing of her inability to see it everywhere, so her self-pity is a rare treat. Nod sympathetically when she broadens her grievances to include her family; the stares and snickers her parents faced in restaurants; how her brother was routinely followed by mall security; how her sister had trouble getting a date for the prom. Say that while these are excellent blemishes on her community, they are relatively benign. Some people, like you, for instance, lived in communities with drugs, gangs, crime, bad schools, police brutality, and the collective view that white people were and would always be racists. Let the conversation end as she concedes that, should you have children, her stereotype is preferable to yours.

Have children, two boys, two years apart, and decide that neither stereotype will do. The ghetto was never an option, but do not be thrilled about raising your sons to be Fonzies. Want a racially diverse, progressive, urban community, but instead move to one that is 96 percent white, conservative, and rural. It is in a college town near Boston where you and your wife land professorships, the primary appeal being that your house is only a block from campus. It is also, the realtor tells you, on the parade route. Buy four lawn chairs. Sit in one next to your wife and sons on the Fourth of July and wave American flags at the procession. Enjoy this. Your boys are happy.

Later that evening, wrestle with this question: How long will your boys be happy in a 96 percent white, conservative, rural town near Boston?

The answer for your older son, now five, is sixty-eight more days.

That is when you come home from teaching one afternoon and your wife informs you that one of his classmates told him that people with his skin color are stinky. Your son reported this incident while crying, but that night he appears to be fine, based on your observations of him, conducted from his bedroom closet. For the twenty minutes you have been in there, he and his little brother have lain in their adjacent beds chatting about cartoon characters and imaginary friends and a new fire truck they wish to own. When they finally fall asleep you sneak out and report the good news to your wife, though you caution that more observations will be necessary. In the meantime, you say, that classmate of his should be disciplined. Curl your fingers into a claw and tell your wife you are twisting off his tiny, five-year-old balls.

"First of all," your wife responds, "the person who said it is a girl. Second, let's not make a big deal out of this. I've already told him that she was just being silly. I'm sure he's already forgotten the whole incident."

Dispute this. Tell her that kids remember these sorts of things, sometimes for decades. Tell her about Congo. Imagine Congo's father learning of his son's nickname and later that night hiding in his closet, watching to see if he cries.

A few weeks pass and your son has not cried again. Decrease but do not suspend the observations. Remain on edge, as there are many kids out there who at any moment could say something potentially harmful with long-term consequences.

This is exactly what happens. And this time the culprit is your older son's little brother. He recently started preschool and has noticed that his skin color more closely resembles the other kids' than his brother's, and that his brother's skin color more closely resembles yours than your wife's, and that your wife's skin color is closer in resemblance to his than to his grandmother's, and that his grandmother's skin color is exactly the same as that of the kids in preschool, except for the brown spots on her hands. He turns to his six-year-old brother and asks, "Why is skin different colors?"

A beat passes before your older son responds, "I don't know."

Wonder if this is the moment to have your first important discussion with your sons about race. You can do it by revisiting that "stinky" comment, for starters, and then by warning them of other insults they'll likely receive, though be sure to note that insults, relatively speaking, are not much compared to what they'll learn studying a history that is not very funny. Determine that yes, the time for this talk has come, and then watch it evaporate when your sons scream bloody murder as you emerge—perhaps too quickly—from their closet. Fail at your attempts to calm them before your wife hurries into their room and catches the full rush of their bodies. She sits with them on the bed as they wail through tears that you frightened them. Your wife gives you a look that foretells a coming drought of affection, and your boys give you looks that make you seriously wonder if you have the capacity to be a good father. Conclude that you probably do not, but decide to give yourself a fighting chance by ending your subjection to race. Tonight the boys will sleep with their mother, and you will sleep alone in their room, but tomorrow evening, while the boys are in the den playing with their new fire truck, find your wife. She will be sitting at the kitchen table grading papers. Scoop her a dish of mint ice cream. Lower yourself across from her. Stare into her eyes and say this: *You have seen how a man was made a slave; you shall see how a slave was made a man.* She will look confused. Explain.

Can You Picture This?
Activism, Art, and Public Scholarship

RACHEL MARIE-CRANE WILLIAMS

In this research-based, autobiographical graphic essay, Rachel Marie-Crane Williams reflects on her work as a writer in various contexts: what does it mean to write for an academic audience when you are trying to enact "real" social change? Is it possible for a writer to reach across the perceived boundaries between "academic" and "activist?" As Williams struggles to present years of research in an effective (if non-traditional) manner, her piece not only calls attention to the injustices present in the U.S. prison system but also to the social act of writing and the conventions of various publication contexts.

can I combine activism, scholarship, and art making in a way that "contribute(s) to the public good and yield(s) artifacts of public and intellectual value" (Ellison &Eatman, 2008)?

Since 1995, I have worked as an artist and scholar in women's prisons. I can't imagine not doing this work. Until recently, I never made artwork that was about my experiences inside the prison walls. I reserved those experiences for my writing as a scholar. But I have always found the impact of scholarly publications to be frustrating. The number of people that read scholarly publications is limited mostly to people who hold positions in academia similar to mine. While they might find my research interesting or informative, rarely does it seem to change the way they perceive the world. Years ago, I came to a point where showing my artwork in galleries and museums was not particularly gratifying. People often experience art as precious, off limits, or removed a few degrees from the "nitty gritty" of everyday life. It might be beautiful or inspiring but rarely are people actually moved beyond the moment of contemplation.

My life in academia was filled with clouds of doubt--

well… that's a little dramatic-- but I did lose sleep over how to satisfy the requirements of my job at a research university, make art, and make a worthwhile contribution that might bring about a change in the prison system and the public's perception of people who are incarcerated.

Through the stories I create I try to offer the reader insight into the prison system, and the lives of women who are incarcerated. In the work I always try to make my position plainly visible.

comics are more than stories; this way of presenting experiences also allows me to succinctly share the sounds, sights, and even smells of prison, as well as the conversations and body language.

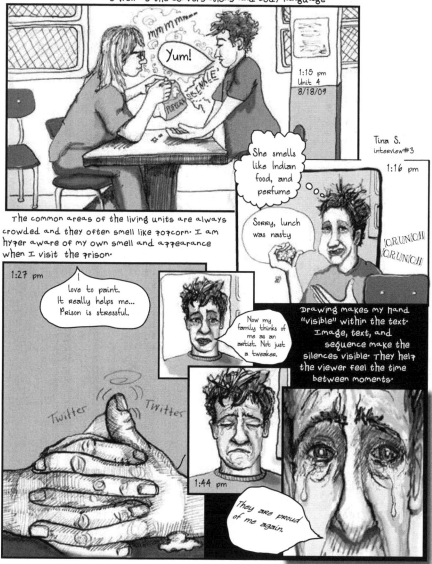

The common areas of the living units are always crowded and they often smell like popcorn. I am hyper aware of my own smell and appearance when I visit the prison.

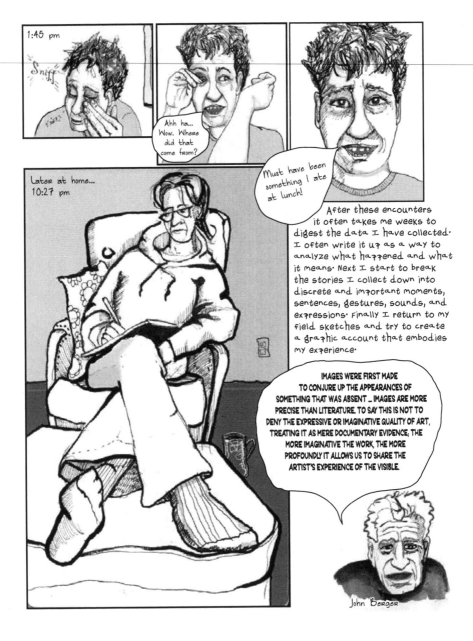

Comics offer so many opportunities to make visible nuances that would be difficult and perhaps less powerful if they were represented by words alone.

Trying to be a facilitator, artist, abolitionist, activist, and scholar in prisons has always been a delicate balancing act between satisfying my academic institution, working to shed a critical light on a system that is terribly flawed, and maintaining a strong relationship with the institution and the women. My ability to go inside the prison depends on trust and institutional support from my university and the prison.

One wrong step... think... balance... breathe

Oh crap!

It is like inching across a tightrope sometimes I waiver, but then I breathe and remind myself to keep trying to slowly and carefully put one foot in front of the other.

People who are incarcerated need people from the outside to bear witness to their struggles, remorse, and endless punishment through our justice and social system. "What is just? What is justice?" What does the spectrum between vengeance and forgiveness look like? All of these things are worthwhile ···I guess I better keep my pencils sharp for the time being· Hmmm··· I wonder if the IRB will ever return my phone calls about comics and research?

*a special thanks to Lois Ahrens, Jefri Palermo, Sean, Jack, and Rylie Kelley, Lori Pompa and the Inside out program, Linda Haack, the women at ICIW, and students and faculty in GWSS and Art·

References

Berger, John· (1972)· Ways of Seeing· London: Penguin Books (p·10)·

Eisner, Elliot· (2008)· Art and Knowledge· In J· Gary Knowles and Andra L· Cole Eds· Handbook of the Arts in Qualitative Research· Los Angeles, CA: Sage, (pp· 3–12)·

Ellison, Julie & Eatman, Timothy· (2008)· Scholarship in public: knowledge creation and tenure policy in the engaged university· www·imaginingamerica·org/TTI/TTI_FINAL·pdf· Syracuse, NY: Imagining America· http://www · · ·"

Fonow, Mary Margaret, and Judith A· Cook· (1991a)· Back to the Future· In Fonow and Cook 1991a, 35–59·

Greene, Maxine (2010)· Prologue· Journal of Educational Controversy [Art, social imagination, democratic education: Dedicated to Maxine Greene· (v·5) (1) (Winter)· http://www·wce·wwu· edu/Resources/CEP/eJournal/v005n001/·

Rachel Marie-Crane Williams
rachel-williams@uiowa·edu

416 JB
Gender Women's and Sexuality Studies/ Media Social Practice and Design
University of Iowa
Iowa City, IA
52242

"Is Your Underwear Flame Retardant?": Sexuality and Sports

DAVE ZIRIN

Examining everything from a Super Bowl coin toss to the history of organized sports in the United States, Dave Zirin explores how ideas about gender and sexuality constrain professional athletes—and our perceptions of them. Zirin, who writes about the politics of sports for The Nation, *crafts a nuanced argument using multiple sources, historical research, and sometimes humorous prose. "'Is Your Underwear Flame Retardant?': Sexuality and Sports" appeared in* Game Over: How Politics Has Turned the Sports World Upside Down, *a 2013 essay collection drawing on Zirin's writing for* The Nation, The Progressive, SLAM Magazine, *and sportsillustrated.com.*

Over the last two years a very youthful, very grassroots women's movement has erupted, going by the name of SlutWalk. It began in January 2011 after a Toronto police officer told students at a campus safety information session at York University, "Women should avoid dressing like sluts in order not to be victimized." The message was that women bring sexual assault on themselves by the way they act or dress. It is a message repeated to women their entire lives, and the response in this particular case was, "Hell no." A march was called. Posters were put up around campus that listed York University "don'ts"—including entries like "Don't go to pub night" and "Don't worry your pretty little head. Don't think too much. Don't get mad and definitely... Don't organize!" They couldn't have known, but they had just started a new movement.[1]

In boisterous demonstrations around the country—and the world—SlutWalk has aimed to smash the age-old idea that women cannot be three-dimensional, sexual human beings. It's a movement against objectification and degradation. It's a movement that calls for a loud rejection of sexist stereotypes and demands sexual freedom for all women. It's a movement against men setting the terms for how women see their bodies, their minds, and their potential. And it's a movement that is very much needed in the world of sports. Look no further than two of the most high-profile female athletes in the country: Danica Patrick and Candace Parker.

In 2008, Danica Patrick accomplished two firsts: she became both the first woman to win an Indy car race and the first race car driver to appear in the men's magazine *FHM*. In *FHM*, Patrick was clad in red leather underwear, with her legs spread on the hood of a car. The pictures were accompanied by a short interview where Patrick answered questions like "Is your underwear flame retardant?" and "Are there times of the month when you are a more aggressive or angry driver?"[2]

Candace Parker also has a cover to her name—one that couldn't contrast more sharply with Patrick's. Parker is arguably the greatest women's basketball player in the world. She will dunk on your head. She also spent a good part of 2009 pregnant. *ESPN The Magazine* put Parker on their cover in glowing maternal white, cradling her belly. The article opens with lavish praise: "Candace Parker is beautiful. Breathtaking, really, with flawless skin, endless legs and a C cup.... She is a woman who plays like a man, one of the boys, if the boys had C cups and flawless skin and perfect, white teeth." The article then brings Danica Patrick into the discussion, noting that "Patrick is nowhere near the best in her field, but she doesn't need to be, because she is hot enough to pose for Maxim. While that works for her, Parker wants more."[3]

First of all, one can only imagine how people would respond to an article about Denver Broncos quarterback Peyton Manning that started, "Peyton Manning is handsome. Breathtaking, really, with flawless skin, endless legs and a medium jock strap he shows off at every turn."

Comparisons aside, though, the entire Danica Patrick–and–Candace Parker dynamic here is frustrating, angering, even infuriating. Most of all, it is very tired. Women athletes have been trapped in the same box for a century. This trap dictates that women must be girls first, athletes second. And, most critically, women athletes must shout at the tops of their lungs that they are absolutely hetero, so straight that their dreams include having pregnant bellies or being on a magazine passed around a frat house.

Mary Jo Kane, a sociologist from the University of Minnesota who specializes in gender and sports, undertook a far-reaching study to understand the effect of sexualizing women athletes. When Kane and her research team showed images of female athletes displaying their bodies to a diverse focus group of both men and women, they found a very basic truth: sex may sell magazines, but it doesn't sell women's sports. As Kane said to me in an interview, "It alienates the core of the fan base that's already there. Women...eighteen to thirty-four and thirty-five to fifty-five are offended by these images. And older males, fathers with daughters, taking their daughters to sporting events to see their favorite female athletes, are deeply offended by these images." As for the young men excited to see Danica Patrick in leather, spread out on a car, "they want to buy the magazines but they didn't want to consume the sports."

This ought to be an earth-shaking revelation for every executive in the Women's Tennis Association, the WNBA, and the LPGA, who have for decades operated under the assumption that a little leg goes a long way. But women's sports, Kane argues, will need more than logic to move away from the abyss of abject objectification: "This is deeper. This is also about what runs in the bone marrow of women's sports, namely homophobia." In other words, sports leagues take as a given that people see women athletes as some 1970s stereotype of a "butch lesbian," so they try to push women athletes about as far from that as possible. If that takes a thong, then so be it.

But to what extent are female athletes themselves at fault? What about those who say that provocative poses are about celebrating their bodies, and that celebration of the "body beautiful" has been a part of sports since ancient Greece? Kane answers, "What muscle group do bare breasts belong to? You can show off your body without being naked in a passive, sexually provocative pose."

This question of breasts as a "muscle group" is about more than whether women's sports is taking itself seriously. It points to whether universities, boosters, and donors take it seriously, as well. And it is, Kane believes, about the future of college athletics, because "the end result of this is that when resources are precious, and you dole out those resources, and you don't take women's athletics as seriously as men's, then there are tangible consequences. Athletic directors get a pass to just not take it seriously."

The Vise

The vise for women athletes is always and forever present: sexism on one side, homophobia on the other. This vise is what crushed an eighteen-year-old South African runner by the name of Caster Semenya.

Caster set a world record in the eight-hundred-meter sprint at the 2009 African Junior Championships. She should be training for the Olympics; instead she spent time on suicide watch. This has everything to do with the twisted way track and field—and the sports world at large—understands gender.

The more Caster won, the more she shaved seconds off her personal bests, the more her drug tests came back negative, the more her competitors whispered:

Her muscles don't look like a woman's. Her hips don't look like a woman's. Her voice doesn't sound like a woman's. She's too fast! Too good! In the culture of women's track and field, there could only be one conclusion: someone this good must be "part man."

The rumors spread, pressure mounted, and international track and field officials proceeded to subject Caster to "gender testing," which included invasive examinations of the eighteen-year-old by a gynecologist, an endocrinologist, and a psychologist. Then, the humiliation: test results were leaked to the press, claiming to show that she has internal testes and no womb or ovaries. (It should be noted that the actual, official test results have never been made public and were deemed confidential.)[4]

It's possible that Caster Semenya is one of the millions of people in the world (one of 1,666 births per year in the United States alone) who are classified as "intersex."[5] Or she may have AIS, androgen insensitivity syndrome, which affects as many as five out of one hundred thousand births.[6] Whatever Caster Semenya's biological makeup, it should be a private issue between her and her doctor—and it certainly shouldn't prevent her from competing or be grounds for derision. Instead, Semenya became a punch line. A news segment about her on MSNBC was preceded by the Aerosmith song "Dude Looks Like a Lady."

What these officials still don't understand, or confront, is that gender—that is, how we comport and conceive of ourselves—is a remarkably fluid social construction. Even our physical sex is far more ambiguous than is often imagined or taught. Medical science has long acknowledged the existence of millions of people whose bodies combine anatomical features that are conventionally associated with either men or women and/or have chromosomal variations of XX or XY. Many of these "intersex" individuals are legally operated on by surgeons who force traditional norms of genitalia onto newborn infants. In what some doctors consider a "psychosocial emergency," thousands of healthy babies are effectively subject to clitoridectomy if a clitoris is "too large" or castration if a penis is "too small" (evidently penises are never considered "too big").[7]

Track and field has had a particular preoccupation with gender, especially when it intersects with race. Fifty years ago, Olympic official Norman Cox proposed that the International Olympic Committee create a separate category of competition for black women, "the unfairly advantaged 'hermaphrodites.'" For years, women athletes had to parade naked in front of Olympic officials for inspection. This gave way to more "sophisticated gender testing" to determine if athletes have what officials still perceive as the ultimate advantage: being a man.

Let's leave aside that being male is not the be-all, end-all of athletic success; wealth, coaching facilities, nutrition, and opportunity determine the development of a world-class athlete far more than a Y chromosome ever could. Essentially, the physical reality of intersex people calls into question fixed notions we are taught to accept about men and women in general, and athletes in sex-segregated sports like track and field in particular. While we are never encouraged to conceive of biology in this way, male and female bodies are more similar than they are distinguishable from each other. And when training and nutrition are equal, it is increasingly difficult to tell the difference (picture, for example, the top male and female Olympic swimmers wearing state-of-the-art one-piece speed suits). Title IX, the 1972 law that imposed equal funding for girls' and boys' sports in schools, has radically altered not only women's fitness and emotional well-being but their bodies as well.

In the Caster Semenya case, there are important questions few in the sports media dared ask. Why should it matter if she is maxing out her every biological advantage? No one claims that basketball star Yao Ming had an unfair advantage because he is seven foot five. No one asked if swimmer Michael Phelps's mammoth, flipper-like feet unfairly skewed the competition. If anything, he was praised for being, as one announcer said breathlessly, "built to swim!" Why isn't Caster Semenya, with her slender hips and powerful muscles, "built to run"? If Semenya's biology is not "normal," it's worth asking, what world-class athlete does have a normal body? As Tommy Craggs of Deadspin wrote,

> Great athletes tend not to come from the vast middle of human life. They're all freaks in one way or another.... But Semenya has nevertheless been portrayed as some lone oddity on the margins, like some Elephant Man of sports, with everyone obsessing like Victorian scientists over the presence of a couple internal testicles. It's funny: People seem to think her very weirdness is grounds enough for stripping her of her medal and drumming her out of track. But this is sports. Her weirdness is perfectly normal.[8]

Clearly, it's the "her" that gets Semenya in trouble. Exceptional male athletes are treated like kings, not sideshow freaks. But for women to join them on the royal dais, they must appear as if they can step seamlessly from the court or track and into the pages of soft-core porn. Freaks need not apply.

The Western media's handling of the Caster Semenya story was at best simplistic and at worst repellent. On various radio shows, it was asked, "Why does she talk like a man?" and "Do you think she's really a dude? Is this a *Crying Game* thing?" Most of these questions reveal more about the questioners' insecurities than about Semenya's situation. The derision was not limited to the confines of sports radio. I appeared on Campbell Brown's now-defunct CNN show, where my co-panelist, Dr. Jennifer Berman, said that suspicion of Semenya's gender was justified because she is "eight feet tall." Caster is five foot seven—and this is hysteria, pure and simple, born out of people's own discomfort with women athletes who don't conform to gender stereotypes.

In South Africa, however, the response could not have been more different. Semenya was greeted by thousands of people in a celebration that included signs and songs from the antiapartheid struggle. She was even embraced by former South African first lady Winnie Mandela. "We are here to tell the whole world how proud we are of our little girl," Mandela told cheering fans. "They can write what they like—we are proud of her."[9]

As Patrick Bond, a leading South African global justice activist, said to me,

To order Semenya tested for gender seems about as reasonable as ordering International Association of Athletics Federations officials like Philip Weiss tested for brain cells—which actually isn't a bad idea given his recent off-field performance. And if Weiss doesn't have a sufficient number of brain cells to know how to treat women athletes, it would only be fair to relieve him of his functions for the good of world athletics.

It's not just national political figures with global profiles who are embracing Semenya. The people have rallied around her fiercely; particularly in the rural, impoverished, subsistence-farming community where Semenya was raised. Her home village, Ga-Masehlong, has an unemployment rate near 80 percent; they only recently acquired electricity. As *The Guardian* wrote:

The loyalty of Semenya's friends and neighbours is striking. South Africa's rural communities are typically regarded as bastions of social conservatism divided into traditional gender roles and expectations of femininity. But there is no evidence that Semenya, an androgynous tomboy who played football and wore trousers, was ostracised by her peers. Instead, they are shocked at what they perceive as the intolerance and prurience of western commentators.

"They are jealous," said Dorcus Semenya, the athlete's mother, who led villagers in jubilant singing and dancing upon Caster's return. "I say to them, go to hell, you don't know what you're saying. They're jealous because they don't want black people improving their status."[10]

It perhaps shouldn't be so surprising that Caster's neighbors recognize the West's "intolerance and prurience." Unlike the United States, South Africa has legalized same-sex marriage, and unlike the United States, South Africa legally prohibits discrimination based on sexuality. By no means is South Africa some sort of LGBT Shangri-la. But this does suggest that the United States could stand to learn a thing or two about discrimination and human sexuality.

There is currently no definitive information regarding Semenya's sexual orientation or gender choice. We should use this opportunity to continue debating the pros and cons of gender segregation in sports, but we must abandon the ludicrous terms that have so far framed this case for a conversation that acknowledges the fluidity of gender in sports and beyond. At this point, all we know for sure is that Semenya identifies herself as an eighteen-year-old woman and that she can run like the wind.

What is the solution, then, for how the International Olympic Committee should deal with this? Scholars Rebecca Jordan-Young and Katrina Karzakis laid out a lucid plan in the *New York Times*. As they wrote:

> First, at the very least, female athletes should be allowed to compete throughout any investigation. Suspending them from competition once questions are raised violates their confidentiality and imposes sanctions before relevant information has been gathered.

> Second, when it comes to sex, sports authorities should acknowledge that while science can offer evidence, it cannot dictate what evidence we should use....

> Testosterone is one of the most slippery markers that sports authorities have come up with yet. Yes, average testosterone levels are markedly different for men and women. But levels vary widely depending on time of day, time of life, social status and—crucially—one's history of athletic training....

> Third, if we want a clear answer to who is eligible for women's competitions, it is time to stop pawning this fundamentally social question off onto scientists....

> Fourth, any policies must be developed through a transparent process with broad input....

Finally, the I.O.C. and other sports governing bodies should denounce gender bashing among athletes, coaches, the news media and fans. Policing women's testosterone would exacerbate one of the ugliest tendencies in women's sports today: the name-calling and the insinuations that an athlete is "too masculine," or worse, that she is a man.[11]

Unfortunately for women athletes, you can't be too tough for fear you'll be called a lesbian. You can't be too aggressive for fear that you will be called mannish. You must be an outdated stereotype of a woman before you are an athlete. These suffocating norms have held for more than a century.

The Babe

Mildred Ella "Babe" Didrikson was the most famous female athlete of the first half of the twentieth century. She won three medals in track and field in the 1932 Olympics and later became the standard for all women golfers. Yet despite her towering athletic accomplishments, Didrikson was denounced as "mannish" and "not-quite female," a "Muscle Moll" who could not "compete with other girls in the very ancient and time honored sport of mantrapping."[12]

Hearing that, in addition to track and field, she also played basketball, football, and numerous other sports, an astonished journalist once asked Didrikson, "Is there anything you don't play?" Without missing a beat, she reportedly answered, "Yeah, dolls."[13]

Didrikson then disappeared and returned in the 1950s, donning long hair, wearing a ton of makeup, and playing golf, which was considered a woman's sport. She also resurfaced married to a mammoth pro wrestler named George Zaharias. Sportswriters loved it, gleefully writing, "Along came a great big he-man and the Babe forgot all her man-hating chatter." One headline read, "Babe Is a Lady Now: The World's Most Amazing Athlete Has Learned to Wear Nylons and Cook for Her Huge Husband."

Why have we covered such a short distance over so many years? Why is there so much sexism and homophobia in sports, even in the twenty-first century? The reasons derive from the ways that formal sports—as apart from informal play—were first promoted in the United States.

Organized sports did not emerge in this country until the end of the nineteenth century. At that time, most women were denied participation, which also meant they were denied access to exercise, a unique form of camaraderie, and the mental training believed necessary to lead the much-heralded New American Century.

In the early 1900s, some wealthy women started to gain access to the country club sports of golf and tennis—but these offered no refuge. Tennis, in particular, was more pain than pleasure. At the time, women were forced to play in corsets so constricting that they would cause the wearers to pass out.

When early women's rights activists began to demand equal access to sports, a cottage industry of quack science developed explaining how sports would cause infertility, nymphomania, everything short of growing a tail. One writer in an 1878 edition of the *American Christian Review* diagrammed the twelve-step downfall of any woman who dared engage in the sinful world of croquet. It is truly a slippery slope:

1. Social party.
2. Social and play party.
3. Croquet party.
4. Picnic and croquet party.
5. Picnic, croquet and dance.
6. Absence from church.
7. Immoral conduct.
8. Exclusion from the church.
9. A runaway match [more croquet].
10. Poverty.
11. Shame and disgrace.
12. Ruin.

The age of the whalebone corset started to crack in part due to the invention of the bicycle. Alarmed, the science community rose up again, proving conclusively that riding a bicycle could implode the uterus. Doctors also claimed that women would be susceptible to what they called the "bicycle face," a condition where excessive riding would leave a permanent scowl consisting of a "protruding jaw, wild staring eyes, and strained expression."[14]

For women activists, access to physical play came to symbolize their very liberation. Pioneering feminist Elizabeth Cady Stanton, in a piece for the women's magazine *The Lily* wholeheartedly rejected claims of a man's "physical superiority," writing, "We cannot say what the woman might be physically, if the girl were allowed all the freedom of the boy, in romping, swimming, climbing, or playing ball." Cady Stanton's argument—that nurture, not nature, determines a man's physical and sporting superiority—was a gutsy one. But it was an argument she and other activists lost: by the 1900s, women had narrowly won the right to play, but in separate and unequal facilities.

Indeed, the first generation of women's gym teachers claimed that sports had to be segregated by gender because only under their watchful eyes could women be prevented from "loss of sexual control" and "emotional stimulation." These teachers were also positioned as the guardians against the dangers of lesbianism as an outgrowth of play. As Susan K. Cahn wrote in *Coming On Strong*, one PE director promised that women's sports would not create "the loud masculinely dressed man-aping individual but the whole hearted rosy cheeked healthy girl."[15]

Yet in these early days, every time a woman showed that she could compete, she excelled. In 1922, Sybil Bauer set the world record in the backstroke, beating the men's record. Then Gertrude Ederle swam the English Channel two hours faster than any man. When Ederle set that record, newspapers said with great trepidation that it was "a battle won for feminism."[16]

But as new sports opened up to women, old stereotypes held them back. The Amateur Athletic Union would integrate beauty pageants into the big athletic tourneys. It was common for PE programs to require that PE majors "have or possess the possibilities of an attractive personal appearance."[17]

This backlash—and the country—got turned on its head during World War II. Just as Rosie the Riveter symbolized a massive shift in the area of work, the All-American Girls Professional Baseball League (AAGPBL) became a symbol of transformation in the world of sports. The league, immortalized in the movie *A League of Their Own*, popularized women's professional baseball in many parts of the country from 1943 to 1955.

There was much to celebrate in the AAGPBL—the fact that women were playing hardball and not softball, the high level of play, and the support it received (at its height, the league drew one million fans in a year). But the players had to wear skirts and follow what management called a "femininity principle," which meant makeup, long hair, and a mandatory evening charm school. Any hint of lesbianism meant prompt dismissal; Josephine D'Angelo, for example, was released immediately after getting a bob haircut.[18]

The AAGPBL was taken apart after the end of the war, when the country set about ushering Rosie the Riveter out of the factory and back to the kitchen and making babies. June Cleaver was the new ideal, and women were whole only in the home. This era was also characterized by McCarthyite raids against LGBT people, mass firings of suspected homosexuals from government jobs, and attacks on gay bars. In turn, virulent homophobia assaulted women's sports in the 1950s, far more explicitly than in the past.

What had previously been coded as fear of the "mannish" athlete or queers now was naked homophobia. At the national 1956 conference of collegiate women physical educators, the guest speaker, Dr. Josephine Renshaw, gave a talk with the benign title of "Activities for Mature Living." The rant warned against the "muscular Amazon with unkempt hair, clod hopper shoes, and dowdy clothing who would become disappointed in heterosexual attachments and see women's sports in a predatory fashion."[19]

This was the terrain upon which women competed (or not) until the late 1960s, when a growing women's movement made demands for equality in society and the world of sports alike. This manifested itself most clearly in the passage of Title IX—the 1972 law stipulating that "no person in the United States shall, on the basis of sex, be excluded from participation in, be denied the benefits of, or be subjected to discrimination under any education program or activity receiving Federal financial assistance"—and the emergence of the great Billie Jean King.

The new movement roared to a big victory when Billie Jean King faced off against Bobby Riggs in their "Battle of the Sexes" tennis match, called by the London *Sunday Times* "the drop shot and volley heard around the world." Riggs, a 1939 Wimbledon champion, had already swept the court with women's champion Margaret Court on Mother's Day in 1973. King, who previously had rejected Riggs's dare to play, accepted his latest challenge. "I thought it would set us back 50 years if I didn't win that match," the twelve-time Grand Slam winner said. "It would ruin the women's tour and affect all women's self-esteem."[20]

The "Battle of the Sexes" captured the entire country's imagination. On September 20, 1973, in Houston, King was carried out on the Astrodome court like Cleopatra, in a gold throne held aloft by four muscular men dressed as ancient slaves. Riggs was wheeled in on a rickshaw pulled by models in tight outfits who were referred to as "Bobby's Bosom Buddies."

Their entrances turned out to be the most competitive part of the day, as King, then twenty-nine, ran Riggs ragged, winning 6–4, 6–3, 6–3. As Neil Amdur wrote in the *New York Times*, "Most important perhaps for women everywhere, she convinced skeptics that a female athlete can survive pressure-filled situations and that men are as susceptible to nerves as women." The great Frank Deford wrote in *Sports Illustrated*, "She has prominently affected the way 50 percent of society thinks and feels about itself in the vast area of physical exercise." He continued, "Moreover, like [Arnold] Palmer, she has made a whole sports boom because of the singular force of her presence."[21]

King was far more than an athlete or a symbol. She was an activist for women's equal rights. In the words of Navratilova, she "embodied the crusader fighting a battle for all of us. She was carrying the flag; it was all right to be a jock."[22] King, who had received $15,000 less than Ilie Nastase did for winning the U.S. Open in 1972, called for a strike by women's players if the prize money wasn't equal by the following year. In 1973, the U.S. Open became the first major tournament to offer an equal winner's purse for men and women. King also fought for a women's players' union and forged the Women's Tennis Association, which elected her its first president in 1973.

It was for her role in the movements of the day that *Life* magazine named her one of the "100 most important Americans of the 20th century." King was the only female athlete on the list, and one of only four athletes. Of the other three, two—Jackie Robinson and Muhammad Ali—are also strongly associated with social movements (Babe Ruth was the third).

As for Title IX, today one in three young girls plays sports; forty years ago, that number was one in thirty-four. Young women who play sports are less likely to suffer from osteoporosis, eating disorders, and depression, among other things. This law has improved the quality of life for tens of millions of women across the country.[23]

The LGBT Landscape

For pro women athletes, sports remains largely a place of denigration, not celebration. Swimsuit issues, cheerleaders, and beer-commercial sexism frame women all too narrowly in a testosterone-addled sports world. Unsurprisingly, homophobia is still a major issue. While some prominent women athletes, like the great basketball player Sheryl Swoopes, have come out of the closet, you can count the number on one hand.

The idea that athletes will routinely come out of the closet in the absence of a broader movement challenging homophobia is pure fantasy. This is why the few challenges to the homophobic status quo in sports must be highlighted and brought out of the "media closet." Take the case of Jen Harris. Jen was one of the leading scorers for the Penn State women's basketball team and a WNBA prospect. Then she was suddenly cut from the team. Jen is a lesbian. And her coach, Rene Portland, a two-time coach of the year whose nickname was "Mom," had three rules: no drugs, no drinking, and no lesbians. [24]

Jen refused to take it and sued for discrimination. Students rallied in support, and soon other Penn State players came forward, revealing a twenty-seven-year history of psychological abuse, humiliation, and discrimination. It's because of the Rene Portlands that Caster Semenya had to be put on suicide watch. It's because of the Rene Portlands that we need a movement for sexual liberation that frames access to athletics as a right and not a privilege. And it's because of brave athletes like Jen Harris that we have a road map of how to fight this level of discrimination in women's sports.

Now, what about the boys? I don't want to shock anybody, but being gay in a men's locker room is not exactly easy. It's difficult to imagine a more oppressive atmosphere. In the world of pro sports, antigay slurs can seem as ingrained as racism was fifty years ago. To be gay is to be weak. To be gay is to be vulnerable. To accept gay teammates is also to accept that all that butt slapping, roughhousing, and co-showering could have other meanings.

Beyond the slurs that have become part of their everyday slang ("That's a nice shirt...no homo"), athletes blithely get away with brazenly homophobic comments. Jeremy Shockey, the gimpy part-time Saints tight end (and full-time jackass), called Coach Bill Parcells a "homo" and said he "wouldn't stand" for a gay teammate. John Smoltz, the pitcher whose two favorite movies (seriously) are *The Passion of the Christ* and *Dumb and Dumber*, volunteered his views on gay marriage (he wasn't asked): "What's next? Marrying animals?"[25]

Players like Mets future Hall of Fame catcher Mike Piazza and Jeff Garcia have felt the need to hold press conferences just to tell the world that they are not gay. Then you have the Evangelical Christian organization Athletes in Action, with connections to groups that promote reparative therapy for gays and lesbians, that is a presence in many locker rooms.

As of today, no active player in the Big Three men's sports—baseball, basketball, and football—has come out of the closet. It's no wonder why, as players would risk financial, if not physical, ruin in doing so. This is why the athletes who have come out of the closet have left it until after they retired. Esera Tuaolo, Dave Kopay, and Ron Simmons of the NFL; John Amaechi of the NBA; and Billy Bean in Major League Baseball all took this route.

One important exception to this history can be found in the late Glenn Burke. While no male athlete in the United States has ever come out as an active player, we should remember Burke as a player who was out to his teammates, if not the public, thirty-five years ago. Burke is the answer to multiple trivia questions: Who was the only rookie to start in the 1977 World Series? Who invented the high five? And who was the first gay Major League baseball player—to our knowledge—to be out of the closet in the presence of his teammates, if not the fans? But Burke's story is as important as it is unknown. He was an Oakland legend, playing both baseball and hoops with pro potential. He was also a young man, growing up in the Bay Area, confident about his sexuality. That confidence, for anyone, was rare back then, but to find it in a male star athlete is remarkable. His confidence was put to the test when he made the big leagues. Dodgers teammates like Dusty Baker, Davey Lopes, Reggie Smith, Rick Monday, and Manny Mota tell the story of a player whose sexuality was noticed, recognized, and even accepted by some teammates but looked on with horror by management. After all, when you wear a red jockstrap in the locker room, people start to talk. The Dodgers organization even offered Burke $75,000 to get married, which is particularly gobsmacking.

Later, when Burke was traded to Oakland, the pressures intensified. Former teammate Claudell Washington tells this anecdote in the brilliant documentary *Out: The Glenn Burke Story*: "[A's manager Billy Martin] was introducing all the [new] players and then he got to Glenn and said, 'Oh, by the way, this is Glenn Burke and he's a faggot.'" By 1980, Burke was out of the game, but the story doesn't end there. *Out* then tells the story of Burke's life after baseball: triumphantly coming out to *Sport* magazine and Bryant Gumbel on the Today show, participating in the first Gay Games in 1982, and being a public figure in San Francisco. Burke's life then took a tragic turn as drugs, petty crime, and the AIDS epidemic claimed his life. He died in 1995 at the too-young age of forty-two.

The grand unanswered question in Burke's story is: how good could he have been without the relentless pressures of homophobia? To hear Dusty Baker tell it, he could have been one of the greats. Today there is a movement to enshrine Glenn Burke in the Baseball Hall of Fame and recognize him as the trailblazer he is. Given that baseball has the only Hall of Fame that explicitly says that they factor in off-field contributions, his enshrinement would be very appropriate.

But Burke's life raises another, very obvious question: why can the locker room be such an unforgiving place? There is a real material reason why men's sports is so homophobic. It's been built into organized sports in the United States from the very beginning. And to understand the roots of homophobia in sports, we have to know our history and look at the foundations of men's sports in our society.

After the Civil War, there was a period of rampant industrial development, expansion, and immigration. The numbers are staggering. From 1860 to 1900, the population of the United States grew from 31 to 75 million. Railroads were built that spanned the country. This was an era of booms for the new rich—robber barons like Rockefeller, Vanderbilt, and Carnegie—and busts for everyone else.[26]

In 1877, as the economy tanked, the reasons for unrest multiplied. Clearly, young immigrant boys needed to be given more than a sweatshop job or a street corner. Robber barons started to invest millions of dollars to make sure sports were an option for this potentially volatile population. They funded and launched the Young Men's Christian Association, or YMCA, about which one historian wrote, "The Y's gospel was play was no longer a sin but a way to glory God...and Jesus was now a stud."[27] By 1880, there were 261 Y's scattered across the U.S. Rockefeller, Carnegie, and Vanderbilt then took a step further and underwrote the first Public Schools Athletic League, which funded sports in urban schools for the first time.

But the sports explosion wasn't just about controlling immigrants and the poor. It was also about shaping young members of the elite class so they would be fit to rule. The robber barons understandably feared that their own pampered, privileged children would be completely unprepared to navigate the violent world they had helped to create. Their concern bordered on the hysterical. As Oliver Wendell Holmes wrote in the *Atlantic Monthly* in the mid-nineteenth century, "I am satisfied that such a set of black-coated, stiff-jointed, soft-muscled, paste-complexioned youth as we can boast in our Atlantic cities never before sprang from the loins of Anglo-Saxon lineage."[28] (I don't think anyone regrets that "sprang from the loins" has left the language.)

Sports were seen as the answer for these stiff-jointed folks, and a word was actually created for those who didn't like sports: "sissy." Elite schools such as Harvard, Yale, and Brown launched intercollegiate football, which came to resemble something out of *Braveheart*, with students literally dying on the field.

If we take a step back, we can discern why today's sports world can be so twisted about masculinity. The heart of the founding of modern athletics was economic elites sending their children to die in Ivy League football games merely because they were terrified that they wouldn't be tough enough to lead conquests abroad and industrial brutality at home. And failure to do so made you a "sissy."

This culture of death was proudly known as Muscular Christianity. Its most prominent spokesperson was an aristocratic boxer named Theodore Roosevelt. Railing repeatedly against sissies everywhere, Roosevelt saw tough athletic training as a way to build the basis for a new American Century.

This can all seem like macho idiocy—and some of it is. But it was not all machismo for machismo's sake. Ideas like Muscular Christianity were about preparing the United States for empire. During this period, the U.S. set out to invade the Philippines, Latin America, and the Caribbean; the value of sports was deeply tied to imperialist notions of conquest and missionary zeal. Albert Spalding (of Spalding sporting goods) spoke proudly about baseball as a kind of helping hand for U.S. empire, writing,

> Baseball has proudly "followed the flag.".... It has followed the flag to the Hawaiian Islands, and at once supplanted every other form of athletics. It has followed the flag to the Philippines, to Puerto Rico, and to Cuba, and wherever a ship floating the stars and stripes finds anchorage today, somewhere on a nearby shore the American national game is in progress.[29]

The U.S. athlete became the embodiment not only of manliness, but of something akin to Conan the Barbarian. It is partly for this reason that there is so much homophobia in sports: it has always been about selling a supremely militaristic, dominant image of the United States back to ourselves. After all, who tossed the coin at the 2009 Super Bowl? It wasn't John Elway or Joe Montana. It was General David Petraeus.

But this militarized, homophobic code of athletics has been challenged again and again.

Tom Waddell, a decathlete at the 1968 Olympics, came out of the closet, got political, and started what he first called the Gay Olympics in San Francisco in 1982. The idea was that they would be open to everyone, regardless of skill and, of course, sexual orientation. This was very daring, and it offended all the right people. The International Olympic Committee (IOC) and the United States Olympic Committee (USOC) sued Waddell and the other organizers to prevent them from using the word "Olympics." They would be the Gay Games. This was the first time the IOC had ever sued for the usage of a word that had been brandished by organizations ranging from the Special Olympics to the Nebraska Rat Olympics. But Waddell wouldn't quit. He also crafted a very different vision of what sports could be. In outlining his mission early in the process, Waddell said, "The Gay Games are not separatist, they are not exclusive, they are not oriented to victory, they are not for commercial gain. They're intended to bring a global community together in friendship, to elevate consciousness and self-esteem."[30]

The opening ceremonies at the first Gay Olympics were led not by a four-star general but by Tina Turner.

In 1986, even though the IOC held a lien on Tom Waddell's house as part of their lawsuits, the games went on as scheduled. They tripled in size, with three thousand athletes attending from eighteen countries to compete in seventeen different sports. There were three times as many women as men in the 1986 power-lifting events. And openly HIV-positive people competed, at a time when the disease was ignored by the Reagan administration and known in great swaths of the country as "the gay plague." Sean O'Neil, a tennis player from San Francisco, said, "I'm playing for all the other people with AIDS."[31]

The 1994 Gay Games IV were held in New York City, this time attracting more than eleven thousand participants in thirty-one events as the largest athletic competition in history. Prior to the games, a political campaign had pushed the Clinton administration to allow HIV-positive individuals from outside the United States to enter the country without special permits to attend the event. That was the first time that was ever allowed. Greg Louganis, a four-time Olympic gold medalist in diving who became HIV-positive, came out at the Gay Games.

While the Gay Games are inspiring for those of us who want to see a level playing field, today there is an even greater reason to be positive. What started with individual acts of resistance has become a broad movement for LBGT rights. And this movement is starting to find voice in the world of sports. In 2009, Baltimore Ravens linebacker and two-time Pro Bowler Brendon Ayanbadejo came out for full marriage equality, saying, "We will look back in 10, 20, 30 years and be amazed that gays and lesbians did not have the same rights as everyone else."[32] Then Saints linebacker Scott Fujita endorsed the October 2009 National Equality March, saying of Brendan Ayanbadejo's remarks,

> I hope he's right in his prediction, and I hope even more that it doesn't take that long. People could look at this issue without blinders on…the blinders imposed by their church, their parents, their friends, or in our case, their coaches and locker rooms. I wish they would realize that it's not a religion issue. It's not a government issue. It's not even a gay/straight issue or a question of your manhood. It's a human issue.[33]

At the 2010 Super Bowl, Fujita took advantage of the media spotlight to speak out for LGBT rights, and his story was picked up by the *New York Times*, the *Boston Globe*, and many other publications. When football players—the ultimate embodiment of Muscular Christianity—speak out, they actively challenge a backward and divisive idea about what it means to be a "real man." That is something we should celebrate.

And many fans do. In a poll published by *Sports Illustrated* in 2005, an astounding 86 percent of fans said that it's "O.K. for male athletes to participate in sports, even if they are openly gay."[34]

There are other reasons to celebrate. As activist Sherry Wolf notes,

> With a stunning 80 percent support, NHL players are practically ready to host Lady Gaga on their Gay Pride float, perhaps reflecting the abundance of players from gay-friendlier Canada. In fact, Blackhawks defenseman Brent Sopel accepted an invitation from the Chicago Gay Hockey Association to stand atop its float alongside his team's Stanley Cup trophy at the 2010 Gay Pride parade. Even 57 percent of NFL players, emblems of the most orthodox hyper-masculinity, say they would play with an openly gay teammate, despite bugaboos about the locker-room showers.[35]

Unfortunately, the media tends to focus on the crassly bigoted statements of players like former NBA all-star Tim Hardaway, who said, "I hate gay people," in response to the 2007 coming-out story of retired NBA player John Amaechi. There was far less publicity when Hardaway later traveled to El Paso, Texas, where he went to college, to stand up for gay rights. A group in El Paso was trying to recall mayor John Cook and two members of the city council for reestablishing domestic-partner benefits for both gay and unmarried couples. Hardaway arrived from Miami to speak at a press conference organized by the No Recall group. "It's not right to not let the gays and lesbians have equal rights here," Hardaway told the crowd. "If I know El Paso, like they came together when the 1966 team won a championship and Don Haskins started those five [black] guys, I know the city will grow and understand that gays and lesbians need equal rights."[36]

Hardaway was referencing UTEP's 1966 national championship, when coach Don Haskins's all-black starting five made history by beating Adolph Rupp's all-white Kentucky squad. Maybe Hardaway came to understand that his earlier position also ran against the currents of change. "My family and friends came to me and were like, 'What are you doing?'" he said. "I talked to them and they made me understand that wasn't right." Amaechi, for one, is understandably skeptical about Hardaway's change of heart, saying, "I hope this is a story of true redemption rather than a savvy p.r. ploy." He added, "Either way, he is at least saying the right words, and that will make a positive difference."

The New "F-Word"

Positive steps aside, there is still a ways to go—and more and more, the struggle for LGBT rights is being fully articulated in the world of sports. On the same day in May 2011 when Chicago Bulls center Joakim Noah was fined for using a homophobic slur against a fan, a commercial for LGBT marriage rights was released featuring Suns all-star Steve Nash. The previous month, the same day Kobe Bryant was caught on camera using the same invective against a referee, Phoenix Suns players Grant Hill and Jared Dudley were filming a public service announcement where they spoke out against using the word "gay" to mean stupid, dumb, or worthy of disrespect.

That May, Suns executive Rick Welts made history when he became the highest-ranking executive to ever come out of the closet. When the most famous Phoenix Sun ever, Charles Barkley, spoke at length in support of Welts, the media obsessed over his comments that he had gay teammates. His retort was sharp: "It bothers me when I hear these reporters and jocks get on TV and say: 'Oh, no guy can come out in a team sport. These guys would go crazy.' First of all, quit telling me what I think. I'd rather have a gay guy who can play than a straight guy who can't play."[37]

There are only two possible conclusions we can draw from this unprecedented collision between the NBA and the politics of LGBT rights. The first is that the Phoenix Suns organization must be the most gay-friendly workplace on earth, festooned with rainbows and good vibes. The other is that while homophobic outbursts are still very much a part of the vocabulary of professional sports, more and more players are calling them out as unacceptable. It was beautifully bracing to hear ESPN announcer Mark Jackson legitimately upset when he heard that Noah's fine was $50,000, only half of Kobe Bryant's fine. "That is a human being [Noah] said that to. You don't speak that way to another human being. Why the double standard?"[38]

The fact that it's Joakim Noah, of all players, who was caught on camera is in and of itself illustrative. Noah spoke out against the war in Iraq. He's called for college players to be paid by the NCAA. He put his name to a statement in defense of the Jena Six (African American teenagers facing decades in prison for a schoolyard fight). I met Noah, and he came across as one of the good guys—a true Jock for Justice. If he would drop an "F-bomb" in the heat of a game, it really says something about how ingrained it is in the language of pro competition (or that, like many of us outside of sports, Noah is progressive on some issues but not others).

But history shows that change will come. I recently had the privilege of screening Peter Miller's documentary that chronicles the use of anti-Semitic language against Jewish players in the early decades of baseball. The "F word" was an all-purpose insult thrown at everyone from Hall of Famer Hank Greenberg to bench guys. But Jewish players challenged fans and opponents, sometimes with their fists, until it was no longer part of the conversation. The same story can be told about Jackie Robinson, Roberto Clemente, and every player of color who had to hear insults in the heat of athletic battle until a combination of public and individual resistance made it an ugly memory.

Fast-forward to today: We have visible struggles for LGBT rights. We have a president who has finally "evolved" to support marriage equality. Hell, Focus on the Family announced that it was throwing in the towel on fighting LGBT marriage, admitting that they'd lost the under-thirty generation.[39] It would certainly help if more players came out of the closet. But one thing is certain: the big leagues can and need to do much more than just levy fines on players who happen to be caught speaking slurs on camera. NBA commissioner David Stern, who is a political liberal and a longtime friend of Rick Welts, said of gay rights, "I don't want to become a social crusader on this issue."[40] No kidding.

We don't need to see David Stern wave the rainbow flag (honestly, if it didn't have a swoosh on it, I don't think he ever would). But the commissioner could make discussion of homophobia part of every rookie orientation. How about a clear indication that homophobic language won't be tolerated any longer? How about statements from the NBA that if any rookies in the room happen to be gay, the NBA will stand as a workplace where their sexuality won't only be "tolerated" but embraced? On some level, the NBA understands that homophobia isn't good business. But for LGBT fans, writers, and players, and their families and friends, this isn't business; it's personal.

One thing is certain for both women *and* men: the vise of homophobia in sports will not loosen unless and until there is a movement off the field and in the streets.

Fighting gender-based prejudice in sports is fighting for a world where sports is about games, fun, and the thrill of teamwork, not about preparing our youth for war. It's about young girls in South Africa having the freedom to run without having to fear who will question their gender; it's about young boys in the United States who can be out and proud without giving up the right to play. It's about living in a world where our dignity and humanity are givens, not something to fight for. My favorite sign at the LGBT Equality

March in DC read, "We hold these truths to be pretty frickin obvious!" This is absolutely right.

In the world of sports, there is still a ways to travel. If nothing else, however, we can see that if sports is the central arena where gender and sexual norms are enforced, then it can also be the place where they can most effectively be challenged. As NHL players say in their new ad campaign aimed at fighting homophobia, "If you can skate, you can play."

Notes

1. Elizabeth Schulte, "Sparks of a new women's movement," *Socialist Worker*, http://socialistworker.org/2011/05/17/a-new-womens-movement.

2. Tucker Center, "Double Standards: Portrayals of Female Athletes in Mainstream Sports Media," September 22, 2009, https://tuckercenter.wordpress.com/2009/09/22/131/.

3. Allison Glock, "The Selling of Candace Parker," *ESPN The Magazine*, http://sports.espn.go.com/espnmag/story?id=3967891.

4. Sportsmail Reporter, "World champion Caster Semenya 'is a hermaphrodite with no womb or ovaries,'" *Daily Mail*, http://www.dailymail.co.uk/sport/othersports/article-1212568/World-champion-Caster-Semenya-hermaphrodite-womb-ovaries-Australian-newspapers-shock-claims-gender-row-runner.html.

5. Intersex Society of North America, "How common is intersex?," http://www.isna.org/faq/frequency.

6. Genetics Home Reference, "Androgen insensitivity syndrome," July 2, 2012, http://ghr.nlm.nih.gov/condition/androgen-insensitivity-syndrome.

7. Sherry Wolf, *Sexuality and Socialism* (Chicago: Haymarket Books, 2009).

8. Tommy Craggs, "Caster Semenya Is a 'Hermaphrodite,' Ballsy Aussie Paper Reports," Deadspin, http://deadspin.com/5356717/caster-semenya-is-a-hermaphrodite-ballsy-aussie-paper-reports.

9. Pumza Fihlani, "Crowds greet gender-test athlete," BBC News, http://news.bbc.co.uk/2/hi/8218530.stm.

10. David Smith, "Caster Semenya row: 'Who are white people to question the makeup of an African girl? It is racism,'" *The Guardian*, http://www.guardian.co.uk/sport/2009/aug/23/caster-semenya-athletics-gender.

11. Rebecca Jordan-Young and Katrina Karkazis, "You Say You're a Woman? That Should Be Enough," *New York Times*, June 17, 2012, http://www.nytimes.com/2012/06/18/sports/olympics/olympic-sex-verification-you-say-youre-a-woman-that-should-be-enough.html.

12. Molly Jay, *Winning Woman: 500 Spirited Quotes About Women and Their Sport* (Philadelphia: Running Press, 2001), 199.

13. Larry Schwartz, "Didrikson was a woman ahead of her time," http://espn.go.com/sportscentury/features/00014147.html

14. Paul Lukas, "From Corsets to Catsuits," ESPN.com, http://sports.espn.go.com/espn/page2/story?page=lukas/050620.

15. Susan K. Cahn, *Coming On Strong: Gender and Sexuality in Twentieth Century Women's Sports* (Cambridge, MA: Harvard University Press, 1998).

16. Ibid.

17. Ibid.

18. Ibid.

19. Ibid.

20. Ibid.

21. Larry Schwartz, "Billie Jean won for all women," ESPN, January 1, 2000, http://espn.go.com/sportscentury/features/00016060.html.

22. Ibid.

23. Ibid.

24. Tara Parker-Pope, "As Girls Become Women, Sports Pay Dividends," *New York Times*, February 15, 2010, http://www.nytimes.com/2010/02/16/health/16well.html.

25. *Training Rules*, dir. Dee Mossbacher, Woman Vision, 2009.

26. Randy Boyd, "First Gays, Then Animals, Then More Cock-Teases," Outsports, http://www.outsports.com/ballin/20032004/0721smoltzbonus.htm.

27. Howard Zinn, *A People's History of the United States: 1492–Present* (New York: Harper Perennial Modern Classics, 2003), 283.

28. Tom Farrey, *Game On: How the Pressure to Win at All Costs Endangers Youth Sports and What Parents Can Do About It*; (ESPN Books, 2009) 106.

29. Elliott J. Gorn and Warren Goldstein, A Brief History of American Sports (Champaign: University of Illinois Press, 2004), 91.

30. Albert G. Spalding, *America's National Game* (New York, 1911), 11.

31. Ann Meredith, "Gay Games II," *Off Our Backs*, October 31, 1986.

32. Ibid.

33. Brendan Ayanbadejo, "Same Sex Marriges: What's the Big Deal?," Huffington Post, April 23, 2009, http://www.huffingtonpost.com/brendon-ayanbadejo/same-sex-marriages-whats_b_190591.html.

34. Dave Zirin, "'Why I Support the National Equality March': NFL's Scott Fujita Speaks Out for Gay Rights," Edge of Sports Radio, October 2009, http://www.edgeofsports.com/2009-10-06-460/index.html.

35. L. Jon Wertheim, "Gays in Sports: A Poll," *Sports Illustrated*, April 18, 2005, http://sportsillustrated.cnn.com/vault/article/magazine/MAG1110762/index.htm.

36. Sherry Wolf, "America's Deepest Closet," August 15, 2011, *The Nation*, http://www.thenation.com/article/162386/americas-deepest-closet.

37. Tim Hardaway Foundation press release, "Tim Hardaway Pledges Support for 'No Recall Group,' Gay Issues," August 23, 2011, http://www.thfla.com/2011/08/tim-hardaway-pledges-support-for-no-recall-group-gay-issues/.

38. ESPN.com news services, "Charles Barkley: I had gay teammates," ESPN.com, http://sports.espn.go.com/nba/news/story?id=6563128.

39. Johnette Howard, "The issues in Wayne Simmonds' version," ESPN. com, September 28, 2011, http://espn.go.com/espn/commentary/ story/_/page/howard110927/wayne-simmonds-alleged-gay-slur-puts-nhl-difficult-position.

40. Tim Murphy, "Focus on the Family Head: 'We've Probably Lost' on Gay Marriage," Mother Jones, May 23, 2011, http://www.motherjones.com/ mojo/2011/05/focus-family-weve-lost-gay-marriage.

41. Henry Abbott, "David Stern predicts openly gay players," ESPN.com, April 15, 2011, http://espn.go.com/blog/truehoop/post/_/id/27380/ david-stern-predicts-openly-gay-players.

Glossary of Rhetorical Terms

audience: the person or people who read, listen to, and/or view a text. A writer may invoke a specific **intended audience** (or even multiple audiences) when creating a text. At the same time, a text often circulates beyond what the writer intends, and there may be other audiences who read the text.

arrangement: the process of arranging or ordering the parts of a written or spoken text; according to the classical Greek rhetorical tradition, the second of the five canons of rhetoric.

circulation: the ways in which texts travel among readers and writers. Circulation may range from a writer sharing a text with one reader, to texts being shared within a specific classroom, to texts circulating within a particular discourse community, to texts being available to a wide public audience. Circulation can rely on analog and/or digital technologies; consider the technologies that enable the following to circulate: print publications like essays in *Opening Conversations*, postal mail, and digital texts like blogs and tweets.

citation: the practice of formally recognizing the author(s) of sources that a writer includes in his/her text. Proper citation style (also called documentation style) will vary depending on genre, discipline, and cultural conventions. Note, for example, the citation practices in Peter Brooks's essay (published in an academic journal) versus Dave Zirin's chapter (excerpted from a trade book for the mass public). In the U.S., it's ethical to attribute sources to their authors. In particular, in *academic* communities, a failure to cite sources that have been summarized, paraphrased, or quoted would constitute **academic dishonesty**.

context: the social and historical settings that shape or otherwise inform something (a person, a topic, an event). The rhetorical situation implies an immediate context. More broadly, context also cuts across time and space to include the places, social groups, social identities, and cultural, social, economic, and political systems that surround us. Those belonging to particular contexts may share particular beliefs or ways of thinking about the world.

delivery: the art of presentation to a public audience; according to the classical Greek rhetorical tradition, the last of the five canons of rhetoric. In oratory, delivery includes vocal performance and physical gestures; in writing, delivery may include design elements offered by a medium.

discourse: a set of speech and/or writing acts that circulate particular kinds of knowledge, ideas, and values. A **discourse community** refers to a group of people who share common ways of writing and speaking, and may even share beliefs and worldviews. While discourse communities are characterized by shared discourse practices, each community has its own diversity and always exists in relation to other communities and wider contexts.

ethos: an appeal to an audience based on the writer's presentation of his/her character (credible, trustworthy, fair minded); according to the classical Greek rhetorical tradition, one of three rhetorical appeals along with pathos and logos.

exigence: the issue, problem, or situation that compel a writer to create a text; an invitation to write. Exigence is an essential part of the rhetorical situation.

invention: the process of finding or discovering *what* one might write, of generating new ideas. While invention is the first of the five canons of rhetoric, according to the classical Greek rhetorical tradition, invention can occur at any stage in the writing process.

kairos: the opportune moment for a text to be delivered. According to the classical Greek rhetorical tradition, this rhetorical concept calls attention to the time and place when the conditions are ripe for the accomplishment of a crucial action. Kairos can also be used to discuss how time, place, writer, and audience work together to make an appropriate argument.

logos: an appeal to an audience based on reason, logic, knowledge, and facts; according to the classical Greek rhetorical tradition, one of three rhetorical appeals along with ethos and pathos.

media (plural of medium): the means of communication. Among artists, media have traditionally referred to the material means of expression—including oil paints, stone sculptures, paper. Within the field of mass communication, media include newspapers, radio, and television. In a digital era of writing, media also refer to digital technologies (e.g., blogs, social media networks, etc.). Each medium comes with affordances and constraints in terms of composing practices, design, and circulation.

pathos: an appeal to an audience based on emotions and the emotional commitments that an audience might have; according to the classical Greek rhetorical tradition, one of three rhetorical appeals along with ethos and logos.

peer review: the sharing of texts among colleagues for the purposes of providing feedback. Peers can provide feedback during any stage of the drafting process: asking questions early on to further develop the writer's ideas; offering content, form, and style suggestions; giving copyediting advice on close-to-finished drafts. Research in writing studies shows that peer review can help students become more aware of their writing options. In academic communities, **peer-reviewed sources** have a specific meaning (see **sources**).

purpose: a writer's reason for creating a text or a reader's reason for reading a text. Writers, like readers, can have many different purposes—to reflect, inform, to persuade, to advocate for social action, etc.—and can often have multiple purposes at the same time. A writer's purpose is a response to a perceived exigence.

research: to find, select, evaluate, and make purposeful use of multiple sources of information and perspectives in response to an exigence (see exigence above). Research is a process that typically begins with curiosity and a question, leads to the collection, evaluation, and synthesizing of sources, and contributes to a writer's purpose (e.g., offering possible solutions, offering a new way of understanding the problem).

revise: to re-see a text in order to generate ideas, extend or complicate meaning, and explore rhetorical options for composing a text.

rhetoric: the art of identifying and using symbolic resources (e.g., words, languages, genres, images) in order to communicate purposefully and effectively within a particular social context.

rhetorical situation: the context in which rhetoric is practiced and a text is created, circulated, and received. The rhetorical situation includes an exigence, a writer or speaker, a topic, and an audience (readers or listeners). The rhetorical situation ought to be understood in relation to the contexts called up by writer, readers, and topic.

source: text-based information, knowledge, and perspectives gathered, examined, and evaluated during the research process. Sources can take a range of forms: books, articles in scholarly and popular periodicals, films, blogs, websites, interviews, surveys, etc. Sources are usually divided into two categories: **primary sources** consist of first-hand knowledge of the researcher gained through observation, interviews, surveys, and experiments; **secondary sources** report and analyze primary sources. Within academic communities, a **peer-reviewed source** has been evaluated by scholars holding expertise within the writer's field of study; evaluation criteria may include accuracy, depth of knowledge, and potential contribution to existing research in the discipline.

style: the art of crafting *how* to express one's ideas; according to the classical Greek rhetorical tradition, the third of the five canons of rhetoric. Because style addresses the personality or even beauty of how a text is written, many assume that style is merely ornamental and not substantive. However, style is integral to the rhetorical effectiveness of a text and can especially contribute to ethos and pathos.

text: a piece of writing or, more broadly, a work that communicates meaning through words, images, and design. A text can be read and interpreted and may include a variety of cultural artifacts (e.g., an essay in *Opening Conversations*, a tweet, an online video, a billboard advertisement).